HOT WATER DETAILS

E.L. WOOLLEY

T.D., F.I.P.H.E., Companion Chartered Institution of Building Services, M.R.S.H.

Lecturer in Building Services,
University of Wales Institute of Science & Technology,
Welsh School of Architecture,
(formerly of Dept. of Civil Engineering & Building Technology)

Edited by
PHIL STRONACH

INTERNATIONAL THOMSON PUBLISHING LTD.,
100 AVENUE ROAD,
LONDON NW3

Published 1986

Building Trades Journal Books, 1986

ISBN 1 85032 0241

A 'BUILDING TRADES JOURNAL' BOOK

Printed in Great Britain by Unwin Brothers Limited
The Gresham Press Old Woking Surrey England
A member of the Martins Printing Group

CONTENTS

Summary of Relevant Legislation 3

      Water Act, 1945 3
      Model Water Byelaws (1966 Edition) 4
      Building Regulations 1985 (England and Wales) 10
      Building Standards (Scotland) (Consolidation) Regulations 1971,
         with 1973 and 1975 Amendments 11
      The Gas Safety Regulations 1972 13
      Regulations for the Electrical Equipment of Buildings 15th
         Edition, 1984 15
      Extract from Building Research Station Digest 16

Metric-Imperial Equivalents 17

Bibliography 21

      British Standards Institution Publications 21
         Codes of Practice 21
         British Standards 21

      Relevant Publications 24

      Government Departments, Councils, Associations, Research
         Establishments, Institutions, etc. 25
      Directory of Manufacturers 26

Detail Number	Detail Title	Page Number
	Fundamentals	
1	Introductory Sheet : the Basic Problems	29
2	Glossary of Terminology Relevant to Hot Water Services	33
3	Model Water Byelaw Requirements	35
4	Basic Circulation : from Physics to Systems	39
	Systems	
5	Direct Systems	41
6	Indirect Systems (Double Feed)	43
7	Indirect Systems (Single Feed)	45
8	Secondary Circulations	47
9	Combined Hot Water and Central Heating	49
10	Systems for Large Buildings	51
11	Unvented Hot Water Systems	53
	Appliances and Fittings	
12	Boilers, Connections and Mountings	55
13	Domestic Cylinders	57
14	Tanks and Cisterns	59
15	Combination Units	61
16	Showers From Centralized Systems	63
17	Instantaneous Showers and Shower Equipment	65
18	Towel Rails	67
19	Spray Taps	69
20	Miscellaneous Fittings	71

Pipe Arrangements

21	Boilers and Primary Circulation	73
22	Cylinder Connections	77
23	Cold Feed and Vent Pipes	79

Hot Water by Gas

24	Methods of Hot Water Supply by Gas	81
25	Gas Circulators	83
26	Gas Storage Heaters: Freestanding	85
27	Instantaneous Water Heaters	87

Hot Water by Electricity

28	Methods of Hot Water Supply by Electricity	89
29	Immersion Heaters	91
30	Storage Heaters: Purpose Made	93
31	Instantaneous Water Heaters	95

Economics of Hot Water

32	Design and Heat Conservation (1): General	97
33	Design and Heat Conservation (2): Cylinder Insulation	99

Introduction to Calculations

34	Tabulated Imperial and SI Units (1): (Rate of Flow, Volume and Mass, Capacity and Mass)	101
35	Tabulated Imperial and SI Units (2): (Temperature Conversions, Heat Flow Rate, Quantity of Heat, Pressure Conversions)	103
36	Example of Sizing a Hot Water System: (Medium Rental House for 5 persons)	105
37	Sizing the Primary Circulation Pipes (By Example)	107
38	Sizing the Distribution Pipes (1): Tables and Charts	109
39	Sizing the Distribution Pipes (2): the Problem	111
40	Sizing the Distribution Pipes (3): a Solution	113

SUMMARY OF RELEVANT LEGISLATION
Water Act, 1945

Section 17 Byelaws for preventing waste, misuse or contamination of water

(1) Staututory water undertakers may make byelaws for preventing waste, undue consumption, misuse, or contamination of water supplied by them.

(2) Byelaws under this section may include provisions:

  (a) prescribing the size, nature, materials, strength and workmanship, and the mode of arrangement, connection, disconnection, alternation and repair, of the water fittings to be used: and

  (b) forbidding the use of any water fittings which are of such a nature or are so arranged or connected as to cause or permit, or be likely to cause or permit, waste, undue consumption, misuse, erroneous measurement or contaminatijon of water, or reverberation in pipes.

(3) If a person contravenes the provisions of any byelaw made under this section, the undertakers may, without prejudice to their right to take proceedings for a fine in respect of such contravention, cause any water fittings belonging to or used by that person which are not in accordance with the requirements of the byelays to be altered, repaired or replaced, and may recover the expenses reasonably incurred by them in so doing from the person in defauly summarily as a civil debt.

(4) Nothing in this section, or any byelaw made thereunder, shall apply to any fittings used on premises which belong to a railway company and are held or used by them for the purposes of their railway, so long as those fittings are not of such a nature or so arranged or connected as to cause or permit or be likely to cause or permit waste, undue consumption, misuse, erroneous measurement or contamination of water supplied by the undertakers, or reverberation in pipes:

Provided that the exemption conferred by this subsection shall not extend to fittings used in hotels or dwelling houses or in offices not forming part of a railway station.

MODEL WATER BYELAWS

(1966 Edition), Ministry of Housing and Local Government

Byelaws made under Section 17 of the Water Act, 1945, by the (name of water 'authority') for preventing waste, undue consumption, misuse, or contamination of water supplied by them.

Interpretation

1. Definitions

In these byelaws, unless the context otherwise requires — 'ballvalve' means any float-operated valve for controlling the inflow of water to a cistern;

'British Standard' means a standard or specification issued by the British Standards Institution a copy of which is available for inspection at the offices of the undertakers at (address of water authority) and 'British Standard Code of Practice' means a code of practice issued and available as aforesaid;

'building' means any structure (including a floating structure) whether of a permanent character or not, and whether movable or immovable, and without prejudice to the generality of the foregoing, includes any caravan, vessel, boat or houseboat;

'capacity' in relation to a storage cistern means the capacity of the cistern measured up to the highest level the water can reach when the ballvalve or other device for controlling the inflow of water is fitted or adjusted in the manner required by paragraph (d) of byelaw 40 or, where paragraph (e) of byelaw 41 applies, by that paragraph;

'closed circuit' means any system of pipes and other water fittings through which water circulates and from which water is not drawn for use, and includes any vent pipe fitted thereto but not the feed cistern or the cold feed pipe;

'corrosion-resisting material' means any material which is highly resistant to any corrosive action to which it is likely to be subjected in the circumstances in which it is used;

'cylinder' means a cylindrical closed vessel capable of containing water under pressure greater than atmospheric pressure;

'distributing pipe' means any pipe (other than an overflow pipe or a flushing pipe) conveying water from a storage cistern, or from a hot water apparatus supplied from a feed cistern, and under pressure from that cistern;

'feed cistern means any storage cistern used for supplying cold water to a hot water apparatus, cylinder to a tank;

'overflowing level' in relation to a warning or other overflow pipe of a cistern, means the lowest level at which water can flow into that pipe from that cistern;

'service pipe' means so much of any pipe for supplying water from a main to any premises as is subject to water pressure from that main, or would be so subject but for the closing of some stopvalve;

'stopvalve' means any device (including a stopcock and stop tap), other than a draw-off tap, for stopping at will the flow of water in a pipe;

'storage cistern' means any cistern, other than a flushing cistern, having a free water surface under atmospheric pressure, but does not include a drinking-trough or drinking-bowl for animals, including poultry;

'tank' means a non-cylindrical closed vessel capable of containing water under pressure greater than atmospheric;

'the undertakers' means the (insert name of relevant authority);

'warning pipe' means an overflow pipe so fixed that its outlet, whether inside or outside a building, is in a conspicuous position, where the discharge of any water therefrom can be readily seen; and

'water fittings' includes pipes (other than mains), taps, cocks, valves, ferrules, meters, cisterns, baths, water closets, soil pans and other similar apparatus used in connection with the supply and use of water.

Note:
These definitions have been given in full, as any attempt to summarise them could lead to misinterpretation. The remainder of the byelaws are summarised.

2. Compliance with British Standards
Worded so that new types of water fittings may be accepted providing basic British Standard requirements are satisfied: e.g. size, nature, materials, strength and workmanship.

Application

---

3. Application of byelaws generally
Deals with many items that persons must not do.

4. Saving for fittings lawfully fitted
Protects existing installations providing previously lawfully fitted.

5. Closed circuits
Only certain byelaws apply to closed circuits (6-8, 10-16, 23, 25, 29(3), 31 and 59-61).

6. Fittings used for industrial or research purposes
Subject to certain provisos and, if not reasonably practicable to do so, most byelaws need not be complied with.

7. Unserviceable fittings and fittings not mentioned in the byelaws
Faulty fittings or incorrect installations to be remedied.

7A. Deterioration through electrolytic action
If likely to occur by use of dissimilar metals, measures must be taken to prevent this.

8. Connections which could cause contamination of mains water
Prohibits cross-connections.

9. Taps for drinking water
In most premises, a convenient draw-off tap is to be provided for supplying drinking water from a service pipe. If not practicable by reason of height, water may be taken from storage cistern if properly protected.

10. Protection from damage from frost
Water fittings to be positioned or protected to reduce risk of damage. Requirements are deemed to be satisfied if work is as recommended in B.S. Code of Practice (C.P.) 99.

11. Protection from damage from other causes.
If liable to be damaged, they must be effectively protected.

12. Accessibility of fittings
Water fittings (this includes *pipes*) to be accessible if reasonably practicable. Provisos are
(a) a chase or duct may be used,
(b) pipes for space heating may be embedded.

13. Disconnection of disused pipes
Pipe supplying a disconnected water fitting to be also disconnected if fitting is not replaced or reconnected within 28 days.

Pipes

---

14. Support of pipes
Adequately supported and aligned to avoid airlock or reverberation in the system.

15. Depth of pipes laid underground
Minimum depth to cover 2 ft 6 in (0.75m) with provisos. (A maximum may be stated in byelaws issued by regional authority, e.g. 4 ft 5 in (1.35m).

16. Protection of pipes from corrosion and contact with contaminating substances
Examples are: ashpit, manure pit, sewer, drain, cesspool, refuse chute, manhole and permeation by gas.

16A. Pipes of wrought iron and steel not to be used

Undertakers may insert this byelaw after consultation with the Ministry. (See latest issue of regional byelaws: it may be re-worded to cover dezincification, for example.)

17. Pipes of lead

Compliance with B.S. required; also includes types of joint. (Regional byelaws may prohibit use of lead.)

18. Pipes of cast iron

Compliance with B.S. required; also test pressure to be not less than double the working pressure.

19. Pipes of steel

Compliance with B.S. required for pipes and fittings for various purposes above **or** below ground.

20. Pipes of copper

Compliance with B.S. required for pipes and fittings for various purposes above **or** below ground.

21. Pipes of asbestos cement

Compliance with B.S. required; also test pressure to be not less than double the working pressure. Compliance with B.S. required for polythene and uPVC. (Stainless steel may also be included in new regional byelaws.)

23. Fittings in closed circuits

Suitable material to be used; also test pressure to be not less than double the working pressure.

Taps and Valves

---

24. Stopvalves on pipes supplying buildings

One example is '... inside and as near as is reasonably practicable to the point where it enters the building'. There are several other positions given, additonally.

25. Stopvalves on outlet pipes from storage cisterns

To be fitted as near to the cistern as is reasonably practicable on draw-off pipes from cisterns over 4 gal (18 litres). If stopvalve cannot be fitted to this pipe, then can be on draw-off pipe from hot water cylinder, e.g. combination units.

26. Location of draining tap

Not to be buried or where the outlet is in danger of being flooded.

27. Standpipes

If standpipe is in 'common use', it must be fitted with non-concussive self-closing tap.

28. Drinking troughs

Subject to certain provisos, requires trough to be fitted with ballvalve suitable protected against damage, interference and contamination.

29. Draw-off taps

Compliance with B.S. required. (New regional byelaws may include plastic bodied draw-off taps.) Draining taps must also comply with B.S.

30. Stopvalves

Compliance with B.S. required. (New regional byelaws may include above-ground and underground requirements.)

31. Operation of stopvalves

Places so that can be readily operated by the means by which it is designed.

32. Ballvalves

Compliance with B.S. required, otherwise various criteria must be met, e.g. high pressure type to close against pressure of 200lbf/in^2 (14 bar); medium pressure: 100lbf/in^2 (7 bar); low pressure: 40lbf/in^2 (3 bar).
All to withstand 300lbf/in^2 (20 bar) when closed. Floats also to comply with B.S. (New regional byelaws may mention both piston and diaphragm ballvalves.)

Storage Cisterns

33. Placing of storage cisterns

If for domestic purposes, they must be placed and equipped for ready inspection and cleansing; and so that the water therein is not liable to be contaminated.

34. Support and covering of storage cisterns

Must be adequately supported and covered (not to be airtight) if used for domestic purposes. (New regional byelaws may include exclusion of light, cover shaped to be not easily dislodged and of material which will not contaminate condensate.)

35. Avoidance of flooding; buried or sunken cisterns

Storage cistern must not be so placed that it is in danger of being flooded. There are special requirements for sunken cisterns.

36. Materials for storage cisterns

To be watertight, of adequate strength and made of certain materials only. (New regional byelaws may exclude lead.)

37. British Standards for storage cisterns

Compliance with B.S. required, if made of mild steel, the grade (A or B), as required by the undertakers, is stated.

38. Capacity of storage cisterns in houses

Minimum sizes for certain cisterns: e.g. if **not** used as a feed cistern, it is 25 gal (115 litres); or if used both as 'feed' and other purposes, 50 gal (230 litres).
(In this byelaw, 'house' means premises separately occupied as a private dwelling.)

39. Storage cisterns to be fitted with ballvalves

States requirements for fixing and positioning ballvalves, their proportions (orifice size, float size and length of lever), etc.

40. Warning pipes on storage cisterns holding not more than 1000 gal (4.5m^3)

If overflow pipe(s) do not act as warning pipe(s), then an efficient warning pipe (or other device) must be fitted. States positioning details, certain dimensions, minimum sizes, etc.

Hot Water Apparatus

42. Distance between hot water apparatus and draw-off taps

Limits length of 'dead legs' as follows:
any pipe not exceeding ¾ in (19mm): max. length 40 ft (12m);
any pipe larger than ¾ in (19mm) but not over 1 in (25mm): 25 ft (7.5m);
any pipe over 1 in (25mm): 10 ft (3m).

43. Positions of outlets in relation to level of water in cylinders and tanks

Outlets are not to be so placed that cylinders and tanks can be drained lower than certain depths.

44. Hot water cisterns not to have ballvalves

Simply prohibits ballvalves as stated. (New regional byelaws may allow ballvalves, if made of suitable materials, etc.)

45. Outlets from feed cisterns to hot water apparatus

This is the cold feed pipe and its function must be to supply the hot water apparatus **exclusively**. Does not apply to instantaneous hot water apparatus. (New regional byelaws may require the outlet to be a minimum of 1 in (25mm) above the bottom of the cistern.)

46. Hot water apparatus not to be connected directly to service pipe

Only certain types of hot water apparatus to be fed directly from the service pipe: e.g. certain gas and electrical hot water appliances.

47. Mixing valves

Certain pipes must not be so connected that certain hot and cold waters (and pressures) come together.

48. Materials for hot water pipes

Permits certain materials to be used as decided by the undertakers: e.g. copper or some other corrosion-resisting material which is not less suitable.

49. Materials for, and support of, hot water cylinders and tanks
Permits certain materials to be used: e.g. copper; and to be adequately supported. If not made of corrosion-resisting materials, they must be effectively protected against corrosion.

50. British Standards for hot water cylinder and tanks
Compliance to B.S. required.

51. Capacity of hot water storage cisterns, cylinders and tanks
Unless forming part of a hot water system which is heated only under thermostatic control, minimum capacity is 25 gal (115 litres).

Baths, Wash Basins and Sinks

---

52. Inlets and outlets of baths, etc.
Inlets must not be connected to outlets. Waste plugs must be provided for certain appliances; exceptions are shower baths, certain appliances with a tap flow rate not exceeding 5 pt per minute (0.06 litre per second).

53. Position of taps on baths, etc.
Taps to discharge $\frac{1}{2}$ in (13mm) above the flood level of the appliance, subject to certain provisos.

Flushing Cisterns

---

54. Waterclosets and urinals to be fitted with flushing cisterns
Flushing cisterns must be used or some other not less efficient and suitable flushing apparatus.

55. Ballvalves and warning pipes on flushing cisterns
Byelaws 39(1), (3), (4) and 40 apply, with any necessary modifications. Excludes automatic flushing cisterns, but includes flushing troughs.

56. Pipes discharging to watercloset pans
Only flush pipes from flushing cisterns to be connected to w.c. pan or urinal. Warning pipes may discharge into the air a minimum 6 in (150mm) above the top edge of pan or urinal.

57. Design and arrangement of flushing cisterns for water closets
Maximum capacity of cistern to be 2 gal (9 litre) and arranged so that after normal use, the contents will effectively clear the pan with one flush. Dual-flush type also permitted. (New regional byelaws may require all flushing cisterns serving washdown w.c. pans to be the dual-flush type in new domestic premises after a certain date.)

58. Design and arrangement of flushing cisterns for urinals
Maximum flush water of 1 gal (4.5 litres) per 2 ft 3 in (700mm) width of slab. Compliance with B.S. required. (New regional byelaws may have 58A, giving a minimum 20-minute interval between flushes and requiring a time switch or other device to limit the hours of usage.

Notice to Undertakers

---

59. Notices to undertakers
(1) Minimum of seven days' notice before fitting or altering any water fitting (except for repair or renewal).

(2) Minimum of seven days' notice before back-filling any excavation in which a pipe is laid to convey any water supplied by undertakers.

(3) Minimum of seven days' notice before first using water for certain domestic purposes otherwise than by meter. (This may not be included in new regional byelaws.)

All notices to be in writing stating expected date to commence work. They shall not, without the consent of the undertakers, begin that work before that date.

60. Penalties

For contravention of any of these byelaws, £400 for **each** offence and a further fine of £50 for each day the offence continues after conviction. (Model Byelaws dated 1966, state £20 and £5 respectively.)

Revocation of Previous Byelaws

61. Revocation of previous byelaws

Previous byelaws revoked (as stated in a Schedule) without prejudice to the completion of any legal proceedings, etc.

Note:

The above summaries should only be regarded as an *aide memoire* or for quick reference to establish the existence or relevance of a particular byelaw. The full and complete byelaws should be studied in detail, understood and complied with.

THE BUILDING REGULATIONS 1985

Approved Document J of Schedule 1 to the Building Regulations. – Heat Producing Applicances – provides guidance to meet the requirements of paragraphs J1, J2 and J3.

J1 | **Air Supply – Walls and roofs**
Heat producing appliances shall be so installed that there is an adequate supply of air to them for combustion and for the efficient working of any flue pipe or chimney.

The requirements in this part apply only to fixed heat producing appliances which: a) are designed to burn solid fuel, oil or gas; or b) are incinerators.

J2 | **Discharge of products of combustion – Chimneys and flue pipes**
Heat producing appliances shall have adequate provision for the discharge of the products of combustion to the outside air.

J3 | **Protection of building**
Heat producing appliances and flue pipes shall be so installed, and fireplaces shall be so constructed as to reduce to a reasonable level the risk of the building catching fire in consequence of their use.

See also Approved Document F1 for guidance on ventilation generally.

Section 73 of the Building Act 1984 gives a local authority special powers where a new building over-reaches an adjacent chimney.

See also Paragraphs B2, B3, and B4 of the Building Regulations 1985, for guidance on fire spread generally.

Paragraphs J1, J2, and J3 Heat producing Appliances

Section 1 | Solid fuel and oil-burning appliances with a rated output of up to 45kW

Part A | Provisions for introducing air to the applicances

Part B | Provisions for discharging the products of combustion
Balanced-flue appliances
Oil-burning applicances — reduced provisions
Flues
Chimneys
Masonry Chimneys
Factory-made insulated chimneys
Flue Pipes

Part C | Provisions for protection against fire and heat
Constructional hearths
Fireplace recesses
Walls
Chimneys
Factory-made insulated chimneys
Flue pipes
Location of appliances

Section 2 | Gas-burning appliances with a rated input up to 60kw

Part A | Provisions for introducing air to the appliances

Part B | Provisions for discharging the products of combustion
Balanced flue appliances
Open-flued appliances
Chimneys
Flue Pipes

Part C | Provisions for protection against heat
Hearths
Shielding of appliances
Chimneys
Flue Pipes

THE BUILDING STANDARDS (SCOTLAND) (CONSOLIDATION) REGULATIONS 1971 WITH 1973 AND 1975 AMENDMENTS

Building and Buildings

Part F: Chimneys, Flues, Hearths and the Installation of Heat-producing Appliances

F1   Application of Part F

Note: Regs. F3 to F20 shall apply to:

(a) any appliance;

    (i) designed to burn solid fuel or oil and having an output rating not exceeding 45 kW, or

    (ii) comprising an incinerator having a combustion chamber capacity exceeding $0.03m^3$, but not exceeding $0.08m^3$, and

(b) any chimney, flue-pipe or hearth used in conjunction with such an appliance.

Regs. F21 to F29 shall apply to:

(a) any appliance:

    (i) designed to burn only gaseous fuels and having an input rating not exceeding 45 kW, or

    (ii) comprising an incinerator having a combustion chamber capacity not exceeding $0.03m^3$, and

(b) any chimney, flue-pipe or hearth used in conjunction with such an appliance.

Regs. F30 shall apply to:

(a) any appliance:

    (i) designed to burn solid fuel or oil and having an output rating exceeding 45 kW, or

    (ii) designed to burn only gaseous fuel and having an input rating exceeding 45 kW, or

    (iii) comprising an incinerator having a combustion chamber capacity exceeding $0.08m^3$, and

(b) any chimney, flue-pipe or hearth used in conjunction with such an appliance.

F2   Interpretation of Part F.

Solid Fuel and Oil-burning Appliances

F3   Construction of chimneys.

F4   Construction of flue-pipes.

F5   Height of chimney stacks and flue-pipes.

F6   Combustible materials in relation to chimneys.

F7   Metal fastenings.

F8   Sealing the outside of chimneys.

F9   Thickness of materials surrounding flues in chimneys.

F10   Lining of flues.

F11   Access to flues.

F12   Flues for appliances.

F13   Thickness of materials surrounding fireplace openings.

F14   Thickness of materials in proximity to free-standing appliances.

F15   Constructional hearths in fireplace openings.

F16   Constructional hearths other than in fireplace openings.

F17   Combustible material under constructional hearths.

F18	Construction of appliances.
F19	Installation of appliances.
F20	Fireguard fittings.
F20A	Additional requirements for insulated metal chimneys.
F20B	Oil-burning appliances.

Gas Burning Appliances

F21	Design and construction of chimneys and flue-pipes.
F22	Flue outlets.
F23	Fastenings in relation to chimneys.
F24	Thickness of materials surrounding flues in chimneys.
F25	Access to flues.
F26	Flues for appliances.
F27	Combustible material in relation to appliances.
F28	Hearths for appliances.
F28A	Installation of gas water-heating appliances in bathrooms.
F29	Gas burning appliances.

Appliances of a High Rating

F30	Chimneys, flue-pipes and hearths and appliances of a high rating.

Part N: Electrical Installations

N1	Application of Part N.
N2	Interpretation of Part N.
N3	Electrical conductors and apparatus.
N4	Fuses, switches and circuit breakers.
N5	Precautions against metal becoming live.
N6	Isolation of systems and apparatus.
N7	Installation of apparatus.
N8	Connection of appliances to supply.
N9	Precautions against special conditions.
N10	Voltages exceeding 250 volts.
N11	Electrical appliances.
N12	Light fittings or appliances in rooms containing baths or showers.
N13	Wiring diagrams.

Part Q: Housing Standards

Q14	Water supply to baths, sinks, tubs and wash-hand basins.

THE GAS SAFETY REGULATIONS 1972

Explanatory Note:

These regulations made by the Secretary of State for Trade and Industry under Section 67 of the Gas Act 1948 will apply generally throughout Great Britain and, except in the Inner London Boroughs, are wholly new. In the Inner London Boroughs, they take the place of certain provisions of the London Gas Undertakings Regulations 1954 made under the London Gas Undertaking (Regulations) Act 1939. Any provisions of those regulations which are inconsistent with or rendered redundant by these regulations ceased to have effect from the date these regulations came into operation, that is to say from 1 December 1972.

Parts II to V lay down certain requirements to be observed by persons installing gas service pipes (II), meters (III), installation pipes (IV), and gas appliances, etc. (V), on consumers' premises. These are designed to ensure that the basic standards necessary to secure safety from the installation are maintained. Part VI imposes certain requirements on the use of gas appliances supplied by Area Gas Boards largely designed to prevent the public being put at risk by the continued use of gas appliances where such use is known to be dangerous or there is reason to believe so. Part VII provides requirements for work done on gas fittings after first installation and Part VIII provides penalties for contraventions (i.e. £400 maximum on summary conviction).

These regulations do not affect any obligation arising under the Building Regulations and byelaws which apply in different parts of Great Britain, and both sets of provisions should be consulted where gas appliances are installed or other gas installation work or alterations done which affect the structure.

Part V: Installation of Gas Appliances

Regulation 44

(1) Any person who installs a gas appliance on any premises shall comply in so doing with the following provisions in this Part of these regulations.

(2) Where such a person carries out the installation in the performance of a contract of service his employer shall ensure that the following provisions in this Part of these regulations are duly complied with.

(3) Where a person installs a gas appliance on any premises forming part of a factory, the occupier shall ensure that the following provisions in this Part of these regulations are duly complied with.

Regulation 45

(1) All gas appliances shall be installed by competent persons.

(2) No gas appliance shall be installed unless:

(a) the appliance and the gas fittings and other works for the supply of gas to be used in connection with the appliance,

(b) the means of removal of the products of combustion from the appliance,

(c) the availability of sufficient supply of air for the appliance for proper combustion,

(d) the means of ventilation to the room or internal space in which the appliance is to be used, and

(e) the general conditions of installation including the connection of the appliance to any other gas fitting,

and such as to ensure that the appliance can be used without constituting a danger to any person or property.

Regulation 46

(1) A person shall not install a gas appliance if the appliance and the gas fittings and any flue or means of ventilation to be used in connection with the appliance do not:

(a) if in Greater London, other than an outer London borough, comply with any such provisions of the London Building Acts and any byelaws made thereunder,

(b) if in other parts of England or Wales, comply with any such provisions of the building regulations, or

(c) if in Scotland, comply with any such provisions of the building standards regulations.,

as are in force at the date of installation of the appliance.

(2) A person who has installed a gas appliance shall forthwith after installation test its connection to the installation pipe to verify that it is gastight and examine the appliance and the gas fittings, etc., to be used in connection with the appliance and make any necessary adjustment in order to ensure:

(a) that the appliance has been installed in accordance with the foregoing provisions of this Part of these regulations,

(b) that the heat input and operating pressure are as recommended by the manufacturer,

(c) that all gas safety controls are in proper working order; and

(d) that, without prejudice to the generality of sub-paragraph (a), any flue system or means of removal of the products of combustion form the appliance and any means of ventilation and of supply of combustion air provided in connectioni with the use of the appliance are in safe working order.

REGULATIONS FOR THE ELECTRICAL EQUIPMENT OF BUILDINGS, 15TH EDITION

(Prepared and issued by The Institution of Electrical Engineers)

Note:

When installations comply with the current edition of the Regulations, they are deemed to fulfil the requirements of the Electricity Supply Regulations Nos. 26, 27, 28, 29, and 31. The supply authorities are only obliged to supply installations which comply, so the I.E.E. Regulations are the effective requirement. The regulations are designed to ensure safety, especially from fire and shock, in the utilisation of electricity in and about buildings.

Part 1: Scope, Object and Fundamental Requirements for Safety
> Scope
> Object and effects
> Fundamental requirements for safety

Part 2: Definitions

Part 3: Assessment of General Characteristics
> Purposes, supplies and structure
> External influences
> Compatibility
> Maintainability

Part 4: Protection for Safety
> Protection against electric shock
> Protection against thermal effects
> Protection against overcurrent
> Isolation and switching
> Application of protective measures for safety

Part 5: Selection and Erection of Equipment
> Common rules
> Cables, conductors, and wiring materials
> Switchgear
> Earthing arrangements and protective conductors
> Other equipment

Part 6: Inspection and Testing
> Initial inspection and testing
> Alterations to installations
> Periodic inspection and testing

EXTRACT FROM BUILDING RESEARCH STATION DIGEST 15

Design

It is common practice to provide the plumbing contractor with copies of drawings prepared in compliance with the local authority's requirements for approval under general building byelaws (now Building Regulations) and on them merely to indicate the positions of sink, bath, basin, etc. These drawings (which need not be to a scale larger than $\frac{1}{8}$ in (1:100) or in some cases $\frac{1}{16}$ in (1:200) to the foot) are not intended to determine the system in all its technical details, and the resulting installation, governed mainly by costs and by the need to comply with the water authority's requirements, may not be wholly satisfactory to the user. It cannot be emphasised too strongly that an installation, to be free of faults and dependable, must be functionally designed in relation to the building it is to serve, and that this calls for considerable understanding of the design principles involved. The builder or plumber should be provided with working drawings showing clearly, on an appropriately large scale, the position and full description of appliances, pipe runs, valves and other fittings, methods of fixing, protection and all other information which may affect the functioning of the system.

METRIC-IMPERIAL EQUIVALENTS

Data Concerning Water

Density
At 4°C (39.2°F) 999.9kg per m³ (usually taken as 1000 kg per m³ or 1 tonne)
  62.428 lb per ft³ (1 lb = 0.454 kg)
At 10°C (50°F) 999.7 kg per m³
  62.411 lb per ft³

Liquid Measure
1 fluid ounce = 28.413cm³ or 28413mm³
1 pint = 0.568 litre (dm³) or 568 ml
1 quart = 1.137 litre (dm³)
1 gallon (Imperial) = 4.546 litre
1 gallon (US) = 3.7853 litre
1 ft³ = 28.32 litre (0.0283m³)
1 yd³ = 0.765m³ or 765 litre
1m³ = 1000 litre (34.315 ft³ or 1.309 yd³ or 1000 000 000mm³)

The Litre
Volume if cubed 100 × 100 × 100mm (0.1 × 0.1 × 0.1m) =
  1 000 000mm³ (0.001m³) or 10^{-3}m³
Area of base if cubed 100 × 100mm = 10 000mm² (0.01m² or 15.5 in² or 0.1076 ft²)

1 dm³ (cubic decimetre)
1000 g or 1 milligram or 1 millilitre
1 kg (kilogram)
0.001 tonne
35.3 oz (ounce)
2.205 lb (pound)
61.02 in³ (cubic inch)
0.035 ft³ (cubic foot)
1.76 pt (pint)
0.22 gallon (Imperial)
0.26423 gallon (US)

Force
1 N/m² = 0.1020mm 'head' or 0.000145 lbf/in² or 0.021 lbf/ft² or 0.01 mbar or 0.004 in 'head'
1mm 'head' = 9.807 N/m² (at 4°C)
1 in 'head' = 249.089 N/m² (at 4°C) or 0.036 lbf/in² or 25.4mm 'head'
1 mbar = 0.402 in 'head' or 100 N/m² or 10.2mm 'head' or 0.0334 ft 'head'
1 ft 'head' = 2989.07 N/m² (at 4°C) or 2.989 kN/m² or 0.434 lbf/in² or 0.305m 'head'
1 kN/m² = 0.145 lbf/in² or 20.8854 lbf/ft²
1 lbf/in² =6894.76 n/m² or 6.895 kN/m² or 2.3 ft 'head' or 68.95 mbar
1 lbf/ft² = 47.88 N/m²
1 metre 'head' = 9.807 kN/m² (at 10°C) or 3.281 ft 'head' or 1.424 lbf/in²
1 bar = 1000 mbar or 10^5N/m² or 100 kN/m² or 14.5 lbf/in² or 33.45 ft 'head' or 10.2m 'head'
1 MN/m² = 1 N/mm²

GENERAL

	Imperial to Metric		Metric to Imperial	
Length	1 inch	25.40mm	1 millimetre	0.03937 in
	1 inch	0.0254m	1 metre	39.37 in
	1 foot	304.8mm	1 metre	3.281 ft
	1 foot	0.3048m	1 metre	1.094 yd
	1 yard	914.4mm	1 metre	0.0497 chain
	1 yard	0.9144m	1 kilometre	3280.99 ft
	1 chain	20.1168m	1 kilometre	1093.66 yd
	1 mile	1.609km	1 kilometre	0.6214 mile
Area	1 inch^2	645.2mm^2	1 millimetre^2	0.00155 in^2
	1 foot^2	0.0929m^2	1 metre^2	10.764 ft^2
	1 yard^2	0.8361m^2	1 metre^2	1.196 yd^2
	1 acre	4047m^2	1 metre^2	0.00025 acre
	1 acre	0.4047 ha	1 hectare (ha) (100 000m^2)	2.471 acre
	1 acre	0.004km^2	1 kilometre^2	247.105 acre
	1 mile^2	258.999 ha	1 kilometre^2	0.3861 mile^2
	1 mile^2	2.59km^2	1 decimetre^3 (litre) (1000 ml)	1.760 pint
Volume	1 inch^3	16387mm^3	1 decimetre^3 (litre) (1000 ml)	0.035 ft^3
	1 inch^3	16.387 cm^3 or ml	1 decimetre^3 (litre) (1000ml)	0.220 Imp. gal
	1 inch^3	0.01639 litre	1 decimetre^3 (litre) (1000ml)	0.2642 US gal
	1 foot^3	28.32 dm^3 or litre	1 metre^3	35.315 ft^3
	1 foot^3	0.02832m^3	1 metre^3	1.308 yd^3
	1 yard^3	764.56 dm^3 or litre		
	1 yard^3	0.7646m^3		
Flow Rate	1 gallon/second	4.546 l/h		
	1 gallon/minute	0.07577 l/s		
	1 gallon/minute	0.272m^3/h		
	1 gallon/hour	4.546 l/h		
	1 gal/person per day	4.546l/p day		
	1 foot^3/second (cusec)	0.02832m^3/s (cumec)	1 litre/second	13.198 gal/min
	1 foot^3/second (cusec)	28.32 dm^3/s (l/s)	1 metre^3/second (cumec)	35.31 ft^3/s (cusec)
	1 foot^3/minute (cumin)	0.03m^3/minute	1 metre^3/second (cumec)	19.01 mgd
	1 foot^3/minute (cumin)	0.0004719m^3/s (cumec)	1 metre^3/hour	3.675 Imp gal/h
	1 foot^3/minute (cumin)	0.4719 dm^3/s (l/s)	1 metre^3/metre^2	183.9 Imp gal/yd^2
	1 million gal/day (mgd)	0.05261m^3/s (cumec)		
	1 gallon/yard^2	0.005437m^3/m^2		
Mass	1 ounce	28.35 g	1 gram	15.432 gr
	1 pound	453.6 g	1 gram	0.035 oz
	1 pound	0.4536 kg	1 kilogram	35.28 oz
	1 cwt	50.802 kg	1 kilogram	2.205 lb
	1 cwt	0.051 tonne	1 kilogram	0.0197 cwt
	1 ton	1016 kg	1 kilogram	0.00098 ton
	1 ton	1.016 tonne	1 tonne (1 Mg or 1000 kg)	0.9842 ton
			1 tonne (1 Mg or 1000 kg)	2204 lb
Density	1 pound/inch^3	27.68 g/cm^3	1 kilogram/metre^3	0.06243 lb/ft^3
	1 pound/foot^3	0.016 g/m^3		
	1 pound/foot^3	16.019 kg/m^3		

Force	1 ounce force	0.278 N			
	1 pound force	4.448 N			
	1 ton force	9.964 kN			
Force Per Unit Length	1 pound f/foot linear	14.5939 N/m	1 newton	0.2248 lbf	
	1 pound f/inch linear	175.127 N/m			
Mass Per Unit Length	1 pound/foot	1.48816 kg/m	1 kilogram/metre	0.67197 lb/ft	
	1 pound/yard	0.49606 kg/m	1 kilogram/metre	2.01591 lb/yd	
Power	1 horse power	745.7 W	1 kilowatt	1.341 hp	
	1 horse power	0.7457 kW			
Motion	1 foot/second	0.3048 m/s			
	1 foot/minute	0.3048m/min	1 metre/second	3.281 ft/s	
	1 foot/minute	0.005m/s	1 metre/second	196.85 ft/min	
	1 mile/hour	0.447m/s	1 kilometre/hour	0.6214 mph	
	1 mile/hour	1.609 km/h			
Temperature	1° Fahrenheit	0.555°C	1° Celsius (Centigrade)	1.8°F	
Quantity of Heat	1 British Thermal Unit (Btu)	1055.1 J (J = Ws = Nm)	1 joule	0.000948 Btu	
	1 Btu	1.0551 kJ	1 kilojoule	0.948 Btu	
	1 kilowatt hour	3.6×10^{6} J			
	1 kilowatt hour	3.6 MJ	1 megajoule	0.2778 kWh	
	1 therm (100,000 Btu)	1.066×10^{8} J	1 kilojoule	0.0000095 therm	
	1 therm	105.506 MJ	1 megajoule	0.0095 therm	
	1 therm	1.055×10^{-1} GJ	1 gigajoule	9.4787 therm	
Heat Flow Rate	1 Btu/hour	0.2931 W (W = Js = Nm/s)	1 watt	3.412 Btu/hour	
	1 Btu/hour	0.000293 kW	1 kilowatt	3412 Btu/hour (1 kJ/s)	
Intensity of Heat Flow Rate	1 Btu/hour ft²	3.155 W/m² (W/m² = J/m²s)	1 watt/metre²	0.317 Btu/ft²h	
	1 watt/ft²	10.76 W/m²	1 watt/metre²	0.0929 watt/ft²	
Thermal Conductivity	1 Btu inch/hour ft²°F	0.1442 W/m²°C (W/m°C = Wm/m²°C)	1 watt/metre°C	6.934 Btu in/ft²h°F	
Thermal Conductance	1 Btu/hour ft²°F	5.678 W/m²°C (W/m²°C = Jm²s°C)	1 watt/metre²°C	0.1761 Btu/h ft²°F	
Thermal Resistivity	1ft² hour°F/Btu inch	6.934m°C/W (m°C/W = m²°C/Wm)	1 metre°C/watt	0.1442 ft²h°F/Btu in	
Thermal Resistance	1 ft² hour°F/Btu	0.1761m²°C/W	1 metre²°C/watt	5.678ft²h°F/Btu	
Specific Heat Capacity (weight basis)	1 Btu/pound°F	4187 J/kg°C	1 joule/kilogram°C	0.00024 Btu/lb°F	
	1 Btu/pound°F	4.187 kJ/kg°C	1 kilojoule/kilogram°C	0.239 Btu/lb°F	
Specific Heat Capacity (volume basis)	1 Btu/ft³°F	67.07 Kj/m³°C	1 kilojoule/metre³°C	0.0149 Btu/ft³°F	

Calorific Value (weight basis)	1 Btu/pound	2.326 kJ/kg	1 kilojoule/kilogram	0.4299 Btu/lb
Calorific Value (volume basis)	1 Btu/gallon	0.232 kJ/litre	1 kilojoule/litre	4.310 Btu/gal
	1 Btu/cubic foot	0.0373 J/cm³	1 joule/cubic centimetre	26.81 Btu/ft³
	1 Btu/cubic foot	37.258 kJ/m³	1 kilojoule/cubic metre	0.0268 Btu/ft³
	1 Btu/cubic foot	37258 J/m³	1 joule/cubic metre	0.0000268 Btu/ft³
	1 therm/gallon	23.298 MJ/dm³	1 megajoule/cubic decimetre	0.0431 therm/gal
	1 therm/gallon	23.208 GJ/m³	1 gigajoule/cubic metre	0.0431 therm/gas

SI Standard Units

Atmospheric pressure $= 101325\ N/m^2$ or 1.01325 bar
Gravity $= 9.80665\ m/s^2$

Decimal multiples and Sub-multiples

Number	Multiple	Prefix	Symbol
1 000 000 000 000	10^{12}	tera	T
1 000 000 000	10^{9}	giga	G
1 000 000	10^{6}	mega	M
1000	10^{3}	kilo	k
100	10^{2}	hecto	h
10	10^{1}	deca	da
0.1	10^{-1}	deci	d
0.01	10^{-2}	centi	e
0.001	10^{-3}	milli	m
0.000 001	10^{-6}	micro	u
0.000 000 001	10^{-9}	nano	n
0.000 000 000 001	10^{-12}	pico	p

BIBLIOGRAPHY

British Standards Institution Publications

Codes of Practice

CP 99: 1972	Frost precautions for water services
CP 310: 1965	Water Supply
CP 324.202: 1951	Domestic electric water-heating installations
CP 342: 1950	Centralised domestic hot water supply
CP 342:	Part 1: 1970 Centralised hot water supply: individual dwellings
	Part 2: 1974 Centralised hot water supply: buildings other than individual dwellings
CP 403: 1974	Installation of domestic heating and cooking appliances burning solid fuel.

British Standards

B.S. 41: 1973 (1981)	Cast iron spigot and socket flue or smoke pipes and fittings.
B.S. 417	Galvanised mild steel cisterns and covers, tanks and cylinders.
	Part 1: 1964 Imperial units
	Part 2: 1973 Metric units
B.S. 567: 1973 (1984)	Asbestos-cement flue pipes and fittings, light quality.
B.S. 699: 1984	Copper cylinders for domestic purposes.
B.S. 715: 1970	Sheet metal flue pipes and accessories for gas fired appliances.
B.S. 759	Part 1: 1984 Specification for valves, mounting and fittings.
	Part 2: 1975 (Obsolescent) Safety valves.
B.S. 779: 1976	Cast iron boilers for central heating and hot water supply (44 kW rating and above).
B.S. 835: 1973 (1984)	Asbestos-cement flue pipes and fittings, heavy quality.
B.S. 843: 1976	Thermal-storage electric water heaters (construction and water requirements).
B.S. 853: 1981	Calorifiers for central heatiing and hot water supply.
B.S. 855: 1976	Welded steel boilers for central heating and indirect hot water supply (44 kW to 3 MW).
B.S. 1010	Draw-off taps and stopvalves for water services (screwdown pattern).
	Part 2: 1973 Draw-off taps and above-ground stopvalves.
B.S. 1212	Ballvalves (excluding floats).
	Part 1: 1983 Piston type
	Part 2: 1970 Diaphragm type (brass body).
B.S. 1289: 1975	Precast concrete flue blocks for domestic gas appliances.
B.S. 1415	Mixing valves.
	Part 1: 1976 Non-thermostatic, non-compensating mixing valves.
B.S. 1563: 1949 (1964)	Cast iron sectional tanks (rectangular).
B.S. 1564: 1975 (1983)	Pressed steel sectional rectangular tanks.
B.S. 1565	Galvanised mild steel indirect cylinders, annular or saddle back type.
	Part 1: 1949 Imperial units.
	Part 2: 1973 Metric units.

B.S. 1566	Copper indirect cylinders for domestic purposes.
	Part 1: 1984 Double feed indirect cylinders.
	Part 2: 1984 Single feed indirect cylinders.
B.S. 1846	Glossary of terms relating to solid fuel burning equipment.
	Part 1: 1968 Domestic appliances.
	Part 2: 1968 (1984) Industrial water heating and steam raising installations.
B.S. 1968: 1953	Floats for ballvalves (copper)
B.S. 2456: 1973	Floats (plastic) for ballvalves for hot and cold water.
B.S. 2767: 1972	Valves and unions for hot water radiators.
B.S. 2777: 1974	Asbestos-cement cisterns.
B.S. 2879: 1980	Draining taps (screw-down patterns).
B.S. 3198: 1981	Combination hot water storage units (copper) for domestic purposes.
B.S. 3377: 1985	Back boilers for use with domestic solid fuel appliances.
B.S. 3378: 1972	Room heaters burning solid fuel.
B.S. 3456	Safety of household electrical appliances.
	Sec. 2.7: 1970 Stationary non-instantaneous water heaters.
	Sec. 2.21: 1972 Electric immersion heaters.
	Sec. 3.9: 1979 Stationary instantaneous water heaters.
B.S. 3955	Part 3: 1979 Electrical controls for domestic appliances, general and specific requirements.
B.S. 3958: 1969-1985	Thermal insulating materials (in six parts).
B.S. 3999	Methods of measuring the performance of household electrical appliances.
	Part 2: 1967 (1985) Thermal-storage electric water heaters.
B.S. 4118: 1981	Glossary of sanitation terms.
B.S. 4213: 1975	Cold water storage cisterns (polyolefin or olefin copolymer) and cistern covers.
B.S. 4433	Solid smokeless fuel boilers with rated outputs up to 45 kW.
	Part 1: 1973 Boilers with undergrate ash removal.
	Part 2: 1969 Gravity feed boilers designed to burn small anthracite.
B.S. 4543: 1976	Factory-made insulated chimneys (in three parts).
B.S. 4994: 1973	Vessels and tanks in reinforced plastics.
B.S. 5154: 1983	Copper Alloy globe, globe stop and check, check and gate valves for general purposes.
B.S. 5258	Safety of domestic gas appliances.
	Part 1: 1975 Central heating boilers and circulators.
	Part 2: 1977 Storage water heaters.
B.S. 5386	Gas burning appliances.
	Part 1: 1976 Gas-burning appliances for instantaneous production of hot water for domestic use.
	Part 2: 1981 Mini water heaters (2nd and 3rd family gases).
B.S. 5388: 1976 (1981)	Specification for spray taps.
B.S. 5410	Code of Practice for oil firing.
	Part 1: 1977 Installations up to 44 kW output capacity for space heating and hot water supply purposes. (Also Parts 2 (44 kW and over) and 3).
B.S. 5412	Specification for the performance of draw-off taps with metal bodies for water services.

B.S. 5413	Specification for the performance of draw-off taps with plastic bodies for water services (in five parts, all dated 1976).
B.S. 5422: 1977	Specification for the use of thermal insulating materials.
B.S. 5440	Code of Practice for flues and air supply for gas appliances of rated input not exceeding 60 kW.
	Part 1: 1978 Flues.
	Part 2: 1976 Air supply.
B.S. 5482	Code of Practice for domestic butaine- and propane-gas burning appliances.
	Part 1: 1979 Installations in permanent dwellings.
B.S. 5546: 1979	Code of Practice for installation of gas hot water supplies for domestic purposes (2nd family gases).
B.S. 5615: 1978	Insulating jackets for domestic hot water storage cylinders.
B.S. 5779: 1979	Specification for spray mixing taps.
B.S. 5918: 1980	Code of practice for solar heating systems for domestic hot water.
B.S. 5970: 1981	Code of Practice for thermal insulation of pipework and equipment (in the temperature range of -100°C to +870°C).
B.S. 5997: 1980	Guide to British Standard Codes of Practice for building services.
B.S. 6461	Part 1 Code of Practice for masonry chimneys and flue pipes.
	Part 2: 1984 Code of Practice for factory-made insulated chimneys for internal applications.

British Standards and Codes of Practice are available from the British Standards Institution, 2 Park Street, London W1A 2BS. Telephone: 01-629-9000

RELEVANT PUBLICATIONS

Building Regulations 1985 (HMSO).

Building Standards (Scotland) (Consolidation) Regulations 1971 (HMSO).

Building Standards (Scotland) Amendment Regulations 1973 (HMSO).

Building Standards (Scotland) Amendment Regulations 1975 (HMSO).

BRE Current Paper CP 44/78: *The Efficiency of Domestic Hot Water Production out of the Heating Season* (G.E. Whittle & P.R. Warren).

BRE Digest 15: *Pipes and Fittings for Domestic Water Supply* (HMSO).

BRE Digest 60: *Domestic Chimneys for Independent Boilers* (HMSO).

BRE Digest 146: *Modernising Plumbing Systems* (HMSO).

BRE Digest 205: *Domestic Water Heating by Solar Energy* (HMSO).

DoE Advisory Leaflet No. 3: *Lagging Hot and Cold Water Systems* (HMSO).

No. 30: *Installing Solid Fuel Appliances (1) — Open Fires and Convectors* (HMSO).

No. 31: *Installing Solid Fuel Appliances (2) — Heaters, Independent Boilers and Cookers* (HMSO).

No. 41: *Frost Precautions* (HMSO).

No. 50: *Chimneys for Domestic Boilers* (HMSO).

Engineering Specifications — Standard Specifications M & E — No. 3: *Heating and Cold Water, Steam and Gas Installations for Buildings* (HMSO).

No. 4: *Central Heating and Hot and Cold Water Installatioons for Dwellings* (HMSO).

Gas Safety Regultions 1972 (S.I. 1972 No. 1178) (HMSO).

Homes for Today and Tomorrow (Parker Morris Report) (HMSO).

Model Water Byelaws (1966 edition) (HMSO).

MoH & LG Design Bulletins: *Service Cores in High Flats* (HMSO).

National Building Studies Research Paper 34: *A Study of Space Heating and Water Heating in Local Authority Flats 1956-59* (HMSO).

Barton, F.J.: *Domestic Heating Data* (H. & V. Publications Ltd.).

BEDA: *Electric Water Handbook — A Guide to Practical Design and Installation* (obsolete).

British Gas: *Gas in Housing — a Technical Guide* (1983 edition).

CIBS: *Domestic Engineering Services* (Report prepared for IVHE, now CIBS).

—: Guide Book B: *Installation and Equipment Data* (IVHE now CIBS).

—: Guide Book C: *Reference Data* (IHVE now CIBS).

Dye, F.W.: *Heating and Hot Water Work* (E. & F. N. Spon, Ltd.).

—: *Hot Water Supply* (E. & F. N. Spon, Ltd.).

Electricity Council: *An Outline Guide to Electric Space and Water Heating.*

—: *An Outline Guide to Electric Space and Water Heating for Small Commercial Premises.*

—: *The Design of Water Heating Systems in New Homes.*

—: *Electric Water Heating.*

Institution of Electrical Engineers: *Regulations for the Electrical Equipment of Buildings* (15th edition).

Institute of Plumbing: *Data Book.*

Solid Fuel Advisory Service: *Solid Fuel Heating.*

GOVERNMENT DEPARTMENTS, COUNCILS, ASSOCIATIONS, RESEARCH ESTABLISHMENTS, INSTITUTIONS, etc.

British Electrotechnical Approvals Board, Mark House, The Green, 9-11 Queen's Road, Hersham, Walton-on-Thames, Surrey KT12 5NA. 093-22 44401-9

British Gas Corporation, 59, Bryanston Street, Marble Arch, London W1A 2AZ 01-723 7030

British Gas Corporation, Research & Development Division, Watson House, Peterborough Road, London SW6 3HN. 01-736 1212

British Oil & Gas Firing Equipment Manufacturers Association, The Fernery, Market Placer, Midhurst, Sussex. 073-081 2782

British Valve Manufacturers Association, 14, Pall Mall, London SW1Y 5LZ. 01-930 7171

British Waterworks Association, 34, Park Street, London W1Y 4BL. 01-499 1092

Building Research Advisory Services. Advisory Centres at:

Building Research Station, Garston, Watford WD2 7JR. 092-73 76612

Birmingham Engineering & Building Centre, Broad Street, Birmingham B1 2DB. 021-643 8961

Princes Risborough Laboratory, Princes Risborough, Aylesbury, Bucks HP17 9PX. 084-44 3101

Fire Research Station, Borehamwood, Herts WD6 2BL. 01-953 6177

Building Research Establishment, Scottish Laboratory, Kelvin Road, East Kilbride, Glasgow G75 0RZ. 041 33941

Building Services Research and Information Association, Old Bracknell Lane, Bracknell, Berks RG12 4AH. 0344-25071-5

Chartered Institution of Building Services, Delta House, 222 Balham High Road, London SW12 9BS. 01-675 5211

Copper Cylinder and Boiler Manufacturers Association, 20, Princess Street, Manchester M1 4LT. 061-236 3668-9

Copper Development Association, Orchard House, Mutton Lane, Potters Bar, Herts EN6 3AP. 77 50711

Department of Energy, Thames House South, Millbank, London SW1P 4QJ. 01-211 3000

Department of Environment, 2 Marsham Street, London SW1P 3EB. 01-212 3434

Domestic Oil Burning Equipment Testing Association Ltd., 2 Savoy Place, Victoria Embankment, London WC2R 0BN. 01-438 3370

Electric Research Association Ltd., Cleeve Road, Leatherhead, Surrey KT22 7SA. 037-23 74151

Electricity Council, Marketing Department, 30, Millbank, London SW1P 4RD. 01-834 2333

Institute of Plumbing, Scottish Mutual House, North Street, Hornchurch, Essex RM11 1RU. 040-24 51236

Institution of Electrical Engineers, Savoy Place, London WC2R 0BL 01-240 1871

Institution of Public Health Engineers, 13 Grosvenor Place, Belgravia, London SW1X 7EN. 01-245 9778

National Building Agency, NBA House, Arundel Street, London WC2R 3DZ. 01-836 4488

National Coal Board, Hobart House, Grosvenor Place, London SW1X 7AE. 01-235 2020

NCB Coal Research Establishment, Stoke Orchard, Gloucestershire. 024-267 3361

National House Building Council, 58, Portland Place, London W1N 4BV. 01-387 7201

National Water Council, 1, Queen Anne's Gate, London SW1H 9BT. 01-930 3100

Property Services Agency, DoE, Lambeth Bridge House, Albert Embankment, London SE1 7SB. 01-211 4478

Shower Information Bureau, Whaddon Works, Cheltenham GL52 5EP. 0242 56317

Solid Fuel Advisory Service, Hobart House, Grosvenor Place, London SW1X 7AE. 01-723 7030

Water Research Centre, Elder Way, Stevenage, Herts SG1 1TH. 0438 2444

DIRECTORY OF MANUFACTURERS

from whom further information may be obtained

Advance Services plc, 77-83 Upper Richmond Road, Putney, London SW15 2TD 01-789 6571

Aga-Rabyburn, Glynwed Appliances Ltd, PO Box 30, Ketley, Telford, Shropshire 0952 3973

Andrews Industrial Equipment Ltd., Dudley Road, Wolverhampton WV2 3DB. (e.g. gas appliances) 0902 58111

Aqualiser Products Ltd., Morewood, London Road, Sevenoaks, Kent TN13 2HU. (showers) 0732 50944

Aquatron (Showers) Ltd., Homer Works, Sterling Road, Shirley, Solihull, West Midlands B90 4NB 021-704 4193

Barking-Grohe, 5-13, River Road, Barking, Essex 1G11 0HD. (mixers and showers) 01-594 7292

Bartol Plastics Ltd., Edlington, Doncaster, Yorkshire DN12 1BY. (e.g. cisterns) 0709 863551

Beeston Boiler Co. (Successors) Ltd., Beeston, Nottingham NG9 2DN. 0602 254271

Belco Manufacturing Co. Ltd., Concord House, 241 City Road, London WC1V 1JD

Braithwaite & Co., Structual Ltd., Neptune Works, Newport, Gwent NPT 2UY. (sectional tanks) 0633 62141

Chaffoteaux Ltd., Concord House, Brighton Road, Salfords, Redhill RH1 5DX. (instantaneous gas) 029-34 72744

Crane Ltd., 11, Bouverie Street, London EC4. (bronze and cast iron ware) 01-353 6511

Damixa Ltd., 10 Woodcock Road East, Warminster, Wilts (mixers and showers) 0985 214683

Davison T. R. Ltd., Coity Road, Bridgend, Mid Glamorgan CF31 1LR. ('Primary' cylinder) 0656 4082

W. H. Dean (High Wycombe) Ltd., Wooburn Green, High Wycombe, Bucks HP10 0HH (gas circulators) 062 85 25011

Delglo Appliances Ltd., Burton Road, Blackpool FY4 4NL. (water storage) 0253 64811

Deltaflow Ltd., Showell Road, Wolverhampton, W. Midlands 0902 733221

Dolphin Showers Ltd., Bromwich Road, Worcester WR2 4BD 0905 422487

Econa (Products) Ltd., Drayton Road, Shirley, Solihull, West Midlands B90 4XA. (pre-fabricated plumbing units)
    021-705 4981

Fibreglass Ltd., Insulation Division, St. Helens, Merseyside WA10 3TR. (cylinder insulation) 0774 24022

Gainsborough Electrical Group, Shefford Road, Aston, Birmingham B6 4PL. (electric instantaneous) 021-359 5631

Gledhill N. & Co. Ltd., Burton Road, Blackpool FY4 4NL. ('Aeromatic' cylinder) 0253 64811

Gledhill Water Storage Ltd., Sycamore Trading Estate, Squires Gate Lane, Blackpool FY4 3RL 0253 401494

Glow-worm Ltd. (as for Radiation-Ascot) (boilers)

Heatpak Ltd., 15, Raynham Road Industrial Estate, Bishops Stortford, Herts. ('Impala' 'Harcoheat'). 0279 55031

Heatrae-Sadia Heating Ltd., Hurricane Way, Norwich Airport, Norwich NR6 6EA. (electric water heating) 0603 44144

Heatstat Ltd., P.O. Box 2, Rankine Street, Johnstone, Renfrewshire PA5 8BE. (indirect cylinders) 0505 21458

Hodgson & Hodgson, Crown Industrial Estate, Anglesey Road, Burton-on-Trent. (cylinder insulation) 0283 64772-4

Ideal Standard Ltd., P.O. Box 60, National Avenue, Kingston-upon-Hull HU5 4JE. (e.g. mixers and showers) 0482 46461

IMI Opella Ltd., Twyford Road, Rotherwas Industrial Estate, Hereford HR2 6JR. (heaters, mixers and showers)
    0432 57331

IMI Santon Ltd., Somerton Works, Newport, Gwent NPT 0XU. (electric water heating) 0633 277711

Johnson & Starley Ltd., Rhosili Road, Northampton NN4 0LZ 0604 62881

Kitson's Insulation Products Ltd., Kitson House, P.O. Box 4, London Road, Barking, Essex. (cylinder insulation)
    01-594 5544

Lennox Industries Ltd., P.O. Box 43, Lister Road, Basingstoke, Hampshire RG22 4AR. (gas storage) 0256 61261

Main Gas Appliances Ltd. (Thorn Group), Gothic Works, Wyre Street, Padiham, Lancs. 0282 72525

Marley Flue, Stifford Road, South Ockenden, Essex. 040-25 6411

Mather & Platt Ltd., Park Works, Newton Heath, Manchester M10 6BA. (sectional tanks) 061-205 2321

Meynell Valves Ltd., Bushbury, Wolverhampton WV10 9LB. (mixers and showers) 0902 28621

New World (Gas Heating) Ltd., Thimble Mill Lane, Aston, Birmingham B6 7QZ. 021-327 1580

Park Sectional Insulating Co. Ltd., Chimney Division, 244, Romford Road, Forest Gate, London E7 9HZ (flues for all
    fuels) 01-534 7695/7435

Peglers Ltd., Belmont Works, Doncaster, S. Yorks DN4 8DF. (plumbers' brasswork) 0302 68581

Perkins Boilers Ltd., Mansfield Road Works, Derby DE2 4BA. 0332-48235

Prometheus Gas Appliances Ltd., Wildemere Road, Banbury, Oxon 0295 61339

Quigley Metal Products Ltd., Oak Street, Quarry Bank, Near Brierly Hill, West Midlands DY5 2JD. (water storage units) 0384 64054

Radiation-Ascot Ltd. (TI Gas Heating), Nottingham Road, Belper, Derby DE5 1JT. 077-382 4141

Stiebel Eltron Ltd., 25-26, Lyveden Road, Brackmills, Northampton NN4 0ED. (electric water heating) 0604 66421

Selkirk Metalbestos, 7, Chesham Place, London, SW1X 5HN. (flues for all fuels) 01-234 0061

Stranks-Monodraught Flues Ltd., Loudwater House, Loudwater, High Wycombe, Bucks. 0494 33128-9

TAC Construction Materials, P.O. Box 22, Trafford Park, Manchester M17 1RU. (cisterns) 061-872 2181

Thermoflue Ltd., Chantry Rise, Llanblethian, Cowbridge, South Glamorgan CF7 7JF. (flues for all fuels) 044-63 2545

Toleries De Grenoble, BP91, Centre de Tri, 38041, Grenoble, Ccedex, France. ('Pacific' electric water heaters)

Topliss Shower Ltd., 18, Victoria Road, Tamworth, Staffs B79 7HR 0827 62621

Triton Aquatherm Ltd., Unit 41, 22, Fourways, Atherstone Industrial Estate, Atherstone, Warwickshire CV9 1LG. (showers) 082-77 5289

True Flue Ltd., 799, London Road, West Thurrock, Grays, Essex RM16 1LR. 040-26 3311

Van Leer (UK) Ltd., General Products Div., West Byfleet, Weybridge, Surrey KT14 6LE. (cisterns) 093-23 41161

Walker Crosweller & Co. Ltd., Whaddon Works, Cheltenham, Gloucestershire GL52 5EP. (water 'mixers') 0242 27953

DESIGN CONSIDERATIONS

GENERAL

The design requirements for all types of buildings, domestic or otherwise, apply equally whether the system is direct or indirect and whether water is heated by solid fuel, gas or oil-fired, or by electricity, and whether the boiler and storage vessel are close-coupled to form a single unit, or are separate entities.

Hot water is required for ablutionary purposes, for the routine cleansing of buildings and apartments and operations such as laundry work, dishwashing, etc. The requirements of an installation for the supply of hot water are that water at the required temperature and in sufficient quantities is available at the draw-off points without delay and that heat is provided for airing linen and heating towel rails. (CP342).

SOME DESIGN CONSIDERATIONS

The following considerations should be taken into account in the planning of hot water installations, as appropriate.

(a) Total consumption
(b) Peak demands
(c) Type of installation, whether local or central
(d) Storage capacity
(e) Method of heating water
(f) Insulation of hot pipes and vessels
(g) Use of circulating system, where appropriate
(h) Choice of materials for installation in relation to the nature of the water.
(j) In connection with pipes and runs:-
(i) mechanical and chemical properties to resist failure,
(ii) prevention of air locks, water hammer, back-siphonage and noise,
(iii) Number of fitments and probable simultaneous demand,
(iv) Available head; and loss of head due to friction in pipes and resistance of meters, bends, fittings, etc,
(v) provision for isolating or emptying parts of the system,
(vi) accessibility for maintenance.

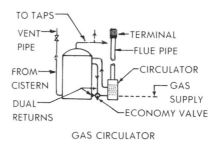

GAS CIRCULATOR

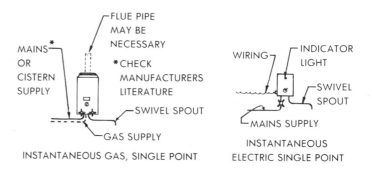

INSTANTANEOUS GAS, SINGLE POINT

INSTANTANEOUS ELECTRIC SINGLE POINT

SOME TYPES MAY SUPPLY MORE THAN ONE POINT

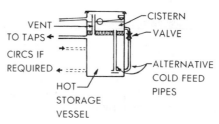

HEAT SUPPLIED BY GAS, ELECTRIC OR BOILER

COMBINATION SYSTEM

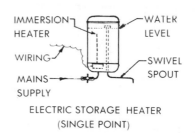

ELECTRIC STORAGE HEATER (SINGLE POINT)

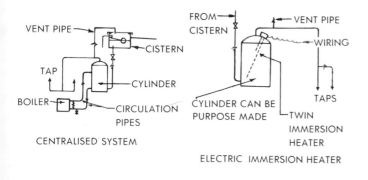

CENTRALISED SYSTEM

ELECTRIC IMMERSION HEATER

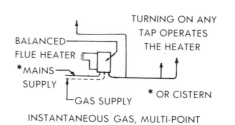

INSTANTANEOUS GAS, MULTI-POINT

REFERENCE DATA
Some conversions are 'rounded off'

Boiler power
'kW from IHVE gal from BS5572

HOT WATER DEMAND, STORAGE AND BOILER POWER							
BUILDING		Maximum Daily Demand per person		Storage per person		Boiler Power to 65°C per person	
		litre	gal	litre	gal	kW	gal
COLLEGES SCHOOLS	Boarding	114	25	23	5	0.7	2.5
	Day	14	3	4.5	1	0.1	0.3
DWELLING HOUSES	Low Rental* (max 950ft² or 88m²)	See particular requirements below					
	Medium Rental* (88m² to 140m²)	114	25	45	10	0.7	3.0
	High Rental* (over 140m²/1500ft²)	136	30	45	10	1.2	4.0
	Factories	14	3	4.5	1	1.2	0.4
FLATS, BLOCKS OF	Low rental* (as above)	68	15	23	5	0.5	1.5
	Medium rental* (as above)	114	25	32	7	0.7	2.5
	High rental* (as above)	136	30	32	7	1.2	3.0
HOSPITALS	General	136	30	27	6	1.5	5.0
	Infectious	227	50	45	10	1.5	5.0
	Infirmaries	68	15	23	5	0.6	2.0
	Infirmaries with laundries	91	20	27	6	0.9	3.0
	Maternity	227	50	32	7	2.1	7.0
	Psychiatric	91	20	23	5	0.7	2.5
	Nurses' homes	136	30	45	10	0.9	3.0
	Hostels	114	25	32	7	0.7	2.5
HOTELS	First class	136	30	45	10	1.2	4.0
	Average	114	25	36	8	0.9	3.0
	Offices	14	3	4.5	1	0.1	0.4
	Sports pavilions with spray showers	36	8	36	8	0.3	1.0

*floor area. NOTE: Hot water demand is given per day of 24 hrs on day of heaviest demand during week. For boiler power given in gallons:- I gal equals 1000 Btu. The boiler power should include for heat losses from towel rails, coils, pipes etc.

PARTICULAR REQUIREMENTS FOR INDIVIDUAL DWELLINGS/FLATS
1 *Storage capacity* :- Base on 45 litres (10gal)/person. Minimum 136 litres (30 gal)
2 *Independent boiler* :- Capacity to heat contents of storage vessel in max. 2½ hours to 65°C (150°F), plus all other loads
3 *Back boiler* :- Cap. 68 litres (15gal) to 27°C (80°F) above feed water temperature in max. 2½ hours 'direct' & 2¾ hours 'indirect'.
4 *Cistern* :- (for H.W. supply only) capacity equal to storage vessel
5 *Outflow* :- with storage temperature 65°C (150°F) hot water should reach open tap at min. 54°C (130°F) within one minute
6 *Towel rail* :- should be provided, plus valve(s) and air cock.

QUANTITIES OF HW USED ASSUMING WATER AT 60°C (140°F)
Bath (per usage) 73.6 litres (16.2). Wash basin (per usage) 14 litres (3.1). Dish washing (per meal) 4.5 litres (1.0). Floor washing and house cleaning (per day) 9.0 litres (2.0). Laundry (per week) 8.2 litres to 24.5 litres (10 to 30). Figures in brackets are gallons. Allow for 20% less H.W. if water temp is 70°C (100°F).

SUGGESTED TEMPERATURES At the draw off point, where applicable		
ITEM	°C	°F
Boiling point at standard conditions	100	212
Industrial use — general	100	212
Laundry work	100	212
Rinsing dishes, utensils, etc	82-88	180-190
Storage temperature*	71	160
Storage temperature (CP342)	66	150
Scalding to the user	66	150
Storage temperature**	60	140
Washing dishes, utensils, pans etc.	† 60	†140
Wash basins, troughs & similar	† 43	†110
Showers (all types)***	43	110
Hot bath****	41	105
Warm bath	37	98
Tepid bath	30	86
Temperate bath	26	78
Cool bath	19	66
Incoming 'mains' temp (average)*****	12	54
Cold bath	7	45

RECOMMENDED RATES OF FLOW		
Appliance or outlet	litre/sec	gal/min
Wash basin tap (15mm/½")	0.15	2.0
Wash basin spray tap	0.04	0.5
Bath tap private (20mm/¾")	0.30	4.0
Bath tap public (25mm/1")	0.60	8.0
Shower with nozzle	0.11	1.5
Shower with 100mm rose	0.30	4.0
Sink tap (15mm/½")	0.19	2.5
Sink tap (20mm/¾")	0.30	4.0
Sink tap (25mm/1")	0.60	8.0
Wash fountain (according to size)	.19 to .38	2.5 to 5.0

*Soft water only
**Hard water
†Minimum temperatures. ***This figure is arguable as opinions differ. Other temperatures quoted vary from 27°C (80°F) to 41°C (105°F) ****Initial temperature would be 43°C (110°F). *****Sometimes taken as 10°C (50°F) for convenience.

SELECTED DEFINITIONS FROM AUTHORITATIVE SOURCES

BOILER A vessel, not open to atmosphere, in which water is heated by direct application of heat to outside of boiler.

BOILER, BACK A boiler fitted at the back of an open fireplace, cooking range, stove or room heater.

BOILER, INDEPENDENT A separate boiler not fitted as part of an open fireplace, cooking range, room heater, etc.

BOWER BARFFING A process for rust proofing cast iron or mild steel in which metal is raised to red heat (900°C) and treated with live superheated steam. The metal takes on a durable layer of black magnetic and other oxide of iron.

CALORIFIER A storage vessel, not open to the atmosphere, in which a supply of water is heated. The vessel contains an element, e.g. a coil of pipe through which is passed a supply of h.w. or steam in such a way that the two supplies do not mix, heat being transferred through the walls of the element.

STORAGE CALORIFIER Stores h.w. as well as a means of heating.

CAPACITY (I) The volume contained in a vessel. (2) Of a storage cistern: the capacity of the cistern measured up to the water line. WATER LINE Highest level water can reach when ballvalve properly adjusted (See Water Byelaws 40 and 4I).

CATHODIC PROTECTION A method of protecting metal pipes or vessels exposed to corrosion. The corrosive action is modified so that the metal to be protected becomes the cathode instead of the anode.

CIRCUIT, CLOSED A system of pipes and fittings in which the same water is circulated and from which no water is drawn off for use, as in a hot water space heating system. (Legally includes the vent pipe but not cold feed pipe.)

CIRCUIT, PRIMARY A circuit in which water circulates between a boiler or other heater, and a h.w. storage vessel.

CIRCUIT, SECONDARY The flow and return pipes through which water circulates from and back to the hot water storage vessel (not boiler). The pipes to the various draw-off points are connected to this circuit.

CISTERN, EXPANSION An open-topped vessel for maintaining the water level in the system and for accommodating increases in volume of water when hot. As it also usually acts as a feed cistern, the term FEED AND EXPANSION CISTERN is often used.

CISTERN FEED Any storage system used for supplying cold water to a hot water apparatus, cylinder or tank.

COMBINATION HOT WATER STORAGE UNIT A hot water supply apparatus, comprising a hot water storage vessel with a cold water feed cistern immediately 'above' it, the two being fabricated together as a compact unit.

CYLINDER A cylindrical closed vessel capable of storing hot water under a pressure greater than atmospheric.

CYLINDER, INDIRECT A cylinder in which water is stored and heated by means of an annular element through which h.w. (from a boiler) is circulated in such a manner that it does not mix with the water stored for use at the taps. Sometimes referred to as CALORIFIER. DIRECT CYLINDER Water for use passes through boiler and is heated directly.

DEAD LEG A length of hot water pipe leading to a draw-off point (e.g. tap), and not forming part of a circuit.

DIVERSITY FACTOR A factor used in the design of pipework to determine the maximum rate of flow to allow for in a pipe. Where there is a large number of taps, it is improbable that all will be in use at the same time. The DF is the probable rate of flow divided by the possible total rate of flow.

ELECTROLYTIC INSULATION To resist transmission of electricty to combat corrosive electrolytic action.

HARDNESS, PERMANENT That part of the hardness of water that remains after the water has been boiled.

HARDNESS, TEMPORARY That part of the hardness of water which can be removed by boiling, when part of the mineral content is precipitated as solid matter. TOTAL HARDNESS Sum of temporary and permanent hardness.

ONE-PIPE CIRCULATION The circulatory flow of a stream of hot water in one direction and a stream of cooler water in the opposite direction at the same time and in the same pipe.

PIPE, COLD FEED A distributing pipe conveying cold water from a cistern to a hot water apparatus.

PIPE, FLOW A pipe in a primary h.w. circuit in which water moves away from the boiler, or a pipe in a secondary h.w. circuit in which the water moves away from the hot water storage vessel.

PIPE, H.W. DISTRIBUTING Any pipe conveying water from a h.w. apparatus supplied from a feed cistern and is under a pressure determined by the height at which the feed cistern is fixed.

PIPE, RETURN Same as above but the water moves vice versa, i.e. back to the boiler, and back to h.w. storage vessel.

PIPE, SAFETY An open pipe, generally run direct from the top of a boiler to a point above the level of the water in the cistern feeding the boiler, and terminates by pointing downwards towards the water in the cistern. (See VENT PIPE).

PIPE, VENT An open pipe taken from any high point of a h.w. apparatus (e.g. top of cylinder) and terminates above the appropriate cistern, pointing in a downward direction. It allows for the escape of air and safe discharge of any steam generated.

PIPE, WARNING An overflow pipe with its outlet in a conspicuous position, terminating inside or outside a building.

SPRAY MIXING TAP A tap supplied with h. and c. and incorporating a mixing device operated by the user. Mixed water is delivered at a restricted rate of flow in the form of a spray. The tap could be supplied with water at pre-set temperature.

SYSTEM, COMBINED A system supplying space heating and domestic hot water from a single source.

SYSTEM, DIRECT A system in which the water supplied to taps has been directly heated in the boiler.

SYSTEM, INDIRECT A system as above, but the water has been indirectly heated in an indirect cylinder.

TANK, HOT WATER Non-cylindrical vessel capable of storing h.w. under pressure greater than atmospheric.

TOWEL RAIL Tubular heating surface usually comprising a series of horizontal rails with vertical ends. Used for airing towels.

VALVE, EMPTYING A tap, cock or valve usually fixed at certain low level positions for draining system, pipe or vessel.

VALVE, REFLUX An automatic valve for preventing the reversal of flow, being opened by the flow and closed by gravity when the flow stops. (Also known as Non-return or Check Valve).

VALVE, SAFETY (OR RELIEF) A device for relieving pressure in excess of that for which the system is designed; it is connected to the boiler or to the return pipe, adjacent to the boiler.

VALVE, THERMOSTATIC MIXING A mixing valve which automatically maintains the mixed water at a pre-selected temperature.

WATER, HARD Water in which soap does not lather freely. WATER, SOFT Water in which soap lathers freely.

WATER, pH An index of the hydrogen ion content ranging from 0 to 14 (below 7 acid; above 7 alkaline).

h = hot   c = cold   w= water

HOT WATER APPARATUS

42 *Distance between hot water apparatus and draw off taps*
Length of any pipe conveying h.w from any h.w. apparatus, h.w. storage cistern, cylinder or tank, or flow and return system to any draw-off tap shall not exceed that specified in respect of that pipe, by reference to the largest diameter of any part of it — see table below.

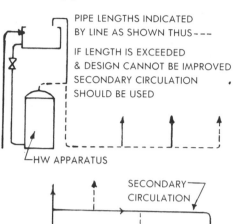

PIPE LENGTHS INDICATED
BY LINE AS SHOWN THUS ---

IF LENGTH IS EXCEEDED
& DESIGN CANNOT BE IMPROVED
SECONDARY CIRCULATION
SHOULD BE USED

HW APPARATUS

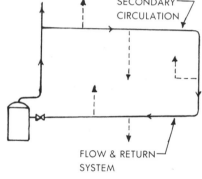

SECONDARY CIRCULATION

FLOW & RETURN SYSTEM

Largest internal diam of pipe	length	
	ft	m
Not exceeding ¾ in (19mm)	40	12.2
Exceeding ¾ but not exceeding 1"	25	7.6
Exceeding 1" (25mm)	10	3.1

TABLE: MAXIMUM LENGTH OF DEAD ENDS

43 *Position of outlets in relation to level of water in cylinders and tanks*
No tap (other than drain tap with removable key) shall be connected to any part of hw system in such a position that by its use the level of the water in the hw storage cistern, cylinder or tank can be lowered (a) below the level of the top of any pipe connecting storage vessel to the heating apparatus; (b) more than ½ cistern depth or ¼ depth of cylinder or tank. Provisos (i) only applies to lowest vessel (ii) does not apply to open-topped vessel directly heated or thermostatic controlled app. by gas, electricity or oil.

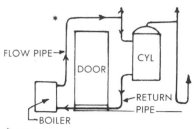

FLOW PIPE→   DOOR   CYL
RETURN PIPE
BOILER
* WATER LEVEL HERE CAN BE LOWERED

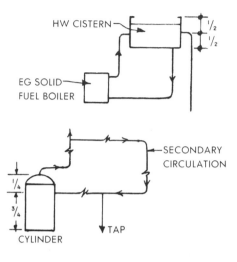

HW CISTERN
½
½
EG SOLID FUEL BOILER
SECONDARY CIRCULATION
CYLINDER
¼
¾
TAP

44 *H.W. Cisterns not to have ballvalve*
No hot water storage cistern shall be fitted with a ballvalve.

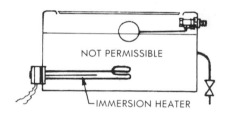

NOT PERMISSIBLE
IMMERSION HEATER

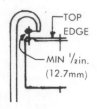

TOP EDGE

MIN ½in. (12.7mm)

45 *Outlets from feed cisterns to hw apparatus*

Every pipe whichy delivers water from a feed cistern to a hw apparatus not of the instantaneous type or to a hw cylinder or tank shall deliver water to that apparatus cylinder or tank only.

FEED CISTERN

VENT PIPE

VALVE

DRAW OFF POINT

COLD FEED PIPE

THIS PIPE TO BE USED FOR NO OTHER PURPOSE

HW DISTRIBUTING PIPE

FLOW PIPE

DRAW OFF POINT

CYLINDER

SERVICE PIPE

RETURN PIPE

BOILER

SAFETY VALVE

DRAIN TAP

FEED & STORAGE CISTERN

FLUE SHOWN DIAGRAMMATIC ONLY

MULTI-PURPOSE PIPE

CW DISTRIBUTING PIPE

SERVICE PIPE

DRAW-OFF POINT

INSTANTANEOUS GAS WATER HEATER

46 *Hot water apparatus not to be connected directly to service pipe*

Where any apparatus draws water from a service pipe etc, the water shall discharge min ½in (12.7mm) above top edge of apparatus. This does not apply to certain gas or electricity hw heaters

47 *Mixing valves*

No mixing valve, pipe or other water fitting in which hw and cw are mixed shall be or remain so connected as to mix either — (a) water supplied from a hw apparatus connected directly to a service pipe, or to a pump delivery pipe drawing water from a service pipe, with cw not supplied directly from a service pipe or a pump delivery pipe drawing water from service pipe *or* (b) water supplied from a hw apparatus not connected directly to a service pipe (or pump delivery pipe, etc) with cw supplied from a service pipe (or pump delivery pipe, etc) with cw supplied from a service pipe (or a pump delivery pipe, etc).

Note: The supplies of hot and cold water, to a mixing valve must have their pressures 'balanced' for example, both hw and cw fed from the same service pipe or from the same cistern.

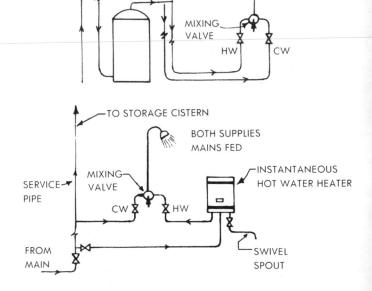

BOTH SUPPLIES FED FROM THE SAME CISTERN

MIXING VALVE

HW   CW

TO STORAGE CISTERN

BOTH SUPPLIES MAINS FED

MIXING VALVE

SERVICE PIPE

CW   HW

INSTANTANEOUS HOT WATER HEATER

FROM MAIN

SWIVEL SPOUT

48 *Materials for hot water pipes*

Every pipe used for conveying hot water shall be of galvanised steel, lead or copper or other corrosion resisting material which is not less suitable. (Where the undertakers wish to prohibit the use of some material, they should submit evidence of the need for this).

49 *Materials for and support of hot water cylinders and tanks*
1 Every hw cylinder or tank shall be constructed of galvanised mild steel, copper or some other not less suitable material. (Undertakers may prohibit use of some material(s)).
2 Where the hw cylinder or tank is not made of corrosion-resisting material it shall be effectively protected against corrosion. Every hw cylinder or tank shall be adequately supported.

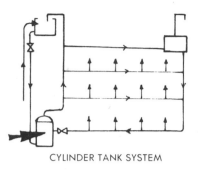

CYLINDER TANK SYSTEM

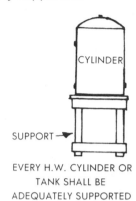

EVERY H.W. CYLINDER OR
TANK SHALL BE
ADEQUATELY SUPPORTED

50 *British Standards for hw cylinders and tanks*
If any of these BS numbers apply, compliance is needed.
417 Galvanised ms cisterns, covers, tanks and cylinders.
1565 Galvanised ms indirect cylinders, annular or S8
699 Copper cylinders for domestic purposes
1566 Pt. I Copper indirect cylinders — Double feed
843 Non-instanaeous electrical water heaters
853 Pt. I Calorifiers of m.s. or cast iron
853 Pt. 2 Calorifiers of copper

51 *Capacity of hw storage cisterns, cylinders or tanks*
Minimum 25 gal (11.4 litres) unless forming part of a hw system in which water is heated only under thermostatic control by electricity, gas or oil *when no minimum applies.*

If the system has two or more storage vessels at different levels, this byelaw only applies to the lowest cylinder or tank.

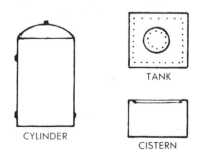

CYLINDER   TANK

CISTERN

38 *Capacity of storage cisterns in houses*
Minimums 25 gal or 114 litre. 50 gal or 228 litre

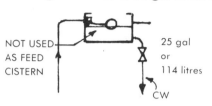

NOT USED AS FEED CISTERN   25 gal or 114 litres   CW

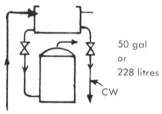

50 gal or 228 litres   CW

CISTERN FOR FEED & OTHER USES

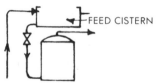

FEED CISTERN

NO MODEL BYE-LAW MINIMUM

SOME OTHER RELEVANT REGULATIONS
7A Deterioration through electrolytic action.
10 Protection from damage from frost.
12 Accessibility of fittings.
23 Fittings in closed circuits.
25 Stopvalves on outlet pipes from storage cisterns.
26 Location of draining taps.
33 Placing of storage cisterns.
34 Support and covering of storage cisterns.
36 Materials for storage cisterns.
37 British Standards for storage cisterns.
39 Storage cisterns to be fitted with ballvalves.
40/41 Cisterns max. 1000 gal (4546 litres)/cisterns over 1000 gal.

CW = COLD WATER
HW = HOT WATER
MS = MILD STEEL
CYL = CYLINDER
SB = SADDLE BACK

ILLUSTRATING THE PHYSICS OF NATURAL CONVECTION

DEFINITIONS

Transportation of heat by movement of heated substance. (Concise Oxford). When a fluid is warmed it expands, its density decreases and it rises, its place being taken by denser, cooler fluid. This is the principle of convection of heat. It is the reason why water circulates in h.w. and heating systems and air moves about in rooms where there is no draught (Dictionary of Building).

To couple the word 'convey' with convection may help 'separate' convection from conduction and radiation. Heat is conveyed or carried. Convection can be said to take place when heat is transmitted through the substance of a body by means of the motion of the heated particles from one point to another. Conduction is heat transmitted through a mass and radiation is heat emission in the forms of rays.

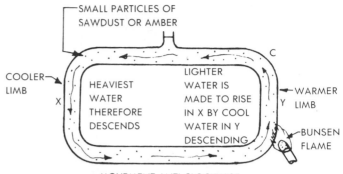

MOVEMENT ANTI-CLOCKWISE

NOTE: No temperature difference between x & y, then no movement. Direction of convection can be changed, depending upon the position of heat source as in B or C. Convection is brisk to commence but slows down as x & y temperatures equalise.

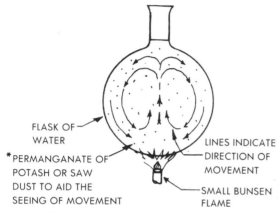

EXPERIMENT SHOWING CONVECTION IN A VESSEL

EXPERIMENT TO SHOW MOVEMENT AND DIRECTION OF CONVECTION IN A TUBE

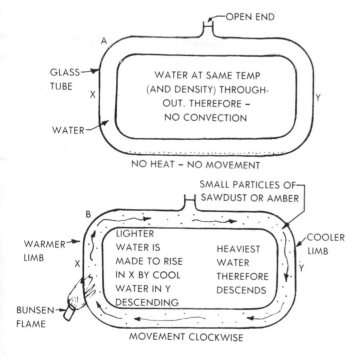

NO HEAT – NO MOVEMENT

MOVEMENT CLOCKWISE

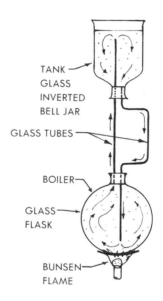

The drawing is a laboratory apparatus to show the circulation that would take place in a hot water system. When water becomes warm it expands and — bulk for bulk — is lighter than cooler water. The heaviest water (by the laws of gravity) will always tend to occupy the lowest position available and the lighter (and warmer) water will be caused to move away, generally upwards. Hot water, therefore, rises but not on its own accord. By arranging a boiler to heat the water, and coupling it by means of two pipes to another vessel, natural convection will cause the water to circulate.

*PLUS SODIUM SULPHITE FORMS BROWN PRECIPITATE OF MANGANESE OXIDE

TEMPERATURE		DENSITY	
°C	°F	kg/m³	lb/ft³
4	39.2	1000.0	62.43
10	50.0	999.7	62.41
16	60.8	998.9	62.36
22	71.6	997.7	62.29
28	82.4	996.2	62.19
34	93.2	994.3	62.07
40	104.0	992.3	61.94
46	114.8	989.8	61.79
52	125.6	987.2	61.63
60	140.0	983.2	61.38
66	150.8	979.9	61.18
72	161.6	976.6	60.97
78	172.4	973.1	60.75
82	179.6	970.6	60.60
90	194.0	965.3	60.26
100	212.0	958.3	59.83

TABLE OF DENSITIES OF WATER
RELATED TO TEMPERATURE

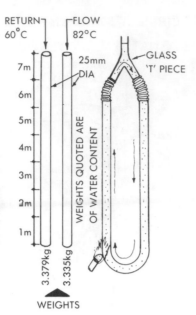

EXPERIMENT TO SHOW THAT THE
LONGER THE VERTICAL COLUMNS,
THE GREATER THE VELOCITY

Calculating circulating pressure:

$$N/m^2 = 9.81 (Dr - Df) \times \text{circulating height.}$$

Dr and Df = density of return and flow in
kg/m³ (N/m³ ÷ 100 = mbar)

Metric: Water at 4°C is taken to weigh 999.9
kg/m³ but is usually taken as 1000kg/m³ or 1
tonne (litre = 1kg)

Imperial: In general terms it has been
assumed that 1 gal of water weighs 10lb with
approximately 6.25 gal/ft³ therefore 62.5
lb/ft³

PRIMARY CIRCS NOT SHOWN   DIAGRAMMATIC

SECONDARY CIRCULATION

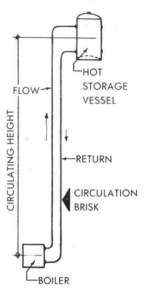

SYSTEMS

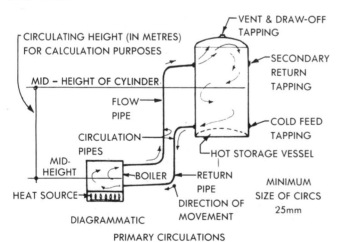

DIAGRAMMATIC

PRIMARY CIRCULATIONS

PRIMARY CIRCS SHOULD BE AS SHORT AS
POSSIBLE WITH THE MINIMUM CHANGES OF
DIRECTION: LONG HORIZONTAL RUNS
SHOULD BE AVOIDED

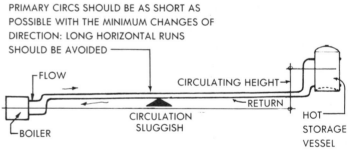

Convection in water is a simple thing to
commence (application of heat only); is very
positive, and movement is rapid in a well
designed system. However, the force at work is
so small in terms of pressure, a simple airlock
will stop circulation.

NOTES: In this system the water supplied to the draw-off points has been directly heated in the boiler. Direct systems should not be used when the temporary hardness of water exceeds 160ppm, unless they can be thermostatically controlled. In such cases an indirect system should be used. With soft corrosive water, a cast iron boiler (unless bower-barffed) for direct supply is not advisable as corrosion of the boiler and discoloration of the water may occur. It is useful to have knowledge of the plumbo and cupro-solvency of the water and the pH value to ensure that the metal used is unaffected by the water supplied. Water can be treated to render it non-corrosive.

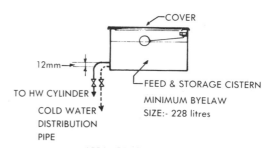

ARRANGEMENT OF COLD SUPPLIES WHEN A FEED & STORAGE CISTERN IS USED

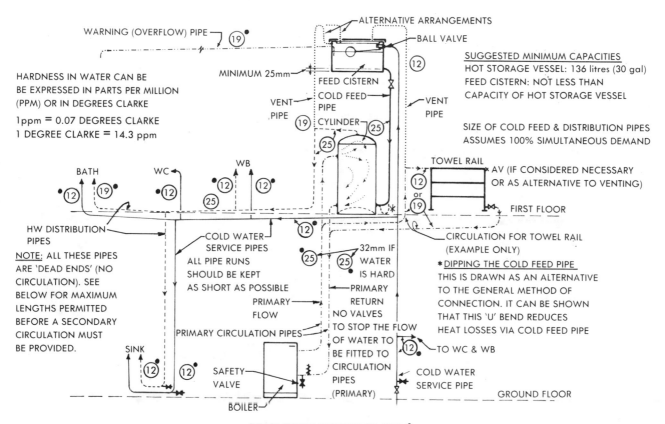

DIRECT SYSTEM (WITH TOWEL RAIL) **A**

HARDNESS IN WATER CAN BE BE EXPRESSED IN PARTS PER MILLION (PPM) OR IN DEGREES CLARKE

1ppm = 0.07 DEGREES CLARKE
1 DEGREE CLARKE = 14.3 ppm

SUGGESTED MINIMUM CAPACITIES
HOT STORAGE VESSEL: 136 litres (30 gal)
FEED CISTERN: NOT LESS THAN
CAPACITY OF HOT STORAGE VESSEL

SIZE OF COLD FEED & DISTRIBUTION PIPES
ASSUMES 100% SIMULTANEOUS DEMAND

PIPE SIZES QUOTED ARE NOMINAL (mm) BORE SIZES AS COMMONLY KNOWN e.g. 19mm OR ¾ in THEY ARE TYPICAL FOR SIMPLE HOUSING SYSTEMS. PIPE SIZING PROCEDURE WILL BE DEALT WITH IN LATER DETAILS.

LEGEND	
————————	COLD FEED PIPE
————————	CW SERVICE PIPE
- - - - - - - - -	HW DISTRIBUTION PIPE
— - — - — - —	CIRCULATION (PRIMARY)
— — — — —	WARNING (OVERFLOW) PIPE
·················	VENT PIPE
— — — — —	STOREY SEPARATION
—⋈—	STOPVALVE
⊢▸◂⊣	DRAIN TAP
———→	DRAW-OFF POINT (EG TAP)
↓T—	THERMOMETER
———→	DIRECTION OF FLOW OR CIRC
×AV	AIR VALVE
⑲●	TYPICAL PIPE SIZE·

● DOT INDICATES SUGGESTED MINIMUM

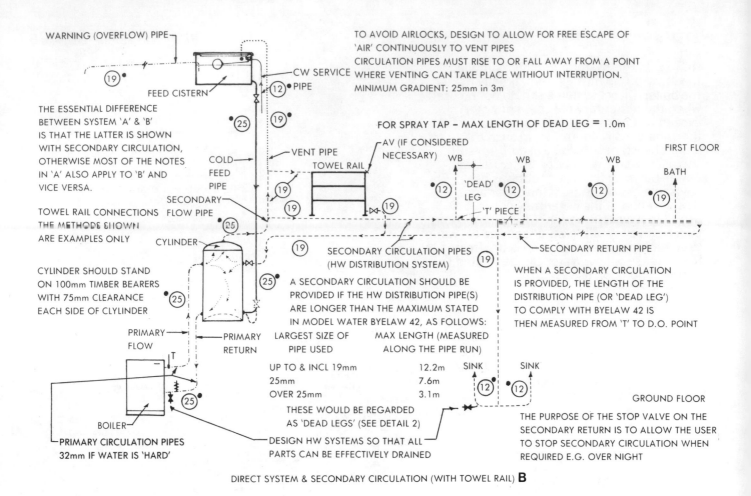

WARNING (OVERFLOW) PIPE

(19)

FEED CISTERN

CW SERVICE PIPE

(12)

(25)   (19)

TO AVOID AIRLOCKS, DESIGN TO ALLOW FOR FREE ESCAPE OF
'AIR' CONTINUOUSLY TO VENT PIPES
CIRCULATION PIPES MUST RISE TO OR FALL AWAY FROM A POINT
WHERE VENTING CAN TAKE PLACE WITHOUT INTERRUPTION.
MINIMUM GRADIENT: 25mm in 3m

THE ESSENTIAL DIFFERENCE
BETWEEN SYSTEM 'A' & 'B'
IS THAT THE LATTER IS SHOWN
WITH SECONDARY CIRCULATION,
OTHERWISE MOST OF THE NOTES
IN 'A' ALSO APPLY TO 'B' AND
VICE VERSA.

TOWEL RAIL CONNECTIONS
THE METHODS SHOWN
ARE EXAMPLES ONLY

CYLINDER SHOULD STAND
ON 100mm TIMBER BEARERS
WITH 75mm CLEARANCE
EACH SIDE OF CLYINDER

COLD
FEED
PIPE

VENT PIPE

TOWEL RAIL

SECONDARY
FLOW PIPE

CYLINDER

(19)

(25)

(19)

(25)

FOR SPRAY TAP – MAX LENGTH OF DEAD LEG = 1.0m

AV (IF CONSIDERED
NECESSARY)

WB   WB   WB   FIRST FLOOR

BATH

(12)   'DEAD'   (12)   (12)   (19)
       LEG

'T' PIECE

(19)

SECONDARY CIRCULATION PIPES
(HW DISTRIBUTION SYSTEM)

(19)

SECONDARY RETURN PIPE

WHEN A SECONDARY CIRCULATION
IS PROVIDED, THE LENGTH OF THE
DISTRIBUTION PIPE (OR 'DEAD LEG')
TO COMPLY WITH BYELAW 42 IS
THEN MEASURED FROM 'T' TO D.O. POINT

PRIMARY
FLOW

T

PRIMARY
RETURN

BOILER

(25)

PRIMARY CIRCULATION PIPES
32mm IF WATER IS 'HARD'

A SECONDARY CIRCULATION SHOULD BE
PROVIDED IF THE HW DISTRIBUTION PIPE(S)
ARE LONGER THAN THE MAXIMUM STATED
IN MODEL WATER BYELAW 42, AS FOLLOWS:

LARGEST SIZE OF PIPE USED	MAX LENGTH (MEASURED ALONG THE PIPE RUN)
UP TO & INCL 19mm	12.2m
25mm	7.6m
OVER 25mm	3.1m

THESE WOULD BE REGARDED
AS 'DEAD LEGS' (SEE DETAIL 2)

DESIGN HW SYSTEMS SO THAT ALL
PARTS CAN BE EFFECTIVELY DRAINED

SINK   SINK

(12)   (12)

GROUND FLOOR

THE PURPOSE OF THE STOP VALVE ON THE
SECONDARY RETURN IS TO ALLOW THE USER
TO STOP SECONDARY CIRCULATION WHEN
REQUIRED E.G. OVER NIGHT

DIRECT SYSTEM & SECONDARY CIRCULATION (WITH TOWEL RAIL) **B**

FURTHER DETAILS OF BOILERS, VESSELS, PIPEWORK, FITTINGS, INSULATION, ETC WILL BE SHOWN ON LATER DETAIL SHEETS
HW – HOT WATER CW – COLD WATER WC – WATER CLOSET WB – WASH BASIN AV – AIR VALVE DO – DRAW-OFF (POINT)

B SYSTEMS

NOTES: In this sytem, the water supplied to draw-off points has been indirectly heated in an indirect cylinder. The primary circulation (with its own feed and expansion cistern, cold feed and vent pipes) forms a closed circuit in which the same water is continuously circulated, and from which no water is drawn off for use. This hot water passes through an annular element (or coil of pipe), within the indirect cylinder and warms the water surrounding it but does not mix with it. Thus the water stored for domestic purposes is heated indirectly. This cylinder is fed from a separate feed cistern with the associated pipework arranged similarly to a direct system. Indirect systems should be used when any temporary hardness in the water exceeds l60 ppm, unless the boiler is thermostatically controlled. A towel rail can be connected to either the closed circuit (primary); or as an independent secondary circulation or part of a larger secondary system — if rail is made of non-ferrous metal (eg. copper or brass)

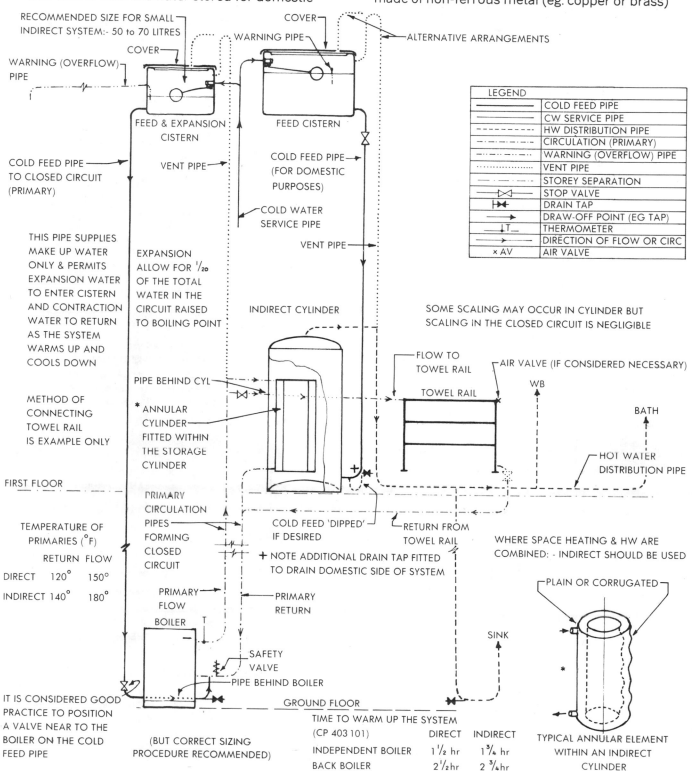

RECOMMENDED SIZE FOR SMALL INDIRECT SYSTEM:- 50 to 70 LITRES

COVER

WARNING PIPE

COVER

ALTERNATIVE ARRANGEMENTS

WARNING (OVERFLOW) PIPE

FEED & EXPANSION CISTERN

FEED CISTERN

COLD FEED PIPE TO CLOSED CIRCUIT (PRIMARY)

VENT PIPE

COLD FEED PIPE (FOR DOMESTIC PURPOSES)

COLD WATER SERVICE PIPE

LEGEND	
─────────	COLD FEED PIPE
─────────	CW SERVICE PIPE
– – – – –	HW DISTRIBUTION PIPE
–·–·–·–	CIRCULATION (PRIMARY)
–··–··–	WARNING (OVERFLOW) PIPE
··········	VENT PIPE
─ · ─ · ─	STOREY SEPARATION
─▷◁─	STOP VALVE
▶◀	DRAIN TAP
────▶	DRAW-OFF POINT (EG TAP)
↓T_	THERMOMETER
────▶	DIRECTION OF FLOW OR CIRC
× AV	AIR VALUE

THIS PIPE SUPPLIES MAKE UP WATER ONLY & PERMITS EXPANSION WATER TO ENTER CISTERN AND CONTRACTION WATER TO RETURN AS THE SYSTEM WARMS UP AND COOLS DOWN

EXPANSION ALLOW FOR ¹/₂₀ OF THE TOTAL WATER IN THE CIRCUIT RAISED TO BOILING POINT

VENT PIPE

INDIRECT CYLINDER

SOME SCALING MAY OCCUR IN CYLINDER BUT SCALING IN THE CLOSED CIRCUIT IS NEGLIGIBLE

METHOD OF CONNECTING TOWEL RAIL IS EXAMPLE ONLY

PIPE BEHIND CYL

* ANNULAR CYLINDER FITTED WITHIN THE STORAGE CYLINDER

FLOW TO TOWEL RAIL

AIR VALVE (IF CONSIDERED NECESSARY)

TOWEL RAIL

WB

BATH

HOT WATER DISTRIBUTION PIPE

FIRST FLOOR

PRIMARY CIRCULATION PIPES FORMING CLOSED CIRCUIT

COLD FEED 'DIPPED' IF DESIRED

RETURN FROM TOWEL RAIL

WHERE SPACE HEATING & HW ARE COMBINED: - INDIRECT SHOULD BE USED

TEMPERATURE OF PRIMARIES (°F)

+ NOTE ADDITIONAL DRAIN TAP FITTED TO DRAIN DOMESTIC SIDE OF SYSTEM

	RETURN	FLOW
DIRECT	120°	150°
INDIRECT	140°	180°

PRIMARY FLOW

PRIMARY RETURN

PLAIN OR CORRUGATED

BOILER

T

SINK

*

SAFETY VALVE

PIPE BEHIND BOILER

IT IS CONSIDERED GOOD PRACTICE TO POSITION A VALVE NEAR TO THE BOILER ON THE COLD FEED PIPE

GROUND FLOOR

(BUT CORRECT SIZING PROCEDURE RECOMMENDED)

TIME TO WARM UP THE SYSTEM (CP 403 101)

TYPICAL ANNULAR ELEMENT WITHIN AN INDIRECT CYLINDER

	DIRECT	INDIRECT
INDEPENDENT BOILER	1¹/₂ hr	1³/₄ hr
BACK BOILER	2¹/₂hr	2 ³/₄hr

The type of system, whether direct or indirect, the choice of materials and the jointing used in the installation should be based on a full knowledge of the character of the water and the experience and recommendations of the local water undertaking. The character of the water may vary from hard to very soft and due account should be taken of the liability of corrosion and the formation of scale or sludge (see CP310). Except for galvanised steel cisterns, copper and galv steel should not be used together in the same installation (CP342 Pt. I)

The requirements for a secondary circulation are the same as for a direct system (Detail 5) whether 'double' or 'single' feed.

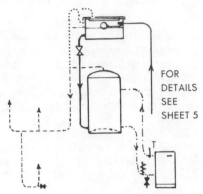

FOR DETAILS SEE SHEET 5

DIRECT SYSTEM SHOWN FOR COMPARISON

REASONS FOR USING AN INDIRECT SYSTEM

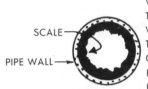

SCALE

PIPE WALL

WHEN HEATED, TEMPORARY HARD WATER DEPOSITS SCALE. THIS CAN RESULT IN OBSTRUCTION OF FLOW PIPE & REDUCED OVERALL EFFICIENCY INDIRECT SYSTEMS REDUCE SCALING TO A LEVEL WHICH IS ACCEPTABLE

SCALING OR FURRING

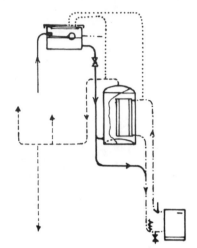

A SINGLE COLD WATER CISTERN MAY REPLACE THE TWO AS SHOWN, EXCEPT WHERE HARDNESS OF THE WATER, BOILER CONSTRUCTION & THE METHOD OF FIXING MAY LEAD TO LOCAL SCALE FORMATION (CP403.101)

SINGLE FEED USING INDIRECT CYLINDER

CERTAIN WATERS USED WITH BOILERS, PIPES & RADIATORS MADE OF FERROUS METAL CAN CAUSE DISCOLOURATION OF WATER DRAWN FROM TAPS. WITH INDIRECT SYSTEM DISCOLOURATION CAN BE CONFINED TO THE CLOSED CIRCUIT & NOT SEEN

DISCOLOURATION OF WATER

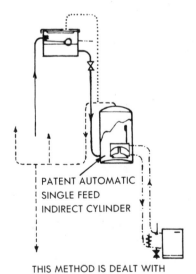

PATENT AUTOMATIC SINGLE FEED INDIRECT CYLINDER

THIS METHOD IS DEALT WITH FULLY ON DETAIL NO. 7

SINGLE FEED USING PATENT CYLINDER

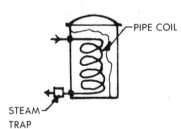

PIPE COIL

STEAM TRAP

STEAM IS AN EXCELLENT HEATING MEDIUM DUE MAINLY TO ITS LATENT HEAT. WASTE OR 'LIVE' STEAM PASSED THROUGH A CALORIFIER PRODUCES HW INDIRECTLY & CHEAPLY

USING WASTE OR 'LIVE' STEAM

MANY DESIGN CONSIDERATIONS APPLY EQUALLY TO INDIRECT SYSTEMS AS FOR DIRECT SYSTEMS, THEREFORE THIS SHEET SHOULD BE STUDIED ALONG WITH DETAIL 5.

HW – HOT WATER. CW – COLD WATER. WB – WASH BASIN.

ALL LAYOUTS ARE DIAGRAMMATIC AND NOT DRAWN TO SCALE

NOTES FROM BS 1566: Part 2 1984 SINGLE FEED INDIRECT CYLINDERS
Single feed indirect copper cylinders are for the storage of hot water, where the water is heated indirectly by the water circulating in an integral primary heater and for which only one feed cistern is required, the feed water to the primary circuit being obtained from within the cylinder through the primary heater. The storage capacities of the cylinders range from 86 litres to 180 litres. The cylinders are all of the type in which the bottom is domed inwards. They are intended for fixing in the vertical position.

Primary heater :- A heater mounted inside a cylinder for the transfer of heat to the stored water from circulating hot water.

Primary water :- The water in the primary circuit including the water in primary heater, boiler, radiators, pipework and the like.

Primary capacity :- The total volume of primary water, the expansion of which is to be accommodated by the primary heater.

Secondary water :- The water in the cylinder and associated pipework that is heated by the primary heater (domestic).

Markings on cylinder :- The letters SF (indicating single feed); also maximum permissible quantity of primary water, water content of primary heater, area of heating surface of the primary heater, and others.

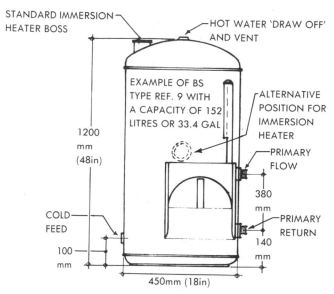

STANDARD IMMERSION HEATER BOSS
HOT WATER 'DRAW OFF' AND VENT
EXAMPLE OF BS TYPE REF. 9 WITH A CAPACITY OF 152 LITRES OR 33.4 GAL
ALTERNATIVE POSITION FOR IMMERSION HEATER
PRIMARY FLOW
1200 mm (48in)
380 mm
COLD FEED
PRIMARY RETURN
140 mm
100 mm
450mm (18in)

STANDARD MODEL BS CLASS 110

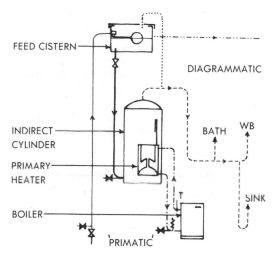

FEED CISTERN
DIAGRAMMATIC
INDIRECT CYLINDER
PRIMARY HEATER
BATH
WB
BOILER
'PRIMATIC'
SINK
T

SINGLE FEED INDIRECT SYSTEM PATENT CYLINDER

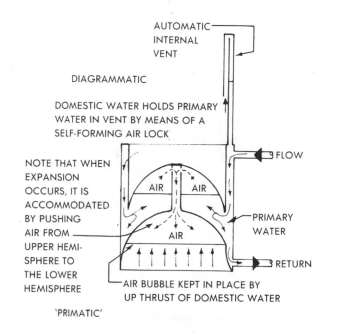

AUTOMATIC INTERNAL VENT
DIAGRAMMATIC
DOMESTIC WATER HOLDS PRIMARY WATER IN VENT BY MEANS OF A SELF-FORMING AIR LOCK
NOTE THAT WHEN EXPANSION OCCURS, IT IS ACCOMMODATED BY PUSHING AIR FROM UPPER HEMI-SPHERE TO THE LOWER HEMISPHERE
FLOW
AIR   AIR
AIR
PRIMARY WATER
RETURN
AIR BUBBLE KEPT IN PLACE BY UP THRUST OF DOMESTIC WATER
'PRIMATIC'

DETAIL OF ONE TYPE OF PRIMARY HEATER WHICH IS SHOWING CONDITIONS TO BE EXPECTED WHEN PRIMARY WATER HAS FULLY EXPANDED

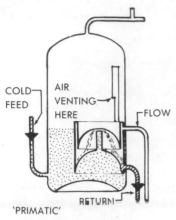

'PRIMATIC'

PRIMARY FILLING

l. Cylinder is filled in the normal way and primary system is filled via the primary heater. As the filling of the cylinder continues, two air seals are automatically formed. The volume of seal is accurately calculated.

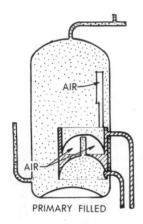

PRIMARY FILLED

2. The two air seals are permanently maintained and self-recuperating in operation. They isolate the primary from the secondary almost as effectively as a mechanical barrier.

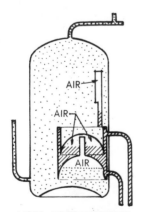

NOTE: AIR TRANSFERRED TO LOWER HEMISPHERE

PRIMARY EXPANDED

3. The expansion volume of total primary water is approx. $\frac{1}{25}$ and is accommodated in the expansion chamber by displacement of air into the lower chamber. Upon contraction the reverse occurs.

The natural force of bouyancy of air forms the seals between the primary and secondary (domestic) systems. The 'Standard' unit will accommodate expansion from 110 litres (24 gal). Other models are available for larger primary systems up to 180 litres (40 gal). Boiling conditions should be avoided, but, if accidental, the unit quickly returns to normal without attention. Performance of 'Standard':- temperature of secondary contents raised 56°C (100°F) in about l hr with primary flow at 82°C (180°F).

BS TYPE REFERENCE	EXTERNAL DIAMETER		EXTERNAL HEIGHT OVER DOME		STORAGE CAPACITY		HEATING SURFACE	NOMINAL SIZE OF CONNECTS
	mm	in	mm	in	litres	gallons	m²	in
3*	400	15.8	1050	41.3	104	22.9	0.63	1
5	450	17.7	750	29.5	86	18.9	0.52	1
7*	450	17.7	900	35.4	108	23.8	0.66	1
8*	450	17.7	1050	41.3	130	28.6	0.78	1¼
9*	450	17.7	1200	47.2	152	33.4	0.91	1¼
10	500	19.7	1200	47.2	180	39.6	1.13	1½

BS DIMENSIONS & DETAILS OF SINGLE FEED COPPER CYLINDERS

* PREFERRED SIZES FOR NEW INSTALLATIONS. HW HOT WATER. CW COLD WATER WB WASH BASIN.

SOME OTHER TYPES
'Aeromatic' cylinder contains two chambers side by side linked by an inverted 'U' tube. One chamber is air-locked & the other (with aperture in base) is filled with water. Heating causes air to move from one chamber to the next allowing expansion to be accommodated. 'Primary' cylinder contains another cylinder similar to 'indirect'. The inner cylinder contains many vertical tubes for the circulation of domestic water. It is filled via an inverted 'U' tube in which an air-lock is formed.

LEGEND	
─────────	COLD FEED PIPE
─────────	CW SERVICE PIPE
- - - - - -	HW DISTRIBUTION PIPE
─·─·─·─	CIRCULATION (PRIMARY)
─··─··─	WARNING (OVERFLOW) PIPE
··········	VENT PIPE
⌇	SAFETY VALVE
─⋈→	STOPVALVE
▶◀	DRAIN TAP
──→	DRAW-OFF POINT (EG TAP)
⌐T⌐	THERMOMETER
──→──	DIRECTION OF FLOW OR CIRC

FOR SINGLE FEED INDIRECT SYSTEM USING ORDINARY CYLINDER, SEE DETAIL 6

MANY DESIGN CONSIDERATIONS APPLY EQUALLY TO INDIRECT SYSTEMS AS FOR DIRECT SYSTEMS, THIS SHEET SHOULD BE STUDIED ALONG WITH DETAIL 5.

OTHER SIZES ARE AVAILABLE, SEE MANUFACTURERS' LITERATURE

INTRODUCTION

A length of hot water distributing pipe leading to a draw-off point (eg tap) and not forming part of a circuit through which hot water can circulate is known as a DEAD LEG. Water Byelaws put a limit on the length according to pipe size, viz. 42. The length of any pipe conveying hot water from any apparatus or flow and return system to any draw-off tap shall not exceed that specified by reference to the largest internal diameter of any part of it (see table below). Byelaw 43 forbids any draw-off point to be so positioned that by its use the level of the water in the hot storage cylinder or tank can be lowered more than one-fourth of the depth of the vessel.

LIMITS OF LENGTHS OF DEAD LEGS

Largest internal diameter of pipe	Max length
Not exceeding ¾in. (19mm)	40 ft (12.2m)
Exceeding ¾in. but not exceeding 1in. (25mm)	25 ft (7.6m)
Exceeding 1in. (25mm)	10 ft (3.1m)

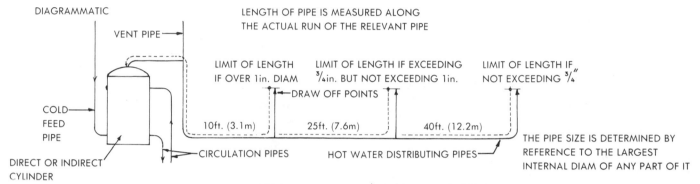

MAX LENGTH OF DEAD LEG FOR SPRAY TAPS SHOULD BE 3ft. (0.9m)

WASTE OF WATER

This is one of the main reasons for restricting the length of 'dead legs'. If no hot water has been used for some time, the water standing in the hw distributing pipe will have cooled off. When hw is required, the water standing in this pipe will most likely be allowed to run to waste until hw arrives from the cylinder. This waste of water can be considerable even if the amount of a single draw-off waste may not appear much as the following calculation shows. Take for example 40ft. (12.2m) of ¾in. (19mm) pipe.

Quantity of water in pipe: $\frac{\pi D^2}{4} \times L = 0.75$ gallons or 3.4 litres.

Assuming this happens 10 times a day per house = 7.5 gal or 34.1 litre.
Amount wasted per annum per house = 2738 gal or 12447 litres.
Assuming 100,000 houses (eg large town) = 274 million gal (1244700m³).
This is equivalent to over 3 weeks' supply for a town of the same size.

WASTE OF ENERGY

Because the water has been heated, the waste of energy is important. When hw has been drawn off, the hottest water in the system is likely to be in the distributing pipe(s). If this pipe is not insulated, in about 5 min the water temperature could be too low to be of any use and may be allowed to run to waste, to obtain hot water. If insulated by simple wrapping, the water may be kept reasonably hot for about 30 minutes with greater chance of it being made use of. For worst theoretical loss of energy and cost, eg 40in. (12.2m) of ¾in. (19mm) pipe, ie 2738 gal (12447 litres) per annum, 2738×10 (lb) $\times 100°F$ (raised from 50° to 150°F) $= \frac{2738000}{3412}$

= say 800kW.
$12447 \times 56°C$ (10° raised to 66°C) $\times 4.2 \div 3600$
= say 800 kW.

SECONDARY CIRCULATIONS

A secondary circulation is defined as a circuit in which water circulates from and back to a hot water storage vessel. Its purpose is to give an 'immediate' supply of hot water at the various fittings and the circulation should be arranged in a position as near to the appliances as possible so that branches are short, otherwise the object is defeated. Heat losses from secondary circulating pipes, heated towel rails, airing cupboard coils should be offset by increasing boiler capacity.

PIPE SIZING

Secondary circuits may be designed for pumped or natural circulation, the latter being preferable. Size flow pipe as a distribution pipe and return pipe so that the temperature drop on the circuit is min 8°C, max 22°C depending upon temperature required at draw-off points. Circulation depends upon heat loss from circuit, circuit pressure and frictional resistance.

ACCEPTANCE TEST

No part of secondary circulation should be less than 43°C when flow from storage vessel is 65°C.

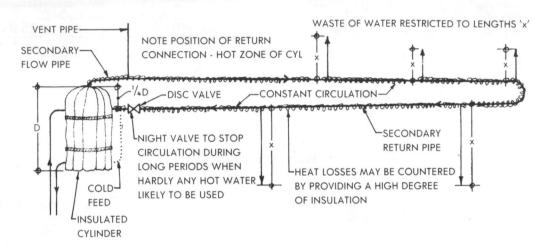

VENT PIPE

SECONDARY FLOW PIPE

NOTE POSITION OF RETURN CONNECTION - HOT ZONE OF CYL

WASTE OF WATER RESTRICTED TO LENGTHS 'x'

¼D — DISC VALVE — CONSTANT CIRCULATION

NIGHT VALVE TO STOP CIRCULATION DURING LONG PERIODS WHEN HARDLY ANY HOT WATER LIKELY TO BE USED

SECONDARY RETURN PIPE

HEAT LOSSES MAY BE COUNTERED BY PROVIDING A HIGH DEGREE OF INSULATION

COLD FEED

INSULATED CYLINDER

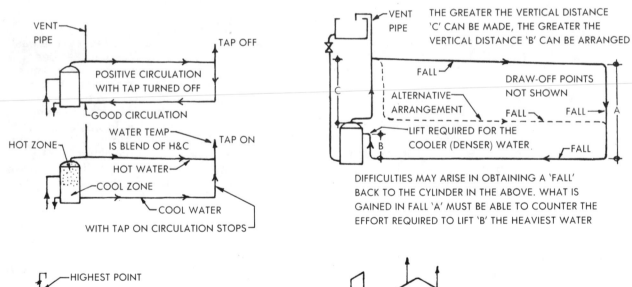

VENT PIPE

POSITIVE CIRCULATION WITH TAP TURNED OFF

TAP OFF

GOOD CIRCULATION

HOT ZONE

WATER TEMP IS BLEND OF H&C

TAP ON

HOT WATER

COOL ZONE

COOL WATER

WITH TAP ON CIRCULATION STOPS

VENT PIPE

THE GREATER THE VERTICAL DISTANCE 'C' CAN BE MADE, THE GREATER THE VERTICAL DISTANCE 'B' CAN BE ARRANGED

FALL

DRAW-OFF POINTS NOT SHOWN

ALTERNATIVE ARRANGEMENT

FALL — FALL

LIFT REQUIRED FOR THE COOLER (DENSER) WATER

FALL

DIFFICULTIES MAY ARISE IN OBTAINING A 'FALL' BACK TO THE CYLINDER IN THE ABOVE. WHAT IS GAINED IN FALL 'A' MUST BE ABLE TO COUNTER THE EFFORT REQUIRED TO LIFT 'B' THE HEAVIEST WATER

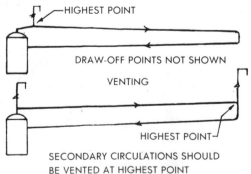

HIGHEST POINT

DRAW-OFF POINTS NOT SHOWN

VENTING

HIGHEST POINT

SECONDARY CIRCULATIONS SHOULD BE VENTED AT HIGHEST POINT

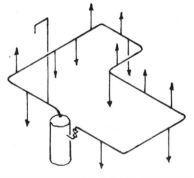

HW = HOT WATER
CW = COLD WATER

SECONDARY CIRCULATION IN ISOMETRIC

INTRODUCTION

Defined simple as 'a system supplying space heating and domestic hot water from a single source'. It usually comprises an indirect hot water supply system (see Detail 6) with the addition of an extension of the primary circulation for supplying hot water to radiators, convectors, heating panels, etc, incorporated in the circuit. Illustrated below are six examples of domestic situations, with slight variations.

AIR MAY CONTINUALLY COLLECT IN THE RADIATOR UNLESS RAD IS FITTED TO BE SELF-VENTING. THIS IS DUE TO CONSTANT CIRC OF FRESH WATER

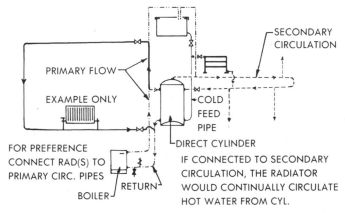

SECONDARY CIRCULATION

PRIMARY FLOW

EXAMPLE ONLY

COLD FEED PIPE

FOR PREFERENCE CONNECT RAD(S) TO PRIMARY CIRC. PIPES

DIRECT CYLINDER

BOILER — RETURN

IF CONNECTED TO SECONDARY CIRCULATION, THE RADIATOR WOULD CONTINUALLY CIRCULATE HOT WATER FROM CYL.

GRAVITY CIRCULATION

USING THE DIRECT SYSTEM

It is possible to connect radiator(s) to a direct system, but expensive copper rads must be used to avoid rust discoloration of the domestic hw. Radiator temperature may be affected by hw draw-off.

VAST IMPROVEMENT IN DESIGN & CONTROLS HAVE RESULTED IN GREAT POPULARITY FOR THIS SYSTEM

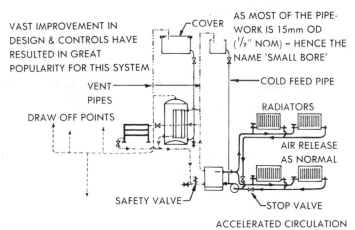

COVER

AS MOST OF THE PIPE-WORK IS 15mm OD ('1/2" NOM) – HENCE THE NAME 'SMALL BORE'

COLD FEED PIPE

VENT PIPES

RADIATORS

DRAW OFF POINTS

AIR RELEASE AS NORMAL

SAFETY VALVE

STOP VALVE

ACCELERATED CIRCULATION

USING THE SMALL BORE SYSTEM

Development of the silent 'pump' removed the noise factor, etc.; enables small pipes to be used ('1/2in. nom); speeded the warm up time, and simplified installation. It revolutionised domestic heating.

*THE UNIT IS A COMBINED HEATING COIL, THERMOSTATIC VALVE & BYPASS TUBE. THE CONTENTS OF THE CYLINDER ARE HEATED TO A PRE-SELECTED TEMPERATURE

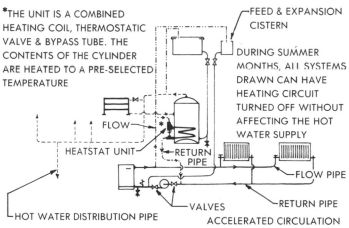

FEED & EXPANSION CISTERN

DURING SUMMER MONTHS, ALL SYSTEMS DRAWN CAN HAVE HEATING CIRCUIT TURNED OFF WITHOUT AFFECTING THE HOT WATER SUPPLY

FLOW

HEATSTAT UNIT

RETURN PIPE

FLOW PIPE

VALVES

RETURN PIPE

HOT WATER DISTRIBUTION PIPE

ACCELERATED CIRCULATION

USING PUMPED CIRCUIT TO CYLINDER

Can be used on any system where there is a pumped primary circuit from a gas or oil fired boiler. Warm up periods I to 3 hours according to the heating coil.

BEFORE NOISELESS 'PUMPS' APPEARED LARGE SYSTEMS WERE PUMPED & SMALLER SYSTEMS RELIED ON GRAVITY CIRC & THE USE OF LARGE DIAMETER PIPES

BOILER THERMOSTAT AND COLD WATER SERVICES NOT SHOWN

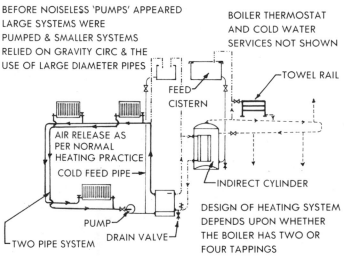

TOWEL RAIL

FEED CISTERN

AIR RELEASE AS PER NORMAL HEATING PRACTICE

COLD FEED PIPE

INDIRECT CYLINDER

PUMP

DRAIN VALVE

TWO PIPE SYSTEM

DESIGN OF HEATING SYSTEM DEPENDS UPON WHETHER THE BOILER HAS TWO OR FOUR TAPPINGS

GRAVITY OR ACCELERATED CIRCULATION

USING THE INDIRECT SYSTEM

With any indirect system rads can be of ferrous-metal (cast iron or mild steel) as the circuit is 'closed' and cannot cause discolouration of the domestic hot water. Systems usually free from air locks.

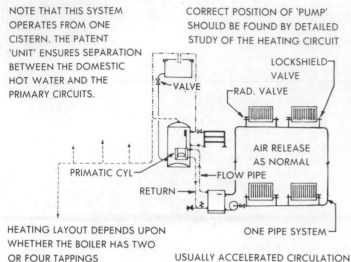

NOTE THAT THIS SYSTEM OPERATES FROM ONE CISTERN. THE PATENT 'UNIT' ENSURES SEPARATION BETWEEN THE DOMESTIC HOT WATER AND THE PRIMARY CIRCUITS.

CORRECT POSITION OF 'PUMP' SHOULD BE FOUND BY DETAILED STUDY OF THE HEATING CIRCUIT

VALVE

LOCKSHIELD VALVE

RAD. VALVE

AIR RELEASE AS NORMAL

PRIMATIC CYL

FLOW PIPE

RETURN

ONE PIPE SYSTEM

HEATING LAYOUT DEPENDS UPON WHETHER THE BOILER HAS TWO OR FOUR TAPPINGS

USUALLY ACCELERATED CIRCULATION

USING THE SINGLE-FEED CYLINDER
This method is suitable for 'small bore' or 'microbore' systems within stated capacities. Operates with equal efficiency for hw with or without a 'pump'. Pump has no adverse effect on unit.

PRESSURISATION BY SEALING THE SYSTEM IS AN 'OPTIONAL EXTRA'. IT ENABLES A WATER TEMPERATURE HIGHER THAN NORMAL TO BE USED. IT ALSO DISPENSES WITH ONE CISTERN AND ALL ASSOCIATED PIPEWORK.

CYLINDERS CAN BE COUPLED IN ANY ONE OF A VARIETY OF WAYS

FROM CYL STAT

CONTROL BOX

MICROBORE TUBE

AIR VALVE

HEATING 'COIL' FOR TOWEL RAIL OR AIRING CUPBOARD

HEATING ELEMENT

BLANKED OFF

DRAIN VALVE

ROOM STAT

MANIFOLD

DOUBLE ENTRY VALVE

MANIFOLD

CLY TEMP CONTROLLED BY THERMOSTAT & MOTORISED VALVE

INJECTOR 'T' IMPROVES CYL CIRCULATION

ACCELERATED CIRCULATION

USING MICROBORE SYSTEM (PRESSURISED)
This sytem has an individual flow and return to each rad from a 22mm manifold using 6, 8, 10 or 12mm OD soft copper tube. Requires more powerful 'pump' than 'small bore'.

CI CAST IRON. CIR CIRCULATION. CYL CYLINDER. HW HOT WATER. MS MILD STEEL. NOM NOMINAL. OD OUTSIDE DIAM. RAD RADIATOR.

NOTE: TOWEL RAILS SHOULD BE SO CONNECTED THAT THEY CAN SERVE THEIR PURPOSE WHEN HEATING IS NOT REQUIRED. THE ABOVE DIAGRAMS ILLUSTRATE A VARIETY OF WAYS OF ACHIEVING THIS.

NOTES

NOTES: Designing for large buildings involves a combination of basic principles but considered in relation to the particular building. Use of secondary circulations to limit length of 'dead' legs; economy in pipework; good thermal insulation; satisfactory flow rates without delay at all times; use of gravity circulation or pumped circuits; excessive static head at lower draw-off points; insufficient delivery potential at high level draw-off taps, etc are points to be considered seriously. Horizontal or vertical zoning may be necessary. Remote d.o. points may be require individual treatment.

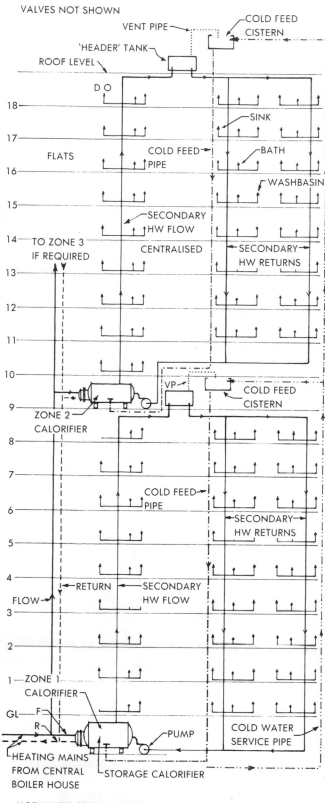

HOT WATER STORAGE COULD BE BASED ON 45 LITRE/FLAT WITH 25% STORED IN 'HEADER' TANK & 75% IN CALORIFIER. COLD FEED CISTERNS TO STORE, SAY, REQUIREMENTS FOR 24 HRS AT 90 LITRE/PERSON

HOT WATER SERVICES IN HIGH-RISE BUILDINGS CENTRALISED SYSTEMS USING ZONED CYL-TANK SYSTEM

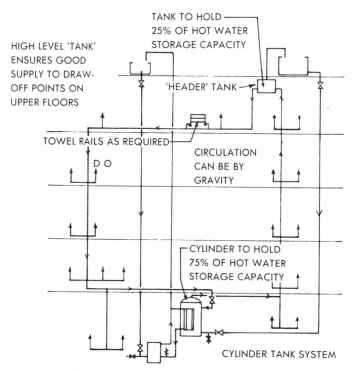

SYSTEM SUITABLE FOR MEDIUM-RISE BUILDINGS CENTRALISED

JUST AS HEATING MAINS WILL PRODUCE A 'HOT' RADIATOR, SO THE SAME MAINS CAN BE USED TO PRODUCE HOT WATER FOR DOMESTIC USE IN ANY PART OF THE BUILDING

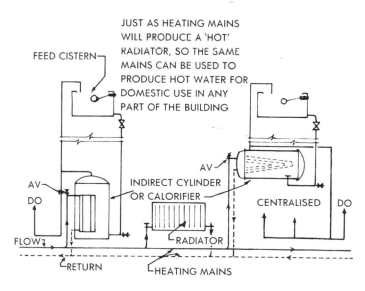

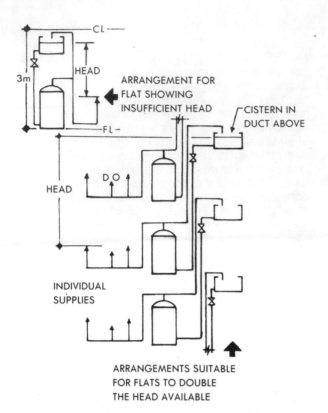

CL

3m

HEAD

FL

ARRANGEMENT FOR
FLAT SHOWING
INSUFFICIENT HEAD

CISTERN IN
DUCT ABOVE

HEAD

D O

INDIVIDUAL
SUPPLIES

ARRANGEMENTS SUITABLE
FOR FLATS TO DOUBLE
THE HEAD AVAILABLE

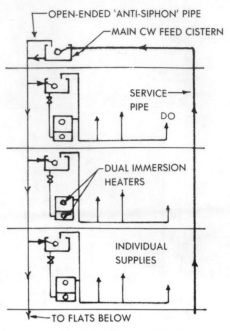

OPEN-ENDED 'ANTI-SIPHON' PIPE

MAIN CW FEED CISTERN

SERVICE
PIPE

DO

DUAL IMMERSION
HEATERS

INDIVIDUAL
SUPPLIES

TO FLATS BELOW

ALL ELECTRICAL SYSTEM USING
'PRESSURE' HEATERS & INDIVIDUAL
BREAK PRESSURE CW FEED CISTERNS

DO DRAW OFF. HW HOT WATER. CW COLD WATER. AV AIR
VENT. VP VENT PIPE. F FLOW PIPE. R RETURN PIPE.

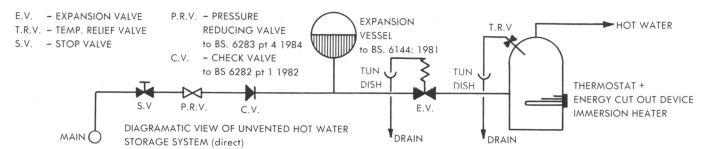

E.V. – EXPANSION VALVE
T.R.V. – TEMP. RELIEF VALVE
S.V. – STOP VALVE

P.R.V. – PRESSURE
REDUCING VALVE
to BS. 6283 pt 4 1984

C.V. – CHECK VALVE
to BS 6282 pt 1 1982

EXPANSION VESSEL
to BS. 6144: 1981

T.R.V

HOT WATER

TUN DISH

TUN DISH

THERMOSTAT + ENERGY CUT OUT DEVICE IMMERSION HEATER

S.V   P.R.V.   C.V.

E.V.

MAIN

DRAIN   DRAIN

DIAGRAMATIC VIEW OF UNVENTED HOT WATER STORAGE SYSTEM (direct)

The Building Regulations 1985 introduced for the first time the use of unvented hot water systems of over 15 litres storage capacity, to be connected directly to the Public Water Supply.

Systems of this type have been in common use throughout the world, but until now this has been resisted in this country for fear of contamination to the public supply.

Part G3 of schedule 1 to the Building Regulations 1985 lists safety requirements for unvented hot water systems (with certain exceptions).

These are:

(i)   Adequate precautions to prevent the temperature of the stored water exceeding 100 deg. C.

(ii)   The discharge of hot water from safety devices to be taken to a point which is visible but will not be a danger to persons nearby.

Unlike hot water storage cylinders fed by cold water storage cisterns, the unvented systems are fed directly from the cold main supply and are not vented to the atmosphere. This allows the hot water storage cylinder to be located in any convenient position in the dwelling because the operating pressure of 2 bar is significantly greater than the pressure normally provided by cistern fed systems. Should the system overheat, however, pressure will increase within the cylinder resulting in a possible explosion unless adequate safety devices are incorporated in the system.

Another advantage is that a mains pressurised system provides balanced pressures at all outlet positions, this being particularly useful for showers, where optimum performance can be achieved.

As pressures are generally greater, pipework sizes can be reduced to reflect this — as well as the elimination of ball valves and cold water cisterns.

Some problems have been found with certain imported systems that are unable to function properly due to the smaller diameter supply pipes in this country. It is considered that the supply is simply not great enough to meet the demands of the present day consumers. The recently formed Water Heater Manufacturers' Association could provide advice for specifiers who wish to use this type of system.

Approved Document G3 lays down the following levels of safety protection.

The discharge pipes to be a suitable metal and the size not less than the safety device outlet. The discharge to be via an air break to a tun dish.

The pipes to be laid in a continuous fall and be no longer than 9m, unless the diameter is increased.

The pipe to discharge into a gully or similar place which will not endanger any persons using the building.

INSTALLATION

Approved Document G3 requires that systems should be installed by an 'Approved Installer' as defined in the British Board of Agrément Certificate.

1)   Install only systems certified by the BBA in accordance with the relevant current BBA certificates.

2)   Employ appropriate management staff and design staff experienced in unvented hot water storage systems.

3)   Employ only registered operatives and trainees on the installation of unvented hot water systems.

4)   Work within an arrangement where they have a clearly defined responsibility for the installations undertaken.

5)   Maintain effective and up-to-date records of all unvented hot water storage system installations undertaken by them.

6)   Provide adequate operative supervision and control to ensure that installations conform to the relevant BBA certificate.

7)   Institute and maintain an arrangement to certify that each unvented hot water storage installation has been carried out in accordance with BBA certificate.

8)   Rectify any installation which they have carried out and which is subsequently shown not to conform to the relevant BBA certificate.

It will be necessary for subsequent repair, maintenance and replacement of components be carried out by BBA approved installers. The system is to be clearly labelled to avoid misunderstanding.

The system must be fully checked through by the installer, followed by an inspection of the Building Control Officer (or Approved Inspector).

It is considered important that the user is made familiar with the workings of the system to enable regular checks to be made. A copy of the Agrément Certificate should be left with the installation.

BACK
OR RANGE BOILER
(SINGLE TAPPINGS)

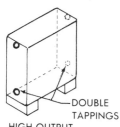

DOUBLE
TAPPINGS

HIGH OUTPUT
BACK BOILER

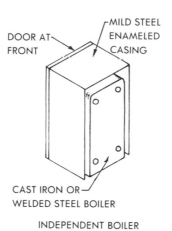

DOOR AT FRONT

MILD STEEL
ENAMELED
CASING

CAST IRON OR
WELDED STEEL BOILER

INDEPENDENT BOILER

BOILERS

A boiler is defined as a vessel, not open to the atmosphere, in which water is heated by the direct application of heat to the outside of the vessel. A 'back' boiler is fitted at the back of an open fireplace, and high output back boiler is fixed as part of a room heater, usually for solid fuel. A range boiler is fitted as part of a solid fuel cooking range. An independent boiler is a separate boiler not fitted as part of the appliances mentioned above (BS 4118). The term 'boiler' is a misnomer as there is no intention for the water to actually boil as it would in a steam boiler.

Irrespective of fuel used, boilers may be classified broadly under 3 headings.

(1)   Back boilers which may be fitted to room heaters, fireplaces or cooking ranges
(2)   Hot water supply boilers which are designed for the direct heating of water actually drawn off. Facilities for inspection and manual descaling are provided.
(3)   Hot water supply boilers which are designed for the indirect heating of the water actually drawn off, by means of an indirect cylinder (CP342 Pt. I).

Where a direct system is used the material of which the boiler is made, or the protective treatment thereof (eg. internal bower-barffing) should be suitable for the water supply and the fuel to be used.

Notes from BS 3377 Back Boilers :- Flow and return tappings shall normally be not less than lin. BSP. The design and construction of the boiler and the position of the flow tapping shall be such that the air is not trapped within the boiler. With top tappings, a dip pipe shall be provided to a position 38mm clear of the bottom. For side tappings, the 38mm (min) clearance of the return is measured to centre of tapping.

Materials :- Mild steel and cast iron (not recommended for direct systems). Copper and aluminium bronze (for soft water areas and direct systems). Stainless steel (use restricted to soft water installations).

Notes from BS 779 Cast Iron Boilers (Independent) :- Boilers for central heating and hot water supply, indirect and direct hw supply (55,000 to 2 million Btu/h rating). For direct; sufficient cleaning holes for inspection and cleaning to be provided.

FLOW AND RETURN CONNECTIONS

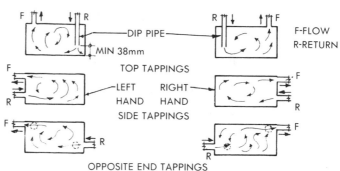

DIP PIPE

MIN 38mm

F-FLOW
R-RETURN

TOP TAPPINGS

LEFT
HAND

RIGHT
HAND

SIDE TAPPINGS

OPPOSITE END TAPPINGS

BACK TAPPINGS SHOWN DOTTED

ALTERNATIVE BACK BOILER TAPPINGS

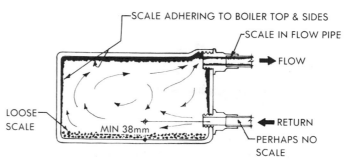

SCALE ADHERING TO BOILER TOP & SIDES

SCALE IN FLOW PIPE

FLOW

LOOSE
SCALE

MIN 38mm

RETURN

PERHAPS NO
SCALE

SECTION THROUGH BACK BOILER.

CIRCULATION WITHIN A BOILER IS DEFINITE AS SOON AS HEAT IS APPLIED. HAVING TWO CONNECTIONS AT DIFFERENT LEVELS ENSURES POSITIVELY WHICH IS THE FLOW AND RETURN PIPE. SECTION SHOWS THE SCALING WHICH WOULD OCCUR IF THE WATER IS TEMPORARY HARD & THE SYSTEM IS DIRECT

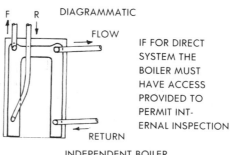

F   R   DIAGRAMMATIC

FLOW

IF FOR DIRECT
SYSTEM THE
BOILER MUST
HAVE ACCESS
PROVIDED TO
PERMIT INT-
ERNAL INSPECTION

RETURN

INDEPENDENT BOILER
(REAR VIEW)

BOILER MAY HAVE TWO OR MORE
TAPPINGS FACING REAR OR SIDEWAYS

MOUNTINGS

These include relief valves, draining taps, thermometers, water temperature controllers, open vent pipe tappings, altitude gauges. Mountings for back boilers are usually restricted to relief valves and draining taps.

Relief valves :- Boilers should be fitted with a direct-acting spring loaded valve mounted directly on the boiler, if possible. For back boilers, the valve should be connected to the return pipe as close to the boiler as possible.

Draining taps :- If cannot be mounted on the boiler, should be connected to lowest point of system, connected to the boiler.

Thermometers :- If cannot be mounted on the boiler it should be fitted in or on the return pipe.

Water temperature controls :- Boilers should have provision for a water temperature controller.

Open vent pipes :- Boilers should have a tapping for an open vent pipe.

Altitude gauges :- Provision should be made for mounting this on the boiler and be fitted with an isolating cock.

Safety controls for automatically fired and controlled boilers :- To comply with relevant BS and CP.

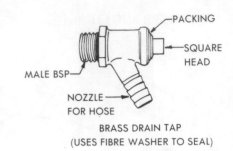

BRASS DRAIN TAP
(USES FIBRE WASHER TO SEAL)

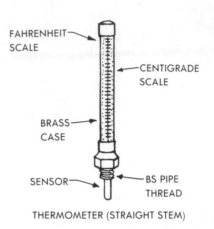

THERMOMETER (STRAIGHT STEM)

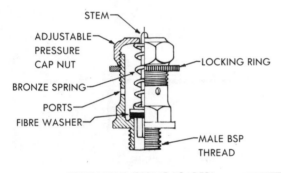

RELIEF VALVE (SPRING LOADED)
SCREW INTO BOILER OR TEE PIECE

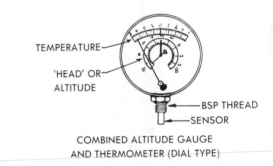

COMBINED ALTITUDE GAUGE
AND THERMOMETER (DIAL TYPE)

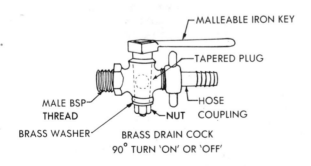

BRASS DRAIN COCK
90° TURN 'ON' OR 'OFF'

56

NOTES FROM CP 342

Hot water storage vessels should preferably be cylindrical; be installed vertically rather than horizontally, with pipe connections made so that advantage is taken of the tendency of heated water to stratify. The draw-off or secondary flow pipe, should be taken from the top of the vessel. Any secondary return pipe should be connected at a point not lower than ¼ of the height down from the top of the vessel. For a direct cylinder the primary flow pipe should be connected at the same height as any secondary return. Cold feed pipe should be connected as near the bottom of the vessel as is practicable and same applies to the primary return. Provision should be made for venting of air from the vessel and also from the heating element of a double feed indirect cylinder. Vessels up to 227 litre (50 gal) may be supported on any normal floor but should be on wood bearers min 100mm in height. Mountings for larger vessels include thermometer but a draining tap is required for DF indirect cylinders and where more than one storage vessel is connected to the boiler.

Available in Grades A, B & C.
A: max working head: 30m*
B: max working head: 18m *
C: max working head: 9m *
* measured from bottom of cylinder to water line of cistern. For OD, add 13mm (welded) or 25mm (riveted). Connections are BSP F parallel threaded hand hole : min. diam. 150mm.

Copper :-

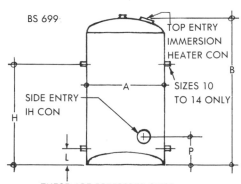

BS 699

● THESE ARE PREFERRED SIZES
FOR NEW INSTALLATIONS
CYLINDER NOT NORMALLY FITTED
WITH HAND HOLE BUT IT MAY BE
PROVIDED BY AGREEMENT BETWEEN
PURCHASER & MANUFACTURER

BS TYPE REF	EXT DIA (A)	HEIGHT (B) OVER DOME	CAPACITY l	CAPACITY gal	HEIGHT OF CONNECTIONS H	L	P	SIZE OF CONNECTIONS
1	350	900	74	16	700	100	150	1"
2	400	900	98	22	700	100	150	1"
3●	400	1050	116	26	800	100	150	1"
4	450	675	86	19	450	100	150	1"
5	450	750	98	22	550	100	150	1"
6	450	825	109	24	625	100	150	1"
7●	450	900	120	26	700	100	150	1"
8●	450	1050	144	32	800	100	150	1¼"
9●	450	1200	166	37	950	100	150	1¼"
10	500	1200	200	44	950	150	200	1½"
11	500	1500	255	56	1200	150	200	1½"
12	600	1200	290	64	950	150	200	2"
13	600	1500	370	81	1200	150	200	2"
14	600	1800	450	99	1350	150	200	2"

DIRECT

Galv mild steel :-

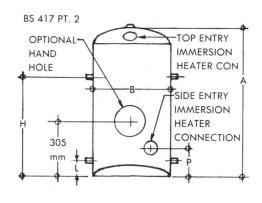

BS 417 PT. 2

BS TYPE REF	INSIDE DIAM B	HEIGHT (A) OVER DOME	CAPACITY l	CAPACITY gal	HEIGHT OF CONNECTIONS H	L	P	SIZE OF CONNECTIONS
YM91	371	762	73	16	584	102	159	1"
YM114	371	991	100	22	762	102	159	1"
YM127	457	787	114	25	584	102	159	1"
YM141	457	838	123	27	635	102	159	1"
YM150	457	914	136	30	686	102	159	1"
YM177	457	1067	159	35	813	102	159	1¼"
YM218	508	1067	195	43	813	102	159	1¼"
YM264	508	1295	241	53	991	102	159	1¼"
YM355	610	1219	332	73	914	127	159	1½"
YM455	610	1600	441	97	1194	127	159	1½"

Available in Grades 1, 2 & 3
1: max working head: 25m*
2: max working head: 15m*
3: max working head: 10m*
1m head of head = 10kN/m²
External BSP F threads may be supplied if required. Seams can be either:- welted, overlapped or butt welded. Note that the diameter given is external — this also applies to copper indirect cylinder.

INDIRECT

Galv. mild steel :-

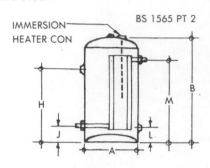

IMMERSION HEATER CON

BS 1565 PT 2

BS SIZE NO	INSIDE DIA (A)	HEIGHT (B) OVER DOME	CAPACITY		HEIGHT OF CONNECTIONS			SIZE OF CONNECTIONS
			l	gal	H	J&L	M	
BSG1M	457	762	109	24	559	140	610	1"
BSG2M	457	914	136	30	686	140	749	1"
BSG3M	457	1067	159	35	813	152	914	1¼"
BSG4M	508	1270	227	50	991	178	1041	1½"
BSG5M	508	1473	273	60	1143	178	1194	1½"
BSG6M	610	1372	364	80	1041	191	1143	2"
BSG7M	610	1753	455	100	1346	191	1524	2"
BSG8M	457	838	123	27	635	140	686	1"

Available in Classes B & C
B: max working head: 18m*
C: max working head: 9m*
Cylinder connections: BSP F internal. Primary heater connections: BSP F external. Hand hole optional. For sizes 1, 2, 3 & 8, distance L = 75mm

Copper :-

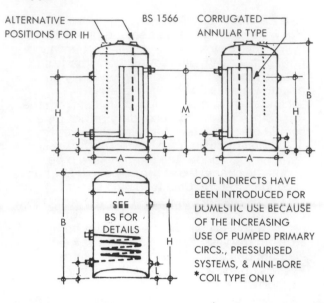

ALTERNATIVE POSITIONS FOR IH

BS 1566

CORRUGATED ANNULAR TYPE

SEE BS FOR DETAILS

COIL INDIRECTS HAVE BEEN INTRODUCED FOR DOMESTIC USE BECAUSE OF THE INCREASING USE OF PUMPED PRIMARY CIRCS., PRESSURISED SYSTEMS, & MINI-BORE
*COIL TYPE ONLY

BS TYPE REF	EXT DIA (A)	HEIGHT (B) OVER DOME	CAPACITY		HEIGHT OF CONNECTIONS				SIZE OF CONNECTIONS
			l	gal	H	J	L	M	
0*	300	1600	96	21	1250	100	100	150	1"
1	350	900	72	16	700	140	100	430	1"
2	400	900	96	21	700	140	100	560	1"
3•	400	1050	114	25	800	140	100	670	1"
4	450	675	84	19	450	140	100	500	1"
5	450	750	95	21	550	140	100	560	1"
6	450	825	106	23	625	140	100	640	1"
7•	450	900	117	26	700	140	100	700	1"
8•	450	1050	140	31	800	150	100	840	1¼"
9•	450	1200	162	36	950	150	100	950	1¼"
10	500	1200	190	42	950	180	150	960	1½"
11	500	1500	245	54	1200	180	150	1110	1½"
12	600	1200	280	62	950	190	150	880	2"
13	600	1500	360	79	1200	190	150	1190	2"
14	600	1800	440	97	3150	190	150	1490	2"

MISCELLANEOUS NOTES
BS 1566 Pt 2 refers to single feed indirect cylinders and lists 6 sizes with capacities ranging from 86 to 180 litres (See Detail No 7). All threads are the parallel type (not taper). Gallons are calculated to the nearest whole gallon. All measurements are in mm unless otherwise stated. The British Standards should be consulted for full details. Min. Byelaw size: 25 gal unless system thermostatically controlled.

Available in Grades 2 & 3
2: max working head: 15m*
3: max working head: 10m*
Cylinder connections: BSP F internal but may be external. Primary heater connections: BSP F external. Hand hole can be provided if required. For horizontally mounted immersion heaters, the primary heater is shortened to allow the heater to be positioned beneath. Also applies to MS indirect.

DF = DOUBLE FEED   OD = OUTSIDE DIAMETER
IH = IMMERSION HEATER   CON = CONNECTION

TANKS
Notes
Model Water Byelaws define a tank as being a non-cylindrical closed vessel capable of containing water under pressure greater than atmospheric as distinct from a cistern which must have a free water surface under atmospheric pressure only. BS 4118 gives the same definition for a hot water tank and CP310 couples hot water cylinder and tank together with the same definition. Therefore the difference between them (re:310) is purely one of shape, but CP341 Pt. 1 states the preference for cylindrical vessels for storing hot water.

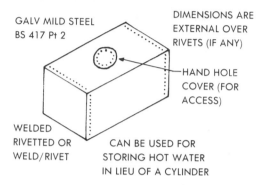

GALV MILD STEEL BS 417 Pt 2

DIMENSIONS ARE EXTERNAL OVER RIVETS (IF ANY)

HAND HOLE COVER (FOR ACCESS)

WELDED RIVETTED OR WELD/RIVET

CAN BE USED FOR STORING HOT WATER IN LIEU OF A CYLINDER

BS TYPE REF	OUTSIDE DIMENSIONS			CAPACITY	
	LENGTH	WIDTH	DEPTH	l	gal
TM114/1	610	432	432	95	21
TM114/2	610	610	305	95	21
TM136/1	610	457	482	114	25
TM136/2	610	610	371	123	27
TM182	686	508	508	155	34

DIMENSIONS OF TANKS TO BS417

Available in 2 Grades : A and B
A: max working heat of water: 4.5m*
B: max working head of water: 3.0m*
*Measured from bottom of tank to water line of cistern. All tanks to have hand hole, min 150mm dia. All '417' tanks, etc, are galvanised after manufacture.

CISTERNS
Notes
A cistern is defined as being a fixed container for water at atmospheric pressure. The water is usually supplied through a ballvalve which is adjusted to shut off when the water reaches the 'water line' which is the highest water level at which a cistern is designed to work. Capacity is the amount of water contained when filled to the water line — not full to the brim. The terms 'nominal' capacity (completely full) and 'actual' (full to water line) should be regarded as obsolescent. Water Byelaws prohibit the direct supply of cold water under pressure from the mains of a water authority to any apparatus in which the water is heated. For exceptions to this — see Water Byelaws. Centralised hot water systems are therefore normally supplied from cold water feed cisterns. A direct system

requires only one feed cistern, whereas an indirect system (unless single feed type) has two in order to keep the water in the primary circuit entirely separate from the water drawn off for use. The capacity of a feed cistern should be at least equal to that of the hot water cylinder; no minimum byelaw capacity is prescribed. A cistern supplying cold water draw-off points may also be used as a feed cistern, then min Byelaw capacity becomes 50 gal (227 l).

GLASS FIBRE CISTERNS ALSO AVAILABLE
CAPACITIES STATED ARE APPROXIMATE

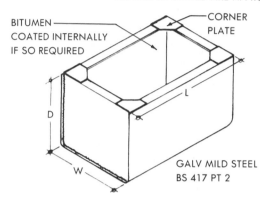

BITUMEN COATED INTERNALLY IF SO REQUIRED

CORNER PLATE

GALV MILD STEEL BS 417 PT 2

TYPE REF BS 417	DIMENSIONS OF CISTERNS			CAPACITY TO WL		DISTANCE WATER LINE FROM TOP	WEIGHT kg	
	LENGTH	WIDTH	DEPTH	l	gal		°A	°B
SCM45•	457	305	305	18	4	111	10	–
SCM70•	610	305	371	36	8	111	14	–
SCM90	610	406	371	54	12	111	17	–
SCM110	610	432	432	68	15	114	18	–
SCM135	610	457	482	86	19	114	20	–
SCM180	686	508	508	114	25	114	23	–
SCM230	736	559	559	159	35	114	35	27
SCM270	762	584	610	191	42	114	38	31
SCM320	914	610	584	227	50	114	43	34
SCM360	914	660	610	264	58	114	46	38
SCM450/1	1219	610	610	327	72	114	52	43
SCM450/2	965	686	686	336	74	114	53	43
SCM570	965	762	787	423	93	146	84	69
SCM680	1092	864	736	491	108	146	86	70
SCM910	1168	889	889	709	156	146	115	87
SCM1130	1524	914	813	841	185	146	124	104
SCM1600*	1524	1143	914	1227	270	146	201	163
SCM2270*	1829	1219	1016	1727	380	146	246	210
SCM2720*	1829	1219	1219	2137	470	190	283	239
SCM4540*	2438	1524	1219	3364	740	254	569	416

Available in 2 Grades: A & B
A: min thickness: 1.6 to 4.8mm
B: min thickness: 1.2 to 3.2mm
Cisterns measured externally over rivets (if any). They shall be either welded, rivetted or partly both, or locked and rolled seams. Top

edges are stiffened in some way (see BS) and all cisterns shall have corner plates except those indicated•. Large size* cisterns are stayed with some arrangement of cross ties. Length of a welded cistern may be increased by max 25mm. Supplied blank unless hole details specified. Weights• are from Braby Ltd. Covers are available.

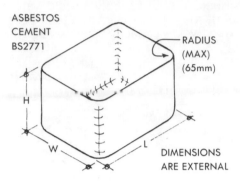

ASBESTOS CEMENT BS2771

RADIUS (MAX) (65mm)

H

W   L

DIMENSIONS ARE EXTERNAL

BS4213 TYPE REF	CAPACITY TO WL		WL FROM TOP	MAX HEIGHT OF CISTERN	MASS kg(min)
	l	gal			
PC4	18	4	111	310	1.36
PC8	36	8	111	380	1.81
PC15	68	15	114	430	2.95
PC20	91	20	114	510	3.18
PC25	114	25	114	560	3.40
PC40	182	40	114	610	6.35
PC50	227	50	114	660	7.03
PC60	273	60	114	660	7.26
PC70	318	70	114	660	9.07
PC100	455	100	114	760	12.70

PLASTIC COLD WATER STORAGE CISTERNS
(MOULDED POLYOLEFIN OR OLEFIN COPOLYMER)
EXAMPLES OF MATERIALS: POLYPROPYLENE & POLYTHENE.
EASILY DRILLED FOR CONNECTIONS. PLAN SHAPE USUALLY
RECTANGULAR OR CIRCULAR COVERS AVAILABLE.

BS 2777 TYPE REF	DIMENSIONS OF CISTERNS			CAPACITY		WL FROM TOP	WEIGHT kg
	LENGTH	WIDTH	HEIGHT	l	gal		
AC27M(6)	323	323	314	17	4	100	6.4
AC45M(10)	481	329	368	28	6	110	13.7
AC90M(20)	532	405	495	62	14	110	21.4
AC114M(25)	634	456	444	80	18	115	23.6
AC136M(30)	634	481	571	114	25	115	30.0
AC182M(40)	710	532	545	136	30	115	33.4
AC227M(50)	634	634	647	188	41	115	39.4
AC273M(60)	786	608	647	227	50	115	44.6
AC364M(80)	938	684	647	300	66	115	54.0
AC455M(100)	989	710	723	381	84	115	61.3
AC591M(130)	1015	862	736	473	104	145	72.0
AC819M(180)	1232	1029	736	701	154	145	104.1

ASBESTOS-CEMENT CISTERN SIZES
CONNECTIONS FOR THE SUPPLY, OVERFLOW & TAKE-OFF PIPES
ARE EASILY DRILLED WITH BRACE & BIT. A.C. COVERS ARE
AVAILABLE.

RELEVANT WATER BYELAWS

33. Placing of storage cisterns
34. Support and covering of storage cisterns
35. Avoidance of flooding: buried or sunken cisterns
36. Materials for storage cisterns
37. BS's for storage cisterns
38. Capacity of storage cisterns in houses
40. Warning pipes on storage cisterns holding not more than 1000 gallons
41. Overflow pipes on storage cisterns holding not more than 1000 gal (4546 l)
(51. Min size of hot storage vessel to be 25 gal (114 l) Unless thermostatically controlled).

1 Kg = 2.2 lb

L = LENGTH
W = WIDTH
D = DEPTH
H = HEIGHT

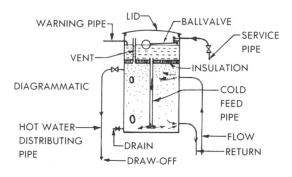

DIAGRAMMATIC

			*		*		*		*
HOT	l	65	85	115	115	130	115	150	115
	gal	15	19	25	25	29	25	33	25
COLD	l	20	25	25	45	45	20	45	115
	gal	4½	5½	5½	10	10	4½	10	25
a		900	900	1075	1200	1300	900	1200	1400
b		400	450	450	450	450	500	500	500
c		580	590	770	770	868	638	810	638
d		303	293	293	420	420	245	370	748
e		368	368	470	470	570	368	570	368
f		500	510	690	690	788	558	730	558

STANDARD DIRECT

NOTES FROM BS 3198
Also known as combination tanks. Although primarily for connecting to pipework, can be obtained for immersion heater or gas circulator. BS size: 25 gal but other sizes are available. During draw-off, replacement water is supplied from cold water feed cistern incorporated in or adjacent to the hot storage vessel. Cistern can be superimposed on (with insulation between) the hot vessel or attached to the side of hot vessel. Interconnections include ¾in. (min) vent pipe which can also act as 'expansion' pipe, outlet from feed cistern to hot storage vessel to connect min lin. up from bottom of feed cistern. Provision shall be made for free venting of air at all times. Draw-off point to connect so that water level cannot be lowered by more than ½ if vessel is open-topped and ¼ if closed vessel. Details of connections for the ballvalve and warning pipe, and depth of the water level are also given.

COMBINING CISTERN & HOT WATER VESSEL PRODUCES A COMPACT UNIT FOR USE PARTICULARLY IN A CONFINED SPACE & FOR LOW INITIAL COST

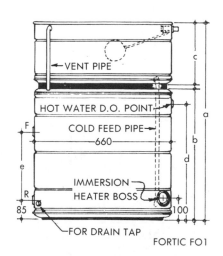

FORTIC FO1

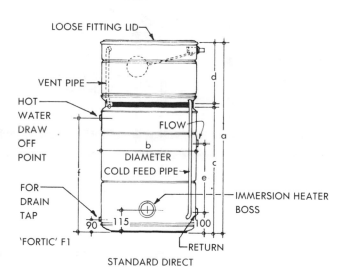

'FORTIC' F1
STANDARD DIRECT

305

660

PLAN VIEW

		*	*
HOT	l	85	115	115
	gal	19	25	25
COLD	l	25	25	45
	gal	5½	5½	10
a		900	1075	1200
b		590	770	770
c		293	293	420
d		515	695	695
e		330	435	435

STANDARD OVAL DIRECT

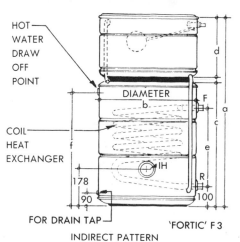

'FORTIC' F 3
INDIRECT PATTERN
REQUIRES SEPARATE COLD FEED TO PRIMARY

HOT				*	*		*		*
	l	65	85	115	115	130	115	150	115
	gal	15	19	25	25	29	25	33	25
COLD	l	20	25	25	45	45	20	45	45
	gal	4½	5½	5½	10	10	4½	10	25
a		900	900	1075	1200	1300	900	1200	1400
b		400	450	450	450	450	500	500	500
c		580	590	770	770	868	638	810	638
d		303	293	293	420	420	245	370	748
e		368	368	470	470	570	368	570	368
f		500	510	690	690	788	558	730	558

INDIRECT PATTERN

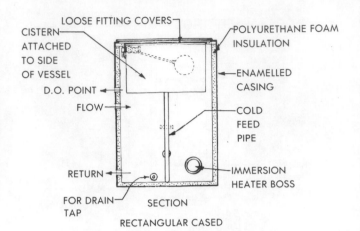

CISTERN ATTACHED TO SIDE OF VESSEL — LOOSE FITTING COVERS — POLYURETHANE FOAM INSULATION — ENAMELLED CASING — D.O. POINT — FLOW — COLD FEED PIPE — RETURN — FOR DRAIN TAP — IMMERSION HEATER BOSS — SECTION

RECTANGULAR CASED

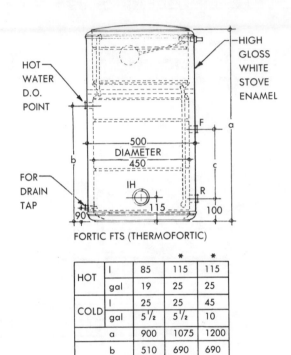

HIGH GLOSS WHITE STOVE ENAMEL — HOT WATER D.O. POINT — 500 DIAMETER 450 — IH — FOR DRAIN TAP — 90 — 115 — 100 — F — R — a — b — c

FORTIC FTS (THERMOFORTIC)

HOT			*	*
	l	85	115	115
	gal	19	25	25
COLD	l	25	25	45
	gal	5½	5½	10
a		900	1075	1200
b		510	690	690
c		330	435	435

INSULATED CASE MODEL

ALL TYPES CAN BE HEATED BY DIRECT CIRCULATION FROM BOILER, OR IMMERSION HEATER OR GAS CIRCULATOR. COIL HEATER EXCHANGERS (INDIRECT) ARE FOR USE EITHER WITH HOT WATER OR STEAM.

OTHER MODELS AVAILABLE.

* THESE SIZES COMPLY WITH BS3198

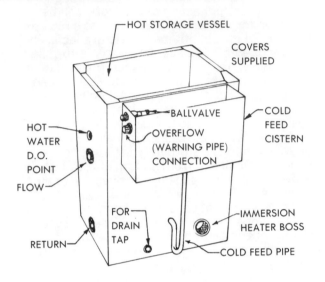

HOT STORAGE VESSEL — COVERS SUPPLIED — BALLVALVE — OVERFLOW (WARNING PIPE) CONNECTION — COLD FEED CISTERN — HOT WATER D.O. POINT — FLOW — FOR DRAIN TAP — RETURN — IMMERSION HEATER BOSS — COLD FEED PIPE

EXTERNAL FINISH PVC COATED GALVANISED MILD STEEL

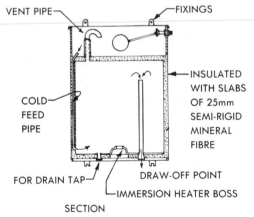

VENT PIPE — FIXINGS — INSULATED WITH SLABS OF 25mm SEMI-RIGID MINERAL FIBRE — COLD FEED PIPE — FOR DRAIN TAP — DRAW-OFF POINT — IMMERSION HEATER BOSS — SECTION

RECTANGULAR CASED, WALL MOUNTED 'SLIMLINE'

DIRECT RECTANGULAR PATTERNS (INDIRECT ALSO AVAILABLE)

ALL DIMENSIONS ARE IN MILLIMETRES UNLESS OTHERWISE STATED.

F: FLOW CONNECTION. R: RETURN CONNECTION. DO: DRAW-OFF (FOR HOT WATER). IH: IMMERSION HEATER BOSS

SOME POINTS IN FAVOUR OF SHOWERS

A shower is claimed to be the most refreshing and hygienic way to bathe, using a continuous spray of clean water delivered at a temperature to suit the user. The operation is quick, simple, convenient and economical e.g. a good shower uses only ¼ of the water required for the average bath. It is considered an easy way and quite safe for use by the elderly or infirm people as compared with using the standard bath. Showering can be carried out in the sitting position. A shower can be installed over an existing or new bath, or separately in almost any part of a typical house occupying floor space from about 0.75m square.

MIXING VALVES

Model Water Byelaw 47:- (See Byelaws for exact wording). No mixing valve, pipe or other water fitting in which hw and cw are mixed, shall be so connected as to mix cold water from a service pipe with hot water from an apparatus not under mains pressure and vice-versa. Pressures must be 'balanced' e.g. from same cistern.

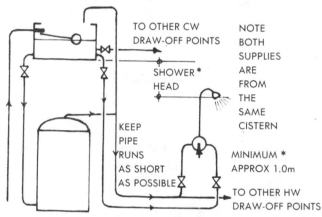

CAPACITY OF STORAGE CISTERNS FOR HOUSES

Model Water Byelaw 38
Capacity of storage cistern (or cisterns connected together) shall be not less than 25 gal (114 litres) if not used as a feed cistern; or 50 gal (228 litres) if used both as a feed cistern and other purposes. For cisterns supplying a hot water apparatus and cold water to a shower, minimum of 50 gal applies.

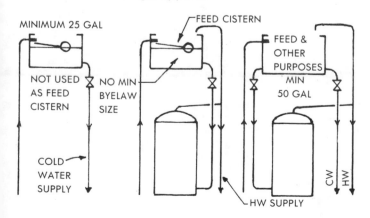

DATA

Shower temperature: 38° to 43°C
Stored water temperature: 60/65°C
Rates of flow: Nozzle: 0.11 litres/s (1.5 gal/min)
*100mm rose: 0.30 litres/s (4 gal/min)
(*regarded as wasteful)
Fixing height: Should be made adjustable with a maximum of about 1.5m above bottom of bath to give shoulder height shower for a 1.8m person.
Minimum Head: Usually taken as 1m ($9kN/m^2$) but 1.5m gives better results — about 0.1 litres/s
Excessive heads: Use pressure reducing valves
Water usage: Say 4 min shower at 0.11 litres/s = about 26 litres (bath: 114 to 136 litres)

MIXING ARRANGEMENTS

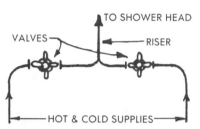

USING TWO VALVES CONTROLLING HOT & COLD SUPPLIES. HAND OPERATION TO OBTAIN BALANCE OF PRESSURE FOR FORCE & TEMP

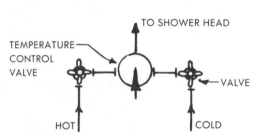

THE TWO VALVES CAN BE PRESET TO GIVE REQUIRED SPRAY FORCE, TO BE RE-ADJUSTED IF REQUIRED. TEMP OBTAINED BY USE OF CENTRE VALVE

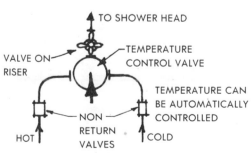

VALVE ON RISER, CONTROLS FLOW RATE, & CENTRE DEVICE CONTROLS THE TEMPERATURE. NON-RETURN VALVES ARE TO PREVENT BACKFLOW

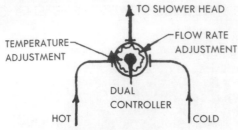

TO SHOWER HEAD

TEMPERATURE ADJUSTMENT

FLOW RATE ADJUSTMENT

DUAL CONTROLLER

HOT

COLD

USING DUAL CONTROLLER, BOTH SPRAY FORCE & TEMPERATURE CAN BE CONTROLLED INDEPENDENTLY OF EACH OTHER. NO OTHER VALVES NEEDED

PROBLEM OF INSUFFICIENT HEAD

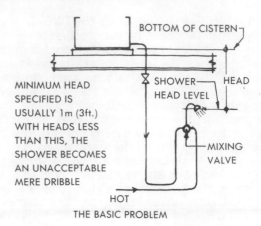

BOTTOM OF CISTERN

MINIMUM HEAD SPECIFIED IS USUALLY 1m (3ft.) WITH HEADS LESS THAN THIS, THE SHOWER BECOMES AN UNACCEPTABLE MERE DRIBBLE

SHOWER HEAD LEVEL

HEAD

MIXING VALVE

HOT

THE BASIC PROBLEM

NOTES FROM THE B.S. CODES OF PRACTICE

CP310. Mixing valves and combined taps for mixing hot and cold water and discharging the mixture through a single outlet should be supplied with hot water and with cold water both under pressure from the same cistern or from cisterns coupled together to act as one; or both under pressure from the same service pipe. One supply should not come from a service pipe and the other from a cistern. These requirements promote the effective control of temperature of the mixed water, especially important with showers and spray fittings, and are necessary because there should be no cross-connections between a service pipe and a distributing pipe. Thermostatic control of temperature for ablutionary fittings is recommended, but is not a substitute for compliance with these requirements.

CP342 Part I. Mixing valves (whether thermostatically controlled or not) ... discharging the mixture through a single outlet, should be supplied with cold water from the same cistern that feeds the hot water system; the cold water should not be under pressure from the mains of a water authority. This requirement assists the effective control of the temperature of the mixed water ... and is necessary because there should be no connection between a pipe under pressure from a cistern and a pipe under pressure from a water main.

Notwithstanding the above, showers can be arranged with both hot and cold water under mains pressure (See Detail 17).

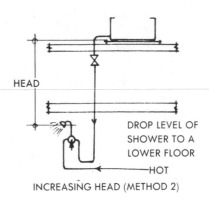

HEAD

RAISE HEIGHT OF CISTERN

HOT

INCREASING HEAD (METHOD 1)

HEAD

DROP LEVEL OF SHOWER TO A LOWER FLOOR

HOT

INCREASING HEAD (METHOD 2)

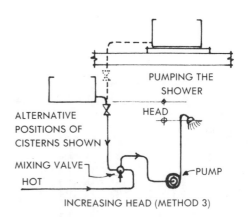

PUMPING THE SHOWER

ALTERNATIVE POSITIONS OF CISTERNS SHOWN

HEAD

MIXING VALVE

HOT

PUMP

INCREASING HEAD (METHOD 3)

COMPLIANCE WITH WATER BYELAWS

Model Water Byelaw 47 (mixing valves) specifically forbids cross-connections between water drawn from a service pipe and water *not* drawn directly from a service pipe. For showers, a common method of compliance is to feed both cold and hot water under the same head and feed from the same cistern. Water to both sides of the 'mixer' is then from the same source and therefore pressures are balanced. It is incorrect to take e.g. the cold water from a service pipe and the hot water from a storage cylinder under cistern pressure. However, Byelaw 47 does not indicate that it is unlawful to take water for a shower directly through an instantaneous hot water heater (without mixing) nor to take cold water from a service pipe and hot water from an instantaneous water heater fed from the same service pipe, thence via a mixing arrangement to a shower head. Pressures are balanced, at least when the shower is on by itself, although the tuning on of another tap will affect the shower operated. If the shower head forms part of a handset attached to a flexible tube and the handset could be immersed in water, an anti-vacuum valve (NRV) should be incorporated to offset the influences of back-siphonage (suction). Without such a valve, 'unclean' water could be drawn into the service pipe producing a potential hazard.

HOT WATER UNDER MAINS PRESSURE

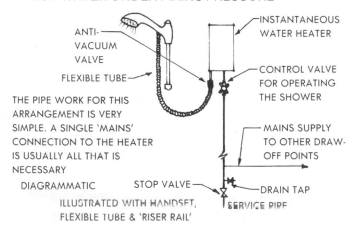

THE PIPE WORK FOR THIS ARRANGEMENT IS VERY SIMPLE. A SINGLE 'MAINS' CONNECTION TO THE HEATER IS USUALLY ALL THAT IS NECESSARY

DIAGRAMMATIC

ILLUSTRATED WITH HANDSET, FLEXIBLE TUBE & 'RISER RAIL'

GENERAL NOTES

Installation must comply with : Relevant Building Regulations, Regional Water Authority Byelaws, I.E.E. Wiring Regs or Gas Regs.
Appliance and installer : Choose an approved appliance and engage an approved contractor for the work.
Water Pressure : A minimum water pressure is necessary to operate appliance (important if cistern fed) and the maximum pressure must also be considered (see manufacturers' instructions). For best results, the shower should be 'on' by itself.
Rating: Higher the rating — the better the shower e.g. 5 kW (21A) 4 pints/minute (0.04 litres/s) 6kW (25A) 4½ pints/minute

HOT AND COLD WATER UNDER MAINS PRESSURE

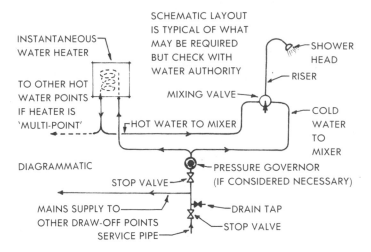

SCHEMATIC LAYOUT IS TYPICAL OF WHAT MAY BE REQUIRED BUT CHECK WITH WATER AUTHORITY

INSTANTANEOUS SHOWERS: POINTS FOR AND AGAINST

FOR

Fixing is simple and economical, using a small appliance plus a minimum of plumbing. Requires water supply (usually 'mains') and electricity or gas connection. Height of cistern therefore not important. A shower can be taken at any time without any thought of stored hot water being available. Hot water ready in seconds and continuous operation allows for several showers in succession. As energy (elec. or gas) is being used only when the shower is operating, running costs are reduced to a minimum. No hot water is stored therefore there is absolutely no heat lost via the hot storage vessel or long pipe runs. Choose highest possible rating of appliance for best results.

AGAINST

The flow rate is considered by some to be insufficient for their personal needs. Temperature may be unstable particularly if another tap is used during the shower operation. Should have several built-in safety devices to prevent scalding, or a suitable mixing arrangement should be used. Outflow temperature can be dependent upon incoming 'mains' temperature (winter as compared with summer) unless compensated for.†

ELECTRICAL INSTANANEOUS HEATERS

Large selection available: 4kW, 5kW, 6kW, 7kW and 8.4kW. Many models incorporate various features. A quick-acting automatic temperature control device should be incorporated. A pressure switch operated by the flow of water is essential (*ie. no water: no elec*). Heaters are splash proof and electrically safe if installed correctly.

  Switch should be double-pole, cord operated*. Conversion efficiency can be taken as 100%.

Varying the rate of flow can be used to vary the temperature. Control may be separate or part of the heater.

GAS INSTANTANEOUS HEATERS

May be single point, or have second outlet, or be multi-point. Can have hand set temp. controller — if not, the built-in thermostat may be set at a temp. too high for a shower eg 60°C (140°F). Therefore 'mixing' arrangements are needed. Appliance efficiency: approximately 75% (may be 'on' for over 5 minutes). Appliance can be 'room-sealed' with balanced flue. Typical performance: 38,000 Btu (11.1 kW) input with hand set controls to give 1 gal/min (0.08 litres/s) at 32°C (90°F) but if turned fully on, the flow rate can be ½ gal/min (0.04 litres/s) at 60°C (140°F)

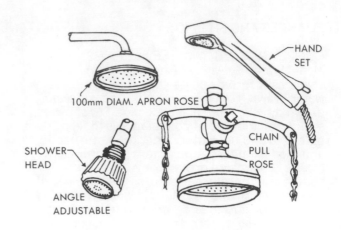

100mm DIAM. APRON ROSE

HAND SET

SHOWER HEAD

ANGLE ADJUSTABLE

CHAIN PULL ROSE

SHOWER POSITIONING IN CUBICLE

SATISFACTORY
SHOWER BOUNCES OFF OPPOSITE WALL & CONTROLS ARE EASILY ACCESSIBLE

UNSATISFACTORY
SPRAY MAY WET FLOOR & CONTROLS CAN ONLY BE REACHED THRO' SHOWER

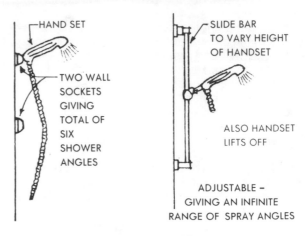

HAND SET

TWO WALL SOCKETS GIVING TOTAL OF SIX SHOWER ANGLES

SLIDE BAR TO VARY HEIGHT OF HANDSET

ALSO HANDSET LIFTS OFF

ADJUSTABLE – GIVING AN INFINITE RANGE OF SPRAY ANGLES

FLEXIBLE HOSE (1.25m)

SHOWER EQUIPMENT

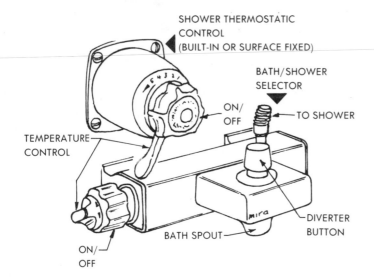

SHOWER THERMOSTATIC CONTROL (BUILT-IN OR SURFACE FIXED)

BATH/SHOWER SELECTOR

ON/OFF

TO SHOWER

TEMPERATURE CONTROL

ON/OFF

BATH SPOUT

DIVERTER BUTTON

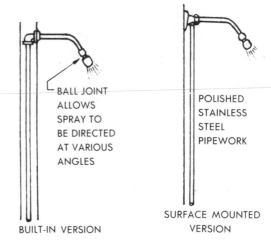

BALL JOINT ALLOWS SPRAY TO BE DIRECTED AT VARIOUS ANGLES

POLISHED STAINLESS STEEL PIPEWORK

BUILT-IN VERSION

SURFACE MOUNTED VERSION

RISER TUBE OR SLIDE BAR

*See I.E.E. Regs.

†Points against are often a matter of opinion and are relevant only to certain models.

SELECTION OF TOWEL RAILS

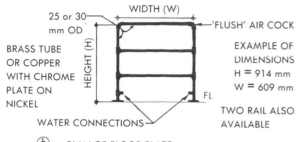

25 or 30 mm OD

WIDTH (W)

HEIGHT (H)

'FLUSH' AIR COCK

BRASS TUBE OR COPPER WITH CHROME PLATE ON NICKEL

EXAMPLE OF DIMENSIONS
H = 914 mm
W = 609 mm

WATER CONNECTIONS

FL

TWO RAIL ALSO AVAILABLE

(b) PLAN OF FLOOR PLATE

THREE RAIL FLOOR MOUNTING

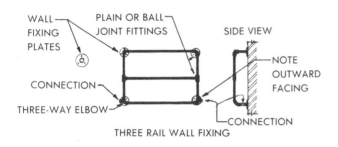

WALL FIXING PLATES

PLAIN OR BALL JOINT FITTINGS

SIDE VIEW

NOTE OUTWARD FACING

CONNECTION

THREE-WAY ELBOW

CONNECTION

THREE RAIL WALL FIXING

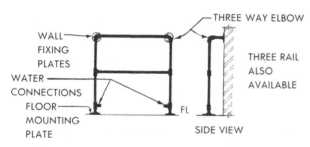

WALL FIXING PLATES

THREE WAY ELBOW

WATER CONNECTIONS

THREE RAIL ALSO AVAILABLE

FLOOR MOUNTING PLATE

FL

SIDE VIEW

TWO RAIL : FLOOR MOUNTING & WALL SUPPORTS

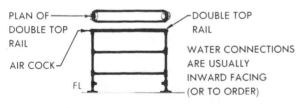

PLAN OF DOUBLE TOP RAIL

DOUBLE TOP RAIL

AIR COCK

WATER CONNECTIONS ARE USUALLY INWARD FACING (OR TO ORDER)

FL

DOUBLE TOP RAIL : FLOOR MOUNTING

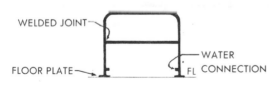

WELDED JOINT

WATER CONNECTION

FLOOR PLATE

FL

SMOOTH LINE CONSTRUCTION : USING NO FITTINGS

EASY FLOW : FLOOR MOUNTING

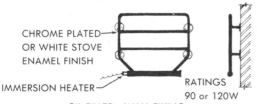

CHROME PLATED OR WHITE STOVE ENAMEL FINISH

IMMERSION HEATER

RATINGS 90 or 120W

OIL FILLED : WALL FIXING

CORROSION

Towel rails without fitted radiators are suitable for open or closed circuits but if fitted with radiators are suitable for closed circuits only. Radiators made of ferrous metal will rust and be the cause of discolouration of the circulating water. This is not noticed if circuit closed.

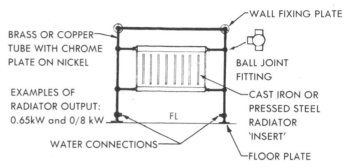

BRASS OR COPPER TUBE WITH CHROME PLATE ON NICKEL

WALL FIXING PLATE

EXAMPLES OF RADIATOR OUTPUT: 0.65kW and 0/8 kW

BALL JOINT FITTING

CAST IRON OR PRESSED STEEL RADIATOR 'INSERT'

FL

WATER CONNECTIONS

FLOOR PLATE

TOWEL RAIL WITH RADIATOR (FLOOR MOUNTED AND WALL SUPPORTS)

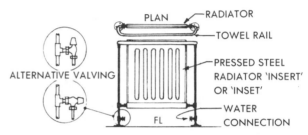

PLAN

RADIATOR

TOWEL RAIL

ALTERNATIVE VALVING

PRESSED STEEL RADIATOR 'INSERT' OR 'INSET'

WATER CONNECTION

FL

TOWEL RAIL WITH RADIATOR: FLOOR MOUNTED

NOTES FROM BS CODES OF PRACTICE

CP342 Centralised Domestic Hot Water Supply: 'Particular requirements for small single family dwellings (about 88m²) (c) There should be ... a heated towel-airing pipe or heated towel rail.' *CP 342 Parts 1 & 2* (Both similarly worded). Towel rails should be provided with control valves (complying with BS 2767) and an air cock and any stay should be of finish equal to that of the towel rail. Towel rails may incorporate a radiator but both should be effectively protected against internal corrosion if connected to a secondary circuit or primary circuit of a direct system.

CP 342 Pt. 1. Pipe coils in airing cupboards ... and towel rails, the use of which may be required outside the heating season, may be connected to a secondary circuit.

CP 342 Pt 1 Towel rails should be of solid drawn brass or copper tubes not thinner than 18 swg highly polished and assembled to give smooth surface of rustless character which cannot damage fabrics. Where a towel rail is supplied as a separate appliance it should be provided with control valve, regulating valve and air cock. All towel rails should be provided with top stays or supports of equal finish to the towel rail. Design should be such that there are not less than two rails in the vertical plane.

CP 342.202 Circulation through towel rails should not be by water heated by electricity — to avoid waste.

CONNECTIONS WITHOUT BY-PASSING

SOME ENGINEERS
PREFER TO CONNECT
A TOWEL RAIL WITHOUT
A RISK OF BY-PASS
WHEN CONNECTING
TO A SIMPLE SYSTEM
OF CIRCULATION

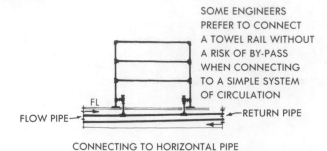

FLOW PIPE ——

—— RETURN PIPE

FL

CONNECTING TO HORIZONTAL PIPE

SIMPLE METHODS
OF CONNECTING
TO PRIMARY OR
SECONDARY FLOW
PIPES ON GRAVITY
CIRCULATION

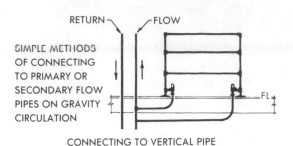

RETURN —   — FLOW

FL

CONNECTING TO VERTICAL PIPE

CONNECTIONS WITH BALANCING ARRANGEMENTS

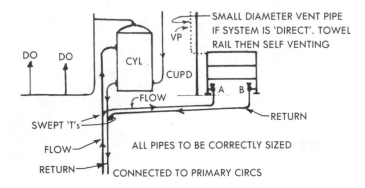

DO   DO

CYL

SMALL DIAMETER VENT PIPE
IF SYSTEM IS 'DIRECT'. TOWEL
RAIL THEN SELF VENTING

VP

CUPD

A   B

— FLOW

SWEPT 'T's

— RETURN

FLOW —

ALL PIPES TO BE CORRECTLY SIZED

RETURN —

CONNECTED TO PRIMARY CIRCS

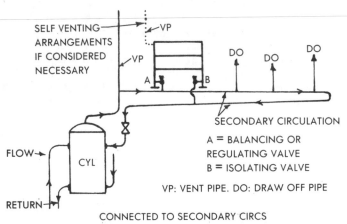

SELF VENTING
ARRANGEMENTS
IF CONSIDERED
NECESSARY

VP

VP

A   B

DO   DO   DO

FLOW →

CYL

RETURN →

SECONDARY CIRCULATION

A = BALANCING OR
REGULATING VALVE
B = ISOLATING VALVE

VP: VENT PIPE. DO: DRAW OFF PIPE

CONNECTED TO SECONDARY CIRCS

POINTS TO CONSIDER

1. Towel rails should not be expected to warm bathroom without rad. insert.
2. Top rail only acts as strip in contact with the towel. The lower tubes effect the drying.
3. Vent pipe from the towel rail can be more satisfactory than an air cock. Air can be a source of nuisance (e.g. on a direct system) with air cocks having to be opened quite frequently: perhaps 3 times a day.

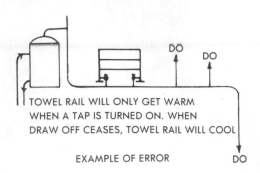

DO   DO

TOWEL RAIL WILL ONLY GET WARM
WHEN A TAP IS TURNED ON. WHEN
DRAW OFF CEASES, TOWEL RAIL WILL COOL

DO

EXAMPLE OF ERROR

ALL TOWEL RAILS ILLUSTRATED
HAVE AIR COCKS FITTED –
EITHER 'FLUSH' OR 'PROUD'

SPRAY MIXING TAP
A tap supplied with hot and cold water and incorporating a mixing device operated by the user. The mixed water is delivered at a restricted rate of flow in the form of a spray.

SPRAY TAP
A tap supplied with water at a pre-determined temperature which it delivers at a restricted rate of flow in the form of a spray. The spray is caused by passing the water through perforated plate.

SPRAY TAP

CP342 PART 2
Where spray taps or spray mixing taps are to be used they should be adjusted to deliver 0.03 litres/s to 0.05 litres/s in order to promote economy of water use. It is recommended that the hot water should be supplied through a pipe with a maximum dead leg length of 1.0m so that there is no appreciable delay in obtaining hot water when the tap is opened. The temperature of the hot water supply to spray taps should be between 38°C and 43°C. When spray mixing taps are used the temperature of the hot water need not exceed 50°C, and it is essential that pressures of H&C are the same.

WATER BYELAW
Byelaw 52(2). Any appliance (incl. a unit of washing trough) with supply incapable of exceeding a flow rate of 5 pints/min, need not be fitted with a plug for the outlet.

BUILDING REGULATION
Approved Document H of the Building Regulations, 1985 recommends a minimum diameter of 32mm shall be provided to a washbasin discharge pipe.

'UNATAP' SPRAY MIXING TAP
The 'UNATAP' offers a different concept in hand washing from the traditional one of filling a wash basin. It generates a fine spray instead of a jet which cleanses the hands more effectively and economically. The temperature of the spray can be regulated from cold to hot by turning the control knob. The control knob or lever operates the piston which proportions the flow of hot and cold water so that they blend. Full flow rate and mid-blend temperature within less than one half turn. Flow rate is almost constant.

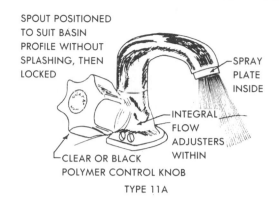

SPOUT POSITIONED TO SUIT BASIN PROFILE WITHOUT SPLASHING, THEN LOCKED — SPRAY PLATE INSIDE — INTEGRAL FLOW ADJUSTERS WITHIN — CLEAR OR BLACK POLYMER CONTROL KNOB

TYPE 11A

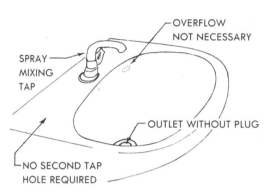

'UNATAP' FITTED TO WASH BASIN

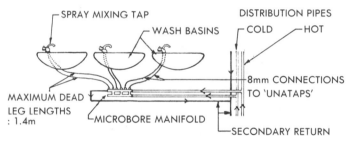

SOFT COPPER CONNECTIONS FROM MICROBORE MANIFOLD

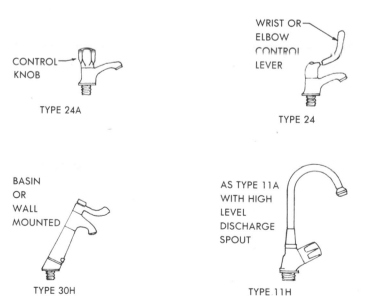

TYPE 24A   TYPE 24   TYPE 30H   TYPE 11H

DESIGN DATA

1. Must have nominally equal pressures (hot and cold)
2. Size of connections are either 2 x 8mm OD or 2 x 10mm OD.
3. Although outflow rate is about $\frac{1}{10}$ of normal discharge rate, Bld Regs require minimum waste pipe size of 32mm
4. Usage time varies with the degree of soiling the hands. Can be 60 sec or less compared with an average of 90 sec for ordinary taps.
5. Flow adjustors can be 'built-in' for preset optimum spray for any pressure within the operating range.
6. There is a minimum and maximum operating pressure for all taps, e.g. min 15 kPa (5ft head) to 700 kPa (233 ft head).
7. Type available with adjustable spout. This enables spout to be adjusted to suit basin contour and locked.
8. Blended temperature of 43°C = $\frac{2}{3}$ at 60° + $\frac{1}{3}$ at 10°C.
9. Secondary circulation always necessary. 3 second delay is design aim i.e. 1.4m of 8mm OD pipe.
10. Flow settings 'UNATAP' optimum: 2.8 litres/m (industrial), 2.4 litres/m (others).

INSTANTANEOUS ELECTRIC

POINTS IN FAVOUR

Water saving. BRE field tests in 1956/7 showed $\frac{2}{3}$ reduction or 68% per person/day. Later a study of 7 wash basins for 1 year revealed usage: ordinary taps 250m³, spray taps 55m³, saving more than $\frac{3}{4}$.

Energy saving. Corresponds to same saving as hot water.

Installation costs. Although spray taps cost more than ordinary taps, savings can be 13% : less storage of water, less boiler power, smaller pipes, incl. waste.

Pay back time. Electricity: 4 months. Gas or oil: 12 months.

Use preference. More agreeable means of hand washing. Opinion samples showed about $\frac{1}{2}$ the men and $\frac{3}{4}$ of the women preferred spray taps.

Hygiene. Reduces possibility of infection (lever type).

Utilisation. Saves time at the wash basin. No wash basin filling and washing is easier. Takes as little as 30% of the normal time. This increases the capacity of the wash room.

Basin design. Simplified e.g. basin acts only as a receiver. Requires only one tap hole, no overflow and no plug necessary. No need to immerse hands in 5 litres of water. Smaller wash basin allows more space to be available.

Microbore. Due to low flow rates, hot and cold water pipes can be 8mm OD (perhaps 10mm) and use of soft copper tube and manifold is possible.

Scaling and corrosion. No problem. Rose easily cleansed.

SUITABLE FOR USE ON ALL MAINS WATER PRESSURES. MAY ALSO BE CISTERN FED PROVIDING SUPPLY IS NOT LESS THAN 100kN/m² (APPROX 35 ft HEAD)

COMBINED ON/OFF VALVE & TEMPERATURE CONTROL

SWIVEL SPOUT

208mm

276mm

111mm

230mm

INLET PIPE LOCATED INSIDE CASING 1½in. BSP F (EXT)

WILL SUPPLY WATER INSTANTLY & CONTINUOUSLY AT HAND WASHING TEMPERATURE AT A RATE OF 0.024 litres/s (2½ pints/min) THROUGH SWIVEL SPOUT AND SPRAY NOZZLE

102mm

PLAN

LOADING 3kW AT 240 v AC

'IMP' BY SANTON LTD

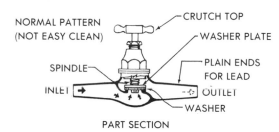

CROSS TOP OR CAPSTAN HEAD
SPINDLE
NOZZLE
EASY CLEAN SHIELD
BSP THREADS
INLET
OUTLET

BIB TAP (SCREW DOWN)

NORMAL PATTERN (NOT EASY CLEAN)
CRUTCH TOP
WASHER PLATE
SPINDLE
PLAIN ENDS FOR LEAD
INLET
OUTLET
WASHER

PART SECTION
STOPVALVE (SCREW DOWN)

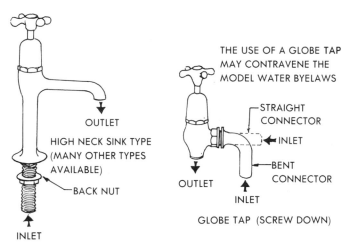

OUTLET
HIGH NECK SINK TYPE (MANY OTHER TYPES AVAILABLE)
BACK NUT
INLET

PILLAR TAP (SCREW DOWN)

THE USE OF A GLOBE TAP MAY CONTRAVENE THE MODEL WATER BYELAWS

STRAIGHT CONNECTOR
INLET
BENT CONNECTOR
OUTLET
INLET

GLOBE TAP (SCREW DOWN)

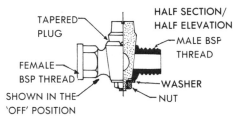

HALF SECTION/ HALF ELEVATION
TAPERED PLUG
MALE BSP THREAD
FEMALE BSP THREAD
WASHER
NUT
SHOWN IN THE 'OFF' POSITION

PLUG COCK

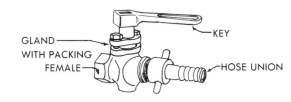

GLAND WITH PACKING FEMALE
KEY
HOSE UNION

GLAND PLUG COCK

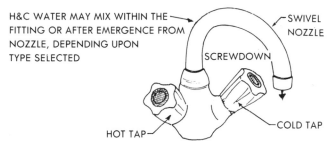

H&C WATER MAY MIX WITHIN THE FITTING OR AFTER EMERGENCE FROM NOZZLE, DEPENDING UPON TYPE SELECTED
SWIVEL NOZZLE
SCREWDOWN
HOT TAP
COLD TAP

SINGLE OUTLET TYPE: TO HAVE BALANCED PRESSURES
DOUBLE OUTLET TYPE: NO MIXING UNTIL WATER EMERGES FROM NOZZLE THEREFORE PRESSURES NEED NOT BE BALANCED

COMBINATION TAP ASSEMBLY

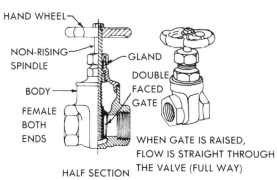

HAND WHEEL
NON-RISING SPINDLE
GLAND
BODY
DOUBLE FACED GATE
FEMALE BOTH ENDS
WHEN GATE IS RAISED, FLOW IS STRAIGHT THROUGH THE VALVE (FULL WAY)

HALF SECTION HALF ELEVATION

FLOW DIRECTION IMMATERIAL UNLESS OTHERWISE INDICATED

GATE VALVES

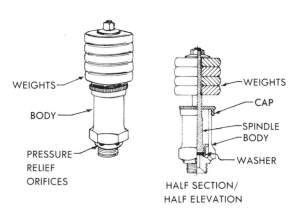

WEIGHTS
BODY
PRESSURE RELIEF ORIFICES
WEIGHTS
CAP
SPINDLE
BODY
WASHER

HALF SECTION/ HALF ELEVATION

DEADWEIGHT SAFETY VALVE

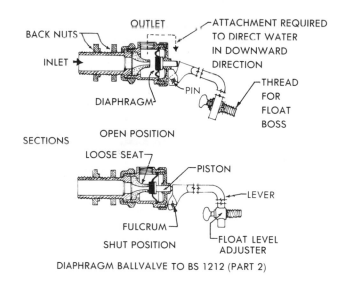

BACK NUTS
OUTLET
ATTACHMENT REQUIRED TO DIRECT WATER IN DOWNWARD DIRECTION
INLET
DIAPHRAGM
PIN
THREAD FOR FLOAT BOSS

OPEN POSITION

SECTIONS

LOOSE SEAT
PISTON
LEVER
FULCRUM
FLOAT LEVEL ADJUSTER

SHUT POSITION

DIAPHRAGM BALLVALVE TO BS 1212 (PART 2)

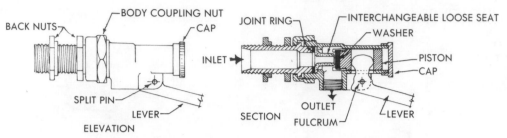

BACK NUTS — BODY COUPLING NUT — CAP

SPLIT PIN — LEVER — ELEVATION

JOINT RING — INTERCHANGEABLE LOOSE SEAT — WASHER

INLET ▶ — PISTON — CAP

OUTLET — FULCRUM — LEVER

SECTION

PISTON TYPE BALLVALVE TO BS1212 (PART 1) (FLOAT NOT SHOWN)

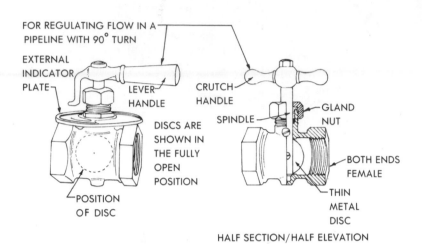

FOR REGULATING FLOW IN A
PIPELINE WITH 90° TURN

EXTERNAL
INDICATOR
PLATE

LEVER
HANDLE

CRUTCH
HANDLE

SPINDLE

GLAND
NUT

DISCS ARE
SHOWN IN
THE FULLY
OPEN
POSITION

BOTH ENDS
FEMALE

POSITION
OF DISC

THIN
METAL
DISC

HALF SECTION/HALF ELEVATION

THROTTLE VALVES: BUTTERFLY TYPE

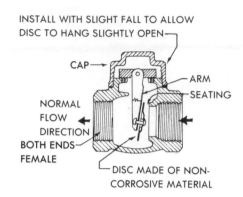

INSTALL WITH SLIGHT FALL TO ALLOW
DISC TO HANG SLIGHTLY OPEN

CAP

ARM

SEATING

NORMAL
FLOW
DIRECTION

BOTH ENDS
FEMALE

DISC MADE OF NON-
CORROSIVE MATERIAL

CHECK VALVE SECTION
METAL DISC – SWING TYPE FEATHERWEIGHT
WILL CLOSE IMMEDIATELY REVERSAL OCCURS

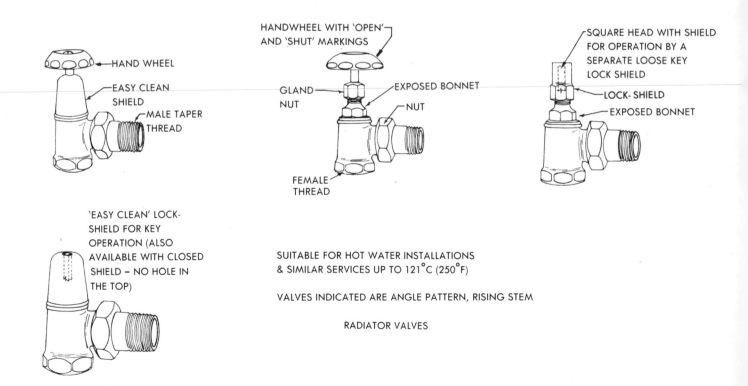

HAND WHEEL

EASY CLEAN
SHIELD

MALE TAPER
THREAD

HANDWHEEL WITH 'OPEN'
AND 'SHUT' MARKINGS

GLAND
NUT

EXPOSED BONNET

NUT

FEMALE
THREAD

SQUARE HEAD WITH SHIELD
FOR OPERATION BY A
SEPARATE LOOSE KEY
LOCK SHIELD

LOCK-SHIELD

EXPOSED BONNET

'EASY CLEAN' LOCK-
SHIELD FOR KEY
OPERATION (ALSO
AVAILABLE WITH CLOSED
SHIELD – NO HOLE IN
THE TOP)

SUITABLE FOR HOT WATER INSTALLATIONS
& SIMILAR SERVICES UP TO 121°C (250°F)

VALVES INDICATED ARE ANGLE PATTERN, RISING STEM

RADIATOR VALVES

OTHER FITTINGS ARE ILLUSTRATED ON DETAIL 12 'BOILERS,
CONNECTIONS & MOUNTINGS'.

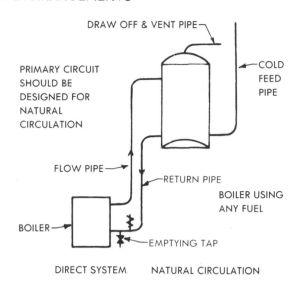

DRAW OFF & VENT PIPE

PRIMARY CIRCUIT
SHOULD BE
DESIGNED FOR
NATURAL
CIRCULATION

COLD
FEED
PIPE

FLOW PIPE

RETURN PIPE

BOILER USING
ANY FUEL

BOILER

EMPTYING TAP

DIRECT SYSTEM   NATURAL CIRCULATION

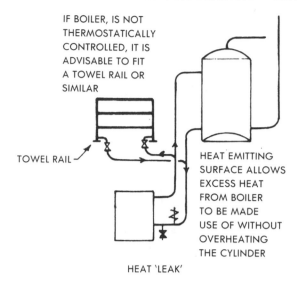

IF BOILER, IS NOT
THERMOSTATICALLY
CONTROLLED, IT IS
ADVISABLE TO FIT
A TOWEL RAIL OR
SIMILAR

TOWEL RAIL

HEAT EMITTING
SURFACE ALLOWS
EXCESS HEAT
FROM BOILER
TO BE MADE
USE OF WITHOUT
OVERHEATING
THE CYLINDER

HEAT 'LEAK'

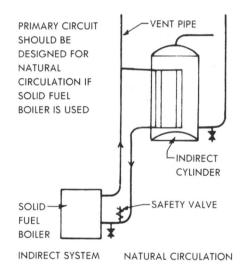

PRIMARY CIRCUIT
SHOULD BE
DESIGNED FOR
NATURAL
CIRCULATION IF
SOLID FUEL
BOILER IS USED

VENT PIPE

INDIRECT
CYLINDER

SOLID
FUEL
BOILER

SAFETY VALVE

INDIRECT SYSTEM   NATURAL CIRCULATION

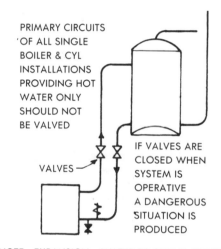

PRIMARY CIRCUITS
'OF ALL SINGLE
BOILER & CYL
INSTALLATIONS
PROVIDING HOT
WATER ONLY
SHOULD NOT
BE VALVED

VALVES

IF VALVES ARE
CLOSED WHEN
SYSTEM IS
OPERATIVE
A DANGEROUS
SITUATION IS
PRODUCED

NOTE:- EXPANSION – WATER TO STEAM: X1700
NO VALVING

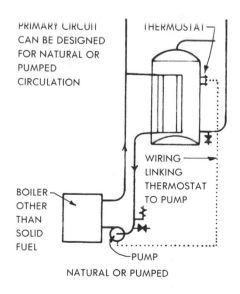

PRIMARY CIRCUIT
CAN BE DESIGNED
FOR NATURAL OR
PUMPED
CIRCULATION

THERMOSTAT

WIRING
LINKING
THERMOSTAT
TO PUMP

BOILER
OTHER
THAN
SOLID
FUEL

PUMP

NATURAL OR PUMPED

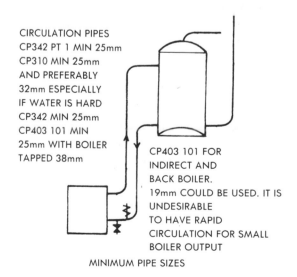

CIRCULATION PIPES
CP342 PT 1 MIN 25mm
CP310 MIN 25mm
AND PREFERABLY
32mm ESPECIALLY
IF WATER IS HARD
CP342 MIN 25mm
CP403 101 MIN
25mm WITH BOILER
TAPPED 38mm

CP403 101 FOR
INDIRECT AND
BACK BOILER.
19mm COULD BE USED. IT IS
UNDESIRABLE
TO HAVE RAPID
CIRCULATION FOR SMALL
BOILER OUTPUT

MINIMUM PIPE SIZES

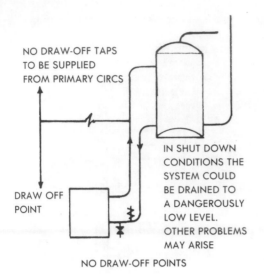

NO DRAW-OFF TAPS TO BE SUPPLIED FROM PRIMARY CIRCS

DRAW OFF POINT

IN SHUT DOWN CONDITIONS THE SYSTEM COULD BE DRAINED TO A DANGEROUSLY LOW LEVEL. OTHER PROBLEMS MAY ARISE

NO DRAW-OFF POINTS

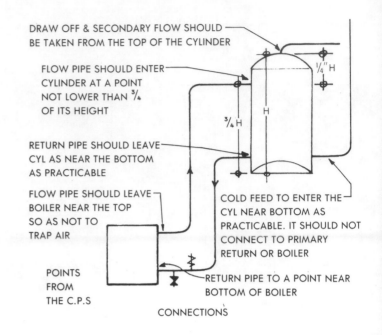

DRAW OFF & SECONDARY FLOW SHOULD BE TAKEN FROM THE TOP OF THE CYLINDER

FLOW PIPE SHOULD ENTER CYLINDER AT A POINT NOT LOWER THAN ¾ OF ITS HEIGHT

RETURN PIPE SHOULD LEAVE CYL AS NEAR THE BOTTOM AS PRACTICABLE

FLOW PIPE SHOULD LEAVE BOILER NEAR THE TOP SO AS NOT TO TRAP AIR

COLD FEED TO ENTER THE CYL NEAR BOTTOM AS PRACTICABLE. IT SHOULD NOT CONNECT TO PRIMARY RETURN OR BOILER

RETURN PIPE TO A POINT NEAR BOTTOM OF BOILER

POINTS FROM THE C.P.S

CONNECTIONS

¼" H

¾ H

H

GRADIENTS ON ALL PIPE RUNS SHOULD NOT BE LESS THAN –

25mm in 3.0m

CP342 STATES A MINIMUM OF 25mm IN 6.0m

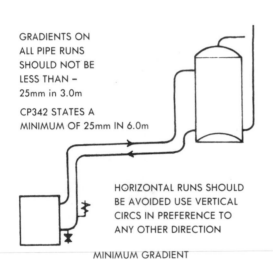

HORIZONTAL RUNS SHOULD BE AVOIDED USE VERTICAL CIRCS IN PREFERENCE TO ANY OTHER DIRECTION

MINIMUM GRADIENT

THIS WAS STANDARD PRACTICE UNTIL A FEW YEARS AGO

NO REALLY HOT WATER AVAILABLE FOR QUITE SOME TIME AFTER STARTING THE BOILER

CONTENTS OF CYLINDER WARMED UP UNIFORMLY

'LAZY' PIPE

THIS METHOD IS REPUTED TO HAVE SOME HOT WATER AVAILABLE IN VERY SHORT TIME BEING DRAWN OFF ALMOST DIRECTLY FROM BOILER

PROBLEM. COLD WATER MAY BY-PASS THE CYL IF TAP IS OPEN FOR A LONG PERIOD FOLLOW

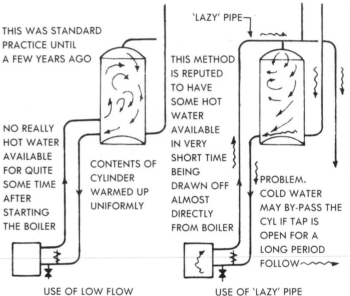

USE OF LOW FLOW

USE OF 'LAZY' PIPE

CYLINDER CONNECTIONS

FOR NATURAL CIRCULATION, CYLINDER, SHOULD BE FITTED AT SUFFICIENT HEIGHT ABOVE THE BOILER TO GIVE ADEQUATE CIRCULATION

HEIGHT IS IMPORTANT WHEN CALCULATING CIRCULATING PRESSURE

DISTANCE 'A' GIVES BETTER CIRCULATING PRESSURE THAN 'B'

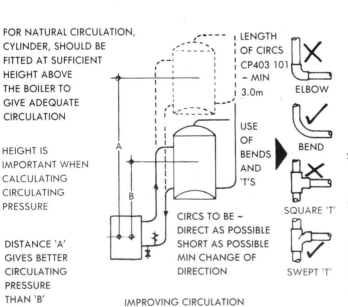

LENGTH OF CIRCS CP403 101 – MIN 3.0m

ELBOW

BEND

USE OF BENDS AND 'T'S

SQUARE 'T'

SWEPT 'T'

CIRCS TO BE – DIRECT AS POSSIBLE SHORT AS POSSIBLE MIN CHANGE OF DIRECTION

IMPROVING CIRCULATION

FLOW NEAR TOP AS POSSIBLE

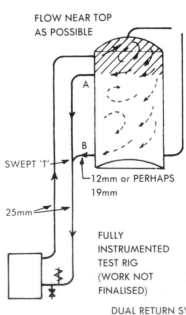

A

B

SWEPT 'T'

12mm or PERHAPS 19mm

25mm

FULLY INSTRUMENTED TEST RIG (WORK NOT FINALISED)

AN EXPERIMENT DESIGNED TO ENABLE SMALL QUANTITY OF HOT WATER TO BE AVAILABLE SOON AFTER THE START OF THE BOILER WATER RETURNS TO BOILER VIA 'A' UNTIL SHADED AREA IS OF EVEN TEMPERATURE THEN 'B' BECOMES THE MAIN RETURN PIPE AND ENABLES THE WHOLE CYL. CONTENT TO HEAT UP. NO VALVE REQUIRED: CHANGE FROM 'A' TO 'B' IS AUTOMATIC

DUAL RETURN SYSTEM

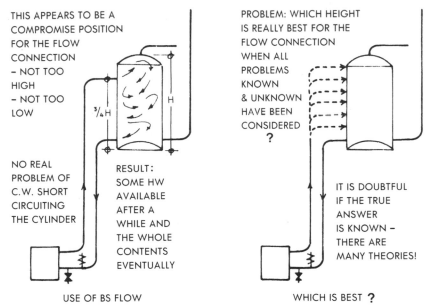

THIS APPEARS TO BE A COMPROMISE POSITION FOR THE FLOW CONNECTION
- NOT TOO HIGH
- NOT TOO LOW

NO REAL PROBLEM OF C.W. SHORT CIRCUITING THE CYLINDER

RESULT: SOME HW AVAILABLE AFTER A WHILE AND THE WHOLE CONTENTS EVENTUALLY

USE OF BS FLOW

PROBLEM: WHICH HEIGHT IS REALLY BEST FOR THE FLOW CONNECTION WHEN ALL PROBLEMS KNOWN & UNKNOWN HAVE BEEN CONSIDERED ?

IT IS DOUBTFUL IF THE TRUE ANSWER IS KNOWN – THERE ARE MANY THEORIES!

WHICH IS BEST ?

CYLINDER CONNECTIONS

MISCELLANEOUS NOTES
Cleaning facilities for primary circulation pipes of a direct system should be provided by means of the use of tees with plugged outlets at changes of direction in combination with union connectors. Flow and return pipes should be separately insulated.

ALL DRAWINGS ARE DIAGRAMMATIC AND NOT DRAWN TO SCALE
CIRC: CIRCULATION. HW: HOT WATER. CW: COLD WATER

STRATIFICATION

Hot water storage vessels should preferably be cylindrical and installed vertically rather than horizontally. The proportion of height (H) to diameter (D) should be such as to increase the possibility of stratification and reduce circulation within the cylinder (particularly off-peak electricity).

Stratification is the term used with reference to water in a hot storage vessel taking up the form of layers of water at different temperatures, although such layers are by no means defined. The hottest water is layered near the top and the coolest at the bottom with a temperature gradient between the two extremes. The further apart the extremes are (e.g. tall vessel as compared with short and position of connections) the better for circulation and draw-off.

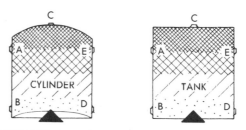

SHORT STORAGE VESSELS GIVE POOR STRATIFICATION

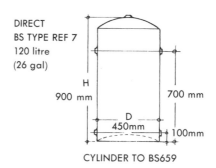

DIRECT
BS TYPE REF 7
120 litre
(26 gal)

H
900 mm   700 mm

D
450mm   100mm

CYLINDER TO BS659

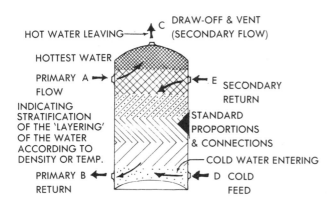

HOT WATER LEAVING — C DRAW-OFF & VENT (SECONDARY FLOW)

HOTTEST WATER

PRIMARY A FLOW

E SECONDARY RETURN

INDICATING STRATIFICATION OF THE 'LAYERING' OF THE WATER ACCORDING TO DENSITY OR TEMP.

STANDARD PROPORTIONS & CONNECTIONS

COLD WATER ENTERING

PRIMARY B RETURN

D COLD FEED

STORAGE TEMPERATURE

It is recommended that in general, the temperature of the stored water should not exceed 65°C (150°F) CP342 Pt. 2. A stored water temperature of 60°C (140°F) is considered sufficient to meet all requirements of CP342 Pt. I. It is recommended that in order to minimise scale and heat loss, the temperature of stored water should not in general, exceed 150°F (65°C).

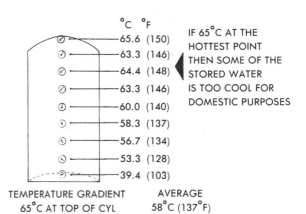

°C	°F	
65.6	(150)	IF 65°C AT THE HOTTEST POINT
63.3	(146)	THEN SOME OF THE
64.4	(148)	STORED WATER
63.3	(146)	IS TOO COOL FOR
60.0	(140)	DOMESTIC PURPOSES
58.3	(137)	
56.7	(134)	
53.3	(128)	
39.4	(103)	

TEMPERATURE GRADIENT   AVERAGE
65°C AT TOP OF CYL   58°C (137°F)

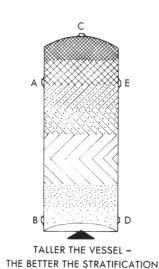

TALLER THE VESSEL –
THE BETTER THE STRATIFICATION

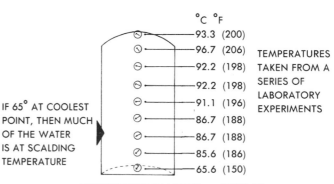

°C	°F	
93.3	(200)	
96.7	(206)	TEMPERATURES
92.2	(198)	TAKEN FROM A
92.2	(198)	SERIES OF
91.1	(196)	LABORATORY
86.7	(188)	EXPERIMENTS
86.7	(188)	
85.6	(186)	
65.6	(150)	

IF 65° AT COOLEST POINT, THEN MUCH OF THE WATER IS AT SCALDING TEMPERATURE

TEMPERATURE GRADIENT   AVERAGE
65°C AT BOTTOM OF CYL   88°C (190°F)

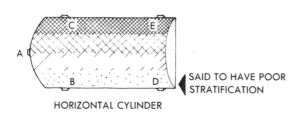

HORIZONTAL CYLINDER

SAID TO HAVE POOR STRATIFICATION

77

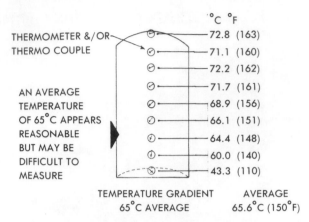

°C	°F
72.8	(163)
71.1	(160)
72.2	(162)
71.7	(161)
68.9	(156)
66.1	(151)
64.4	(148)
60.0	(140)
43.3	(110)

THERMOMETER &/OR THERMO COUPLE

AN AVERAGE TEMPERATURE OF 65°C APPEARS REASONABLE BUT MAY BE DIFFICULT TO MEASURE

TEMPERATURE GRADIENT 65°C AVERAGE AVERAGE 65.6°C (150°F)

THE AGREED DESIGN TEMPERATURE APPEARS TO BE 65°C, BUT A HW VESSEL CANNOT HOLD WATER AT THE SAME TEMPERATURE THROUGHOUT

HORIZONTAL CYLINDERS v VERTICAL CYLINDERS

The CP recommendation is that cylinders should be installed vertically rather than horizontally. However there may be an advantage in having the storage space for linen, etc, at a lower lowel (ie cylinder fitted near to ceiling) instead of alongside and above the cylinder, beyond the normal reach of many people. The necessary supports must be considered and a suitable airing temp. may not be reached.

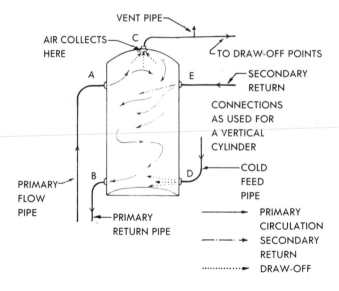

VENT PIPE

AIR COLLECTS HERE

TO DRAW-OFF POINTS

SECONDARY RETURN

CONNECTIONS AS USED FOR A VERTICAL CYLINDER

COLD FEED PIPE

PRIMARY FLOW PIPE

PRIMARY RETURN PIPE

→ PRIMARY CIRCULATION
–·–·→ SECONDARY RETURN
·········► DRAW-OFF

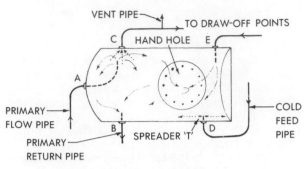

VENT PIPE

TO DRAW-OFF POINTS

HAND HOLE

PRIMARY FLOW PIPE

COLD FEED PIPE

PRIMARY RETURN PIPE

SPREADER 'T'

ILLUSTRATING A METHOD OF CONNECTING TO A CYLINDER FIXED IN THE HORIZONTAL PLANE. MANY PEOPLE WHO HAVE EXPERIENCED THE USE OF THE HORIZONTAL CYLINDER REPORT A SATISFACTORY SUPPLY OF HOT WATER. NOTE THAT SOME PIPEWORK IS NEEDED INSIDE THE CYL.

FUNCTION OF CONNECTION

A. *Primary flow pipe.* To convey water and free gases from 'boiler' to storage vessel. Should connect about ¼ down from top.

B. *Primary return pipe.* To convey water from cyl to 'boiler'. Should connect about 100-150mm from bottom to clear sedimentation etc.

C. *Draw-off (secondary flow) and vent pipe.* Vents free gases and conveys water to draw-off points or secondary circ.

D. *Cold feed pipe.* Conveys cold water from feed cistern to cyl. Connect as for B.

E. *Secondary return pipe.* Connect as for A.

COLD FEED PIPES
DESIGN NOTES

I. Delivering water from a feed cistern to a hot water apparatus (except instantaneous type), cylinder or tank shall be the sole purpose of a cold feed (CF) pipe.

2. CF pipes should be sized to meet the probable demand of the draw-off taps, with a minimum size of 25mm.

3. A stopvalve should be provided on the CF pipe as near the cistern as reasonably practicable and in a convenient and accessible position. A further stopvalve may be provided adjacent to the hot storage vessel. To reduce frictional losses, the valve should be of the fullway type. Such valve(s) will avoid waste of water and of time; reduce inconvenience, etc, when repairs are needed.

4. The CF pipe connection should be positioned so as to minimise the mixing between hot and cold water in the storage vessel. Ideally, storage vessel should be fitted with a suitable horizontal spreader within the hot vessel. Recommendations are to incorporate such a spreader if the working head on the system exceeds l0m (water), and velocity at point of entry to max. of 0.45m/sec.

5. Connection to cistern to be min. 25mm above bottom of cistern (to be above sediment). Others treated similarly.

6. CF pipe should be insulated for various reasons, eg, delay freezing, condensation troubles, and to reduce heat loss.

7. A separate CF pipe from feed and expansion cistern should feed the primary circuit of an indirect system (unless 'single feed' cyl) Opinions differ regarding valving.

8. CF pipe not to connect to primary return pipe or boiler.

DEFINITION: A DISTRIBUTING PIPE CONVEYING COLD WATER FROM A CISTERN TO A HOT WATER APPARATUS (N PT: FEED PIPE*) BS4118

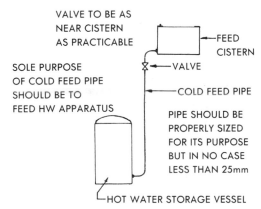

VALVE TO BE AS NEAR CISTERN AS PRACTICABLE

FEED CISTERN

VALVE

SOLE PURPOSE OF COLD FEED PIPE SHOULD BE TO FEED HW APPARATUS

COLD FEED PIPE

PIPE SHOULD BE PROPERLY SIZED FOR ITS PURPOSE BUT IN NO CASE LESS THAN 25mm

HOT WATER STORAGE VESSEL

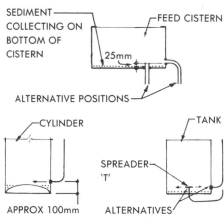

SEDIMENT COLLECTING ON BOTTOM OF CISTERN

FEED CISTERN

25mm

ALTERNATIVE POSITIONS

CYLINDER

TANK

SPREADER 'T'

APPROX 100mm   ALTERNATIVES

SEDIMENT CAN STAY UNDISTURBED

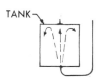

CONNECTION TOO LOW FEED WATER DEFLECTED UPWARDS TO MIX WITH HW

FEED WATER ENTERING AT TOO HIGH VELOCITY (MAX 0.45m/sec)

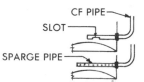

TANK

VERTICAL INFLOW WILL CAUSE WHOLE-SALE MIXING. TO CURE: FIT SPREADER T

CF PIPE

SLOT

SPARGE PIPE

IDEAS TO ALLOW COLD WATER TO ENTER DIFFUSED

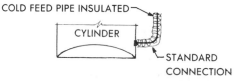

COLD FEED PIPE INSULATED

CYLINDER

STANDARD CONNECTION

AS CYL GETS WARM NEAR THE BOTTOM SO WATER IN CF PIPE ALSO GETS QUITE HOT DIPPING CF PIPE REDUCES THERMAL LOSSES

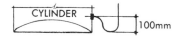

CYLINDER   100mm

EXAMPLE OF CF CONNECTION DIPPED TO FLOOR LEVEL & IS QUITE EFFECTIVE NEED FOR INSULATION NOT SO GREAT

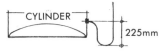

CYLINDER   225mm

A 225mm DIP IS MORE EFFECTIVE THAN 100mm DIP

VENT PIPES
DESIGN NOTES

1. The function of a vent pipe (VP) is to allow the continual release of air, prevent build-up of poressure and to contain surge. Normal expansion takes place via CF pipe; abnormal by VP and/or CP pipe. A VP is a safety pipe.

2. One pipe should not serve as both cold feed and vent pipe.

3. A VP should be provided from the top of the hot storage vessel or from the highest point of the secondary system. Potential air pockets should be avoided and immediately after leaving the vessel, the VP should run 300 to 600mm in the horizontal plane in order to reduce one-pipe circulation which causes considerable heat loss from a vertical VP. Pipe should then rise to discharge point. Separate VP should be provided for the primary circuit of indirect system, unless cyl is 'single feed' type.

4. Size recommended for rating up to and incl. 60 kW is 25mm but 19mm should suffice for small dwelling.

5. VP should terminate where discharge will not cause problems and preferably through the side of the feed cistern above level of the overflow. Alternatively, VP may terminate over cistern with outlet downwards.

6. VP connected to a natural circ. system should rise above the cistern overflow at least 150mm plus 12mm for every 300mm in height of the overflow level above the lowest point of the cold feed pipe.

7. Precautions should be taken against freezing of VP and insulation is also needed to reduce heat loss.

8. Subsidiary VP(s) elsewhere may be needed (usually 19mm).

DEFINITION: A PIPE IN A HOT WATER APPARATUS, FOR THE ESCAPE OF AIR & FOR THE SAFE DISCHARGE OF ANY STEAM GENERATED (N-: PTS: EXHAUST PIPE, EXPANSION PIPE)* BS4118

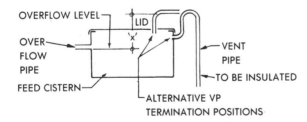

OPEN VENT PIPES SHOULD RISE ABOVE THE OVERFLOW LEVEL OF CISTERN AT LEAST 150mm PLUS 12mm IN HEIGHT OF THE OVERFLOW LEVEL ABOVE THE LOWEST POINT OF THE COLD FEED PIPE (SEE DISTANCE 'x' ABOVE)

HEIGHT OF VENT TERMINATION FOR NATURAL CIRCULATION

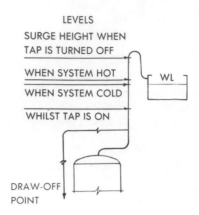

LEVELS

SURGE HEIGHT WHEN TAP IS TURNED OFF
WHEN SYSTEM HOT
WHEN SYSTEM COLD
WHILST TAP IS ON
DRAW-OFF POINT

VENT PIPE SERVES THREE PURPOSES

1. ALLOWS 'AIR' TO ESCAPE FREELY AT ALL TIMES
2. ACTS AS SAFETY PIPE IF THERE IS A BUILD UP OF PRESSURE
3. ACCOMMODATES SURGE THEREFORE HW DOES NOT SPILL OVER INTO CISTERN

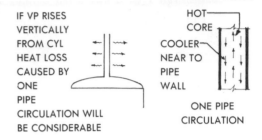

IF VP RISES VERTICALLY FROM CYL HEAT LOSS CAUSED BY ONE PIPE CIRCULATION WILL BE CONSIDERABLE

HOT CORE COOLER NEAR TO PIPE WALL

ONE PIPE CIRCULATION

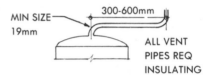

MIN SIZE 19mm   300-600mm

ALL VENT PIPES REQ INSULATING

TAKING THE VENT PIPE HORIZONTALLY FOR 300 to 600mm REDUCES ONE PIPE CIRCULATION

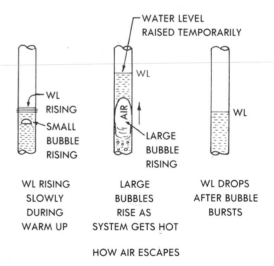

WL RISING SLOWLY DURING WARM UP

LARGE BUBBLES RISE AS SYSTEM GETS HOT

WL DROPS AFTER BUBBLE BURSTS

HOW AIR ESCAPES

SEE ALSO MODEL WATER BYLAWS
WL = WATER LINE   CYL = CYLINDER   HW = HOT WATER
* N-PTS NON-PREFERRED TERMS

SELECTION OF APPLIANCES

A wide range of gas water heaters is available. These differ in design, construction, heating capacity, the method of application & installation. They may be broadly divided into 'storage' and 'instantaneous' types. This detail deals mainly with domestic applicances.

STORAGE METHODS

In this type, water is heated & stored until required. The storage vessel may not necessarily be an integral part of the appliance. Hot water can be withdrawn at the maximum rate of flow up to the limit of the hot storage capacity. Thermostatically controlled.

INSTANTANEOUS METHODS

The cold water is heated as it passes thro' the appliance directly to the point of usage. Flow will continue as long as required at any chosen hot water temperature. The rate of delivery will depend upon the gas rate & initial water temperature

The basis on which choice should be made involves consideration of maximum demand for hot water, rate of delivery, amount & frequency of use of each draw-off point, water characteristics, & pre-disposition of the actual user.

SINGLE POINT

This serves one point only or two adjacent points e.g. by means of a swivel spout. Generally the water control tap is on the inlet & the heater is not normally constructed to withstand high water pressure. Therefore no restrictions on the outlet is permissible unless approved.

DUAL PURPOSE
Single or multi point
This is a hybrid arrangement where it is possible to supply a swivel spout attached to the appliance & an additional one or two outlets e.g. shower &/or wash basin as there are taps on the outlet. The appliance must be able to withstand pressure in the pipe to which it is connected.

MULTIPOINT

A multipoint heater serves one or more points which may be remote from it. Main burner is turned on by an automatic valve operated by the flow of water which occurs when a tap is turned on. As the taps are on the outlet side of the appliance, it must withstand the connected pressure

Output temperature is dependent upon flow rate: increase in flow rate: drop in temperature or decrease in flow rate: rise in temp.

SINK TYPE

Input (Energy)	Output (Flow rate)
11.1 kW	2.6 l/min
38,000 Btu/h	0.57 gal/min

SINK (BOILING TYPE)

Output (Flow/Rate)
1.5 - 1.8 l/min
2.5 - 3.0 pints/min
May not now be available

BATH TYPE

Input (Energy)	Output (Flow Rate)
20.5 kW	5.23 l/min
70,000 Btu/h	1.15 gal/min

'SINK TYPE'

Input (Energy)	Output (Flow/Rate)
11.7 kW	2.7 l/min
40,000 Btu/h	0.59 gal/min

'BATH' TYPE

Input (Energy)	Output (Flow Rate)
29.3 kW	7.4 l/min
100,000 Btu/h	1.63 gal/min

SINK/WASH BASIN/SHOWER TYPE
Input (Energy) 11.1 kW (38,000 Btu/h) Output (Flow Rate) 2.6 l/min (0.57 gal/min)
Input (Energy) 20.5 kW (70,000 Btu/h) Output (Flow Rate) 5.23 l/min (1.15 gal/min)

NOTE: Flow rates quoted are based on a temperature rise of approx. 44°C (80°F) as the water flows through the gas appliance, except boiling models & if otherwise stated.

USING GAS BOILER
This is using a gas-fired boiler, connected to hot storage vessel, using the direct or indirect system of hot water supply. The boiler can also provide hot water for central heating (using the indirect system). Availability of hot water is dependent upon the rating of the boiler(s) which could be said to be unlimited.

USING GAS CIRCULATOR
This appliance could be referred to as a small boiler because normal fixing is by flow & return pipes coupled to a HW storage vessel, existing or new or installed as a purpose-made unit it is often fitted alongside cylinder in an airing cupboard. May have dual returns to allow choice of quantity of 'hot' water stored.

USING FACTORY-MADE UNITS
These are purpose-made storage units & are multipoint being intended to supply hot water e.g. to say 3 draw-off points in a domestic situation. The appliance may include an integral cold water feed cistern. Apart from a wide range of sizes, they can be interconnected allowing for even larger storage. Whilst actual capacity is important, rate of recovery is often paramount.

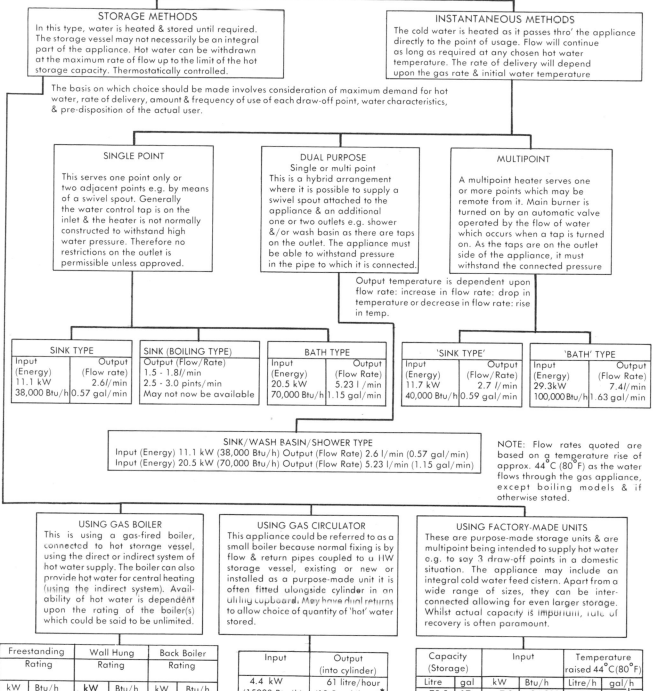

Freestanding Rating		Wall Hung Rating		Back Boiler Rating	
kW	Btu/h	kW	Btu/h	kW	Btu/h
20	68,000	10.26	35,000	11.7	40,000
1465	5 million	20.51	70,000	14.7	50,000

Examples selected from a vast range

Input	Output (into cylinder)
4.4 kW (15000 Btu/h)	61 litre/hour (13.5 gal/hour)*

Example only   Raised 44.5°C (80°)
*Note: Not flow rate

Capacity (Storage)		Input		Temperature raised 44°C (80°F)	
Litre	gal	kW	Btu/h	Litre/h	gal/h
75.5	17	7.3	24,900	105	25‡
286.4	63	105.5	360,000	1542	339 ‡

Examples selected from a vast range. Capacity is actual contents of vessel. Recovery rate often exceeds capacity.‡

NOTE: The term input has been used to denote the 'energy' being used by the appliance (in kW or Btu/h) and output indicates what the consumer is obtaining in flow rate terms. Rating (for boilers) is also input in the sense used here. Capacities must not be confused with inputs or outputs.

Metric flow rates should be stated in litre/second but for straight comparison with imperial gallons, litre per minute has been used. To convert l/sec to gal/min: x 13.198 & gal/min to l/sec: x 0.07577. Average incoming cold water temp can be taken as 10°C (50°F). 1 gal = 4.546 l. 1 pint = 0.57 l.

The above is not the complete range of appliances available but is representative of the equipment most readily available. See manufacturers' literature for full details.

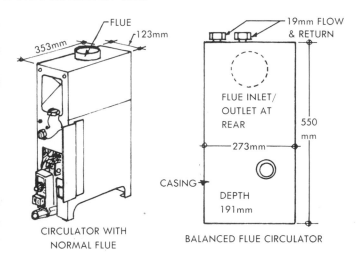

CIRCULATOR WITH NORMAL FLUE

FLUE INLET/ OUTLET AT REAR

19mm FLOW & RETURN

CASING

DEPTH 191mm

BALANCED FLUE CIRCULATOR

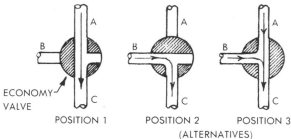

A: FROM HIGH LEVEL RETURN (R_1). B : FROM LOW LEVEL RETURN (R_2) C: TO CIRCULATOR

ECONOMY VALVE

POSITION 1   POSITION 2   POSITION 3
                         (ALTERNATIVES)

POSITION 1 FOR HW DEPTH 'x',
POSITIONS 2 AND 3 FOR DEPTH 'y'

PRINCIPLE OF ECONOMY VALVE

NOTES

Gas circulators are essentially small gas-fired boilers connected to separate h.w. storage vessels or may be used in conjunction with a system heated by an alternative fuel. They can be fixed almost anywhere in the home — on a kitchen or bathroom wall; under the sink; in a separate cupboard or attached to the storage vessel itself. Gas circulators heat water to a predetermined temperature and water in the storage vessel is maintained at the required temp. by automatic thermostatic control. Only 'room sealed' circulators may be installed in bathrooms. Flues from circulators, when fitted in an airing cupboard, should be protected against combustible materials such as clothes. In a way, the circulator is the gas industry's answer to the elec. immersion heater.

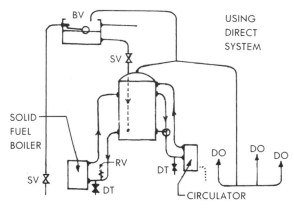

USING DIRECT SYSTEM

SOLID FUEL BOILER

DUAL INSTALLATION

CF: COLD FEED PIPE
SV: STOP VALVE
DT: DRAINING TAP
DO: DRAW-OFF POINT
BV: BALL VALVE
RV: RELIEF VALVE (SAFETY)
CYLINDER AND PIPEWORK SHOULD BE INSULATED TO THE HIGHEST POSSIBLE STANDARD

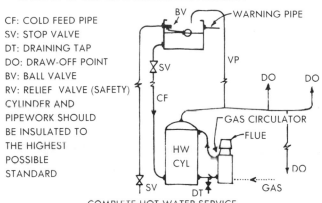

COMPLETE HOT WATER SERVICE

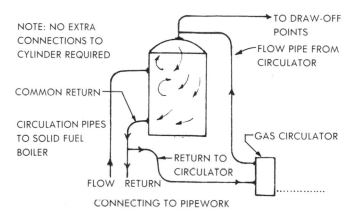

NOTE: NO EXTRA CONNECTIONS TO CYLINDER REQUIRED

COMMON RETURN

CIRCULATION PIPES TO SOLID FUEL BOILER

TO DRAW-OFF POINTS

FLOW PIPE FROM CIRCULATOR

GAS CIRCULATOR

RETURN TO CIRCULATOR

FLOW   RETURN

CONNECTING TO PIPEWORK

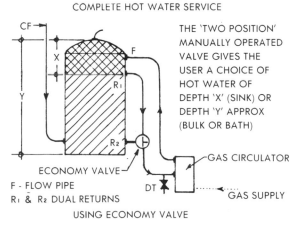

THE 'TWO POSITION' MANUALLY OPERATED VALVE GIVES THE USER A CHOICE OF HOT WATER OF DEPTH 'X' (SINK) OR DEPTH 'Y' APPROX (BULK OR BATH)

F - FLOW PIPE
R_1 & R_2 DUAL RETURNS

USING ECONOMY VALVE

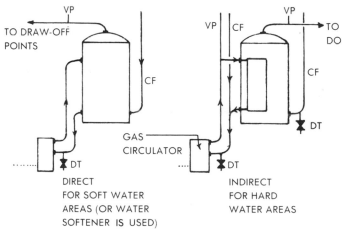

DIRECT FOR SOFT WATER AREAS (OR WATER SOFTENER IS USED)

INDIRECT FOR HARD WATER AREAS

DIRECT & INDIRECT

DESIGN DATA

Rating Typical 4.4 kW (or 15 mJ/h) or (15000 Btu/hour).

Hot water output. (eg) 61 litres/h (13.5 gal/h) raised 44.5°C (80°F)

Thermostat settings (eg.) direct system 65°C (150°F). Indirect system 82°C (180°F). May be preset but are adjustable.

Pipework Size. Usually 22mm OD (BS2871) but may be 28mm OD for an indirect system.

Length. (eg max total length of flow and return: 9m to 15m.

Slope. 25mm (1in.) in 3m (10ft)

Bends. Use swept (large radius)

Ratio. Horizontal to vertical is recommended 3:1 max

Circulating head. For min vertical distance between flow connections, follow manufacturers' instructions.

Flow connections to cylinder. Connect within 75mm (3in.) of top.

TYPE OF SYSTEM. Up to 16° Clark, direct system usually all right; 16°-21° better to use indirect; over 21° indirect should be used.

Water pressure. Not for 'mains'.

Ignition. Power may be required.

Draining tap. Fix at low point if not incorporated elsewhere.

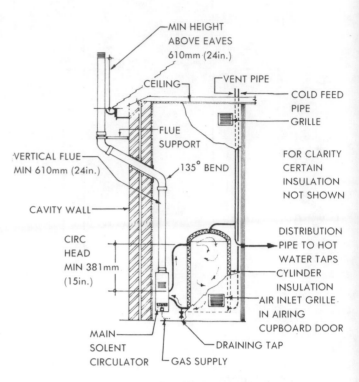

TYPICAL AIRING CUPBOARD APPLICATION
INSTALLATIONS TO COMPLY WITH LOCAL GAS BOARD DEMANDS

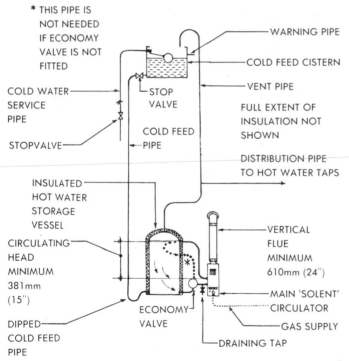

DIRECT SYSTEM INCORPORATING ECONOMY VALVE

FLUE CONSIDERATIONS

If 'balanced flue', fit appliance to any suitable external wall. Connect to top centre of rear of circulator : size 129mm (5.1in.) and max length 381mm (15in.). Flue terminal suitable for wall thickness of 76mm (3in.) to 380mm (15in.). If 'normal flue', size is usually 76mm (3in.) and min. vertical length of 610mm (24in.) recommended. Bends 135° preferable to 90°. Flue terminal to be at or above ridge of pitched roof or 610mm (24in.) above the eaves or parapet wall of flat roof. Relevant Building Regulations etc, must be complied with.

ALL GAS INSTALLATIONS SHOULD COMPLY WITH CURRENT REGULATIONS, CODES OF PRACTICE & WORK DONE BY CORGI MEMBER.

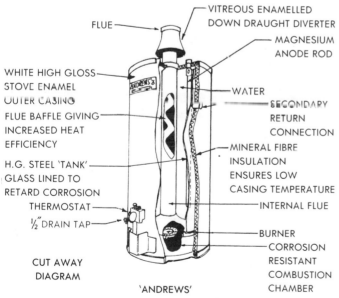

STORAGE HEATER

DESCRIPTION
Storage water heaters are completely self-contained units that combine a gas burner and a well-insulated water cylinder. Ample hot water can be supplied for a dwelling, commercial or industrial building, etc. The temperature is controlled by a thermostat. Hot water can be withdrawn at the max. rate of flow up to the limit of the storage capacity. The delay before further hot water is available depends upon the recovery rate of the appliance.

MODEL WATER BYELAW 46
The delivery of water into the air, ½in. above the top edge of a h.w. apparatus (if fed from a service pipe) does not apply to a gas water heater which has a max. of 3 gal. capacity *or* is capable of holding more than 3 gal. but not more than 15 gal and is fitted with a device which will prevent or limit back siphonage. Also (i) the design working pressure to be correct, (ii) to be no leakage between gas and water, (iii) water space is enclosed (except vent and draw-offs), (iv) to be ½in. gap between tap nozzles and flood level of sanitary appliance.

SOME COMMON FEATURES
1. For installation, only gas, cold feed, flue and hot water connections are required.
2. Enamelled outer jacket.
3. High efficiency insulation between hot cyl. and outer jacket.
4. Tappings provided for safety valve, drain tap and secondary return.
5. Replaceable magnesium anode(s) fitted internally for additional protection against corrosion.
6. Glass lined storage cylinders and flue ways similarly treated.
7. Operation is automatic and the temperature control is variable.
8. Ventilation of space occupied by the heater is essential — always follow manufacturers' instructions.

FIXING NOTES
In general, storage water heaters should not be connected directly to a service pipe but fed from a feed cistern. If in doubt, contact local water authority. Cistern must be at a height sufficient to give a satisfactory flow rate to all taps. Gas supply is at the base, and both cold feed and h.w. connections are top connections. Floor beneath the heater must be level and flat, and able to take the weight of the *full* heater. Clearance around and above the heater is needed for maintenance and servicing. Continuous vertical flues are recommended but should commence by 2ft. vertical in any case.

MODEL NUMBER	STORAGE CAPACITY	RECOVERY RATE	HEAT INPUT	GAS FLOW RATE
	litre (gal)	litre/h(gal/h)	kW(Btu/h)	m^3/h (ft^3/h)
16/23	75.5(16.6)	105.0(23.1)	7.3(25000)	0.69(24.5)
25/37	113.7(25.0)	170.5(37.5)	11.72(40000)	1.1(39.2)
33/38	151.4(33.3)	173.2(38.1)	16.16(41500)	1.14(40.7)
41/55	189.1(41.6)	252.3(55.5)	17.5(60,000)	1.6(58.8)
62/69	284.1(62.5)	315.0(69.3)	22.0(75000)	2.1(73.5)
69/188	312.8(68.8)	858.7(188.9)	58.6(200,000)	—
63/388	286.4(63.0)	1542.2(338.5)	105.5(360000)	—

HEATER HEIGHT	DIMENSIONS DIAMETER	FLUE DIAMETER	WEIGHT (FULL)	WORKING PRESSURE
mm (in)	mm (in)	mm (in)	kg (lb)	bar (psi)
1123(44¼)	406(16)	76(3)	114(250)	10.3(150)
1200(47¼)	457(18)	76(3)	160(350)	10.3(150)
1244(49)	508(20)	76(3)	210(462)	10.3(150)
1492(58¾)	508(20)	101(4)	256(562)	10.3(150)
1632(64¼)	622(24½)	101(4)	386(850)	10.3(150)
1765(69½)	711(28)	152(6)		
1816(71½)	711(28)	203(8)		

NOT YET AVAILABLE AWAITING BRITISH GAS APPROVAL

THE TABLES GIVE SOME DETAILS FROM THE LARGE SELECTION OF HEATERS LISTED MODEL 16/23 WILL PROVIDE A FULL W.B. FOR EACH OF 20 USERS IN 5 MINUTES; 45 USERS OVER 1 HOUR; OR 2 HOT BATHS IN 1 HOUR

FLUE

VITREOUS ENAMELLED DOWN DRAUGHT DIVERTER

MAGNESIUM ANODE ROD

WHITE HIGH GLOSS STOVE ENAMEL OUTER CASING

WATER

SECONDARY RETURN CONNECTION

FLUE BAFFLE GIVING INCREASED HEAT EFFICIENCY

MINERAL FIBRE INSULATION ENSURES LOW CASING TEMPERATURE

H.G. STEEL 'TANK' GLASS LINED TO RETARD CORROSION

INTERNAL FLUE

THERMOSTAT

½" DRAIN TAP

BURNER

CORROSION RESISTANT COMBUSTION CHAMBER

CUT AWAY DIAGRAM

'ANDREWS'

GAS FIRED WATER STORAGE HEATER

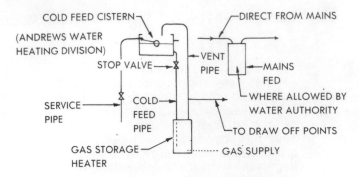

COLD FEED CISTERN
(ANDREWS WATER HEATING DIVISION)
STOP VALVE
SERVICE PIPE
COLD FEED PIPE
GAS STORAGE HEATER
VENT PIPE
DIRECT FROM MAINS
MAINS FED
WHERE ALLOWED BY WATER AUTHORITY
TO DRAW OFF POINTS
GAS SUPPLY

SIMPLE DIRECT SYSTEM (CISTERN FED)

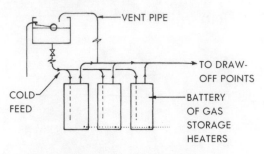

VENT PIPE
COLD FEED
TO DRAW-OFF POINTS
BATTERY OF GAS STORAGE HEATERS

ARRANGEMENT FOR LARGE DEMAND WITH
FREQUENT USE NEEDING FAST RECOVERY

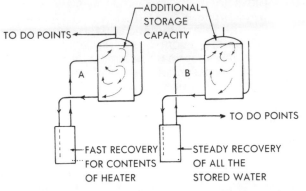

TO DO POINTS
ADDITIONAL STORAGE CAPACITY
A
B
TO DO POINTS
FAST RECOVERY FOR CONTENTS OF HEATER
STEADY RECOVERY OF ALL THE STORED WATER

LAYOUTS FOR LARGE DEMAND WITH INFREQUENT USE

CHOICE

Different households have different requirements, and peak demand is considerably greater than average weekly demand. Whilst a large storage capacity combined with a quick recovery rate will give the best service additional factors such as capital cost, overall size and availability of a flue may lead to a choice of a system with a lower standard of service. A limited output heater can be offset by connecting to large well insulated cylinder.

ALL DRAWINGS ARE DIAGRAMMATIC

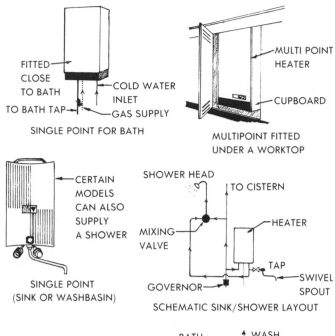

FITTED CLOSE TO BATH
COLD WATER INLET
TO BATH TAP
GAS SUPPLY

SINGLE POINT FOR BATH

MULTI POINT HEATER
CUPBOARD

MULTIPOINT FITTED UNDER A WORKTOP

CERTAIN MODELS CAN ALSO SUPPLY A SHOWER

SINGLE POINT (SINK OR WASHBASIN)

SHOWER HEAD
TO CISTERN
MIXING VALVE
HEATER
GOVERNOR
TAP
SWIVEL SPOUT

SCHEMATIC SINK/SHOWER LAYOUT

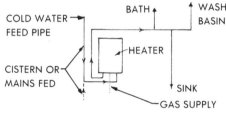

COLD WATER FEED PIPE
BATH
WASH BASIN
HEATER
CISTERN OR MAINS FED
SINK
GAS SUPPLY

SCHEMATIC LAYOUT OF MULTI-POINT & 3 HW DRAW OFF POINTS

DESCRIPTION

These heaters will give a continuous flow of hot water at any time within a few seconds of turning on any tap to which the heater is connected. For any particular hot water temperature, the rate of delivery will depend upon the gas rate and the initial water temperature. The heat input into these heaters is constant, most heaters being designed to give a 45°C (81°F) temperature rise, but it is usually possible to obtain a greater flow at a lower temperature without any drop in the efficiency of the heater. There are sink and bath heaters which serve one point only; multipoint models providing full domestic hot water service, and heaters specifically designed for shower use. Other features may include water governor, thermostat, etc.

WATER SUPPLY

For mains connection, obtain permission from local water authority. Always check that minimum working pressure is sufficient to operate the heater, eg. min. 35kN/m² (5lb/in²), but low pressure models available.

GAS SUPPLY

Meter must be capable of passing the gas supply to the heater, eg, 105 MJ/h (100,000 Btu/h or 100 ft³/h natural gas) in addition to other requirements.

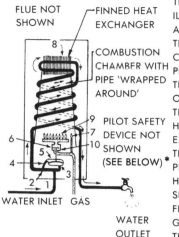

FLUE NOT SHOWN
FINNED HEAT EXCHANGER
COMBUSTION CHAMBER WITH PIPE 'WRAPPED AROUND'
PILOT SAFETY DEVICE NOT SHOWN (SEE BELOW) *
WATER INLET   GAS
WATER OUTLET

THIS SKETCH IS MAINLY TO ILLUSTRATE, IN BASIC FASHION, ARRANGEMENT SHOWING THE INCOMING WATER COLLECTING HEAT BY THE PIPE BEING WRAPPED AROUND THE COMBUSTION CHAMBER ON ITS WAY TO AND AWAY FROM THE HEAT EXCHANGER HOWEVER, IT IS WITHIN THE EXCHANGER WHERE MOST OF THE HEAT TRANSFER TAKES PLACE. FLOW THROUGH THE HEATER ONLY TAKES A FEW SECONDS. ONLY WHEN WATER FLOWS THRO' THE HEATER CAN GAS PASS TO THE MAIN BURNER THEREFORE NO WATER – NO GAS

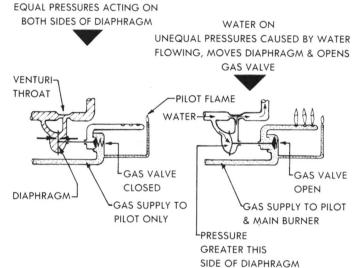

WATER OFF
EQUAL PRESSURES ACTING ON BOTH SIDES OF DIAPHRAGM

WATER ON
UNEQUAL PRESSURES CAUSED BY WATER FLOWING, MOVES DIAPHRAGM & OPENS GAS VALVE

VENTURI THROAT
PILOT FLAME
WATER
DIAPHRAGM
GAS VALVE CLOSED
GAS SUPPLY TO PILOT ONLY
GAS VALVE OPEN
GAS SUPPLY TO PILOT & MAIN BURNER
PRESSURE GREATER THIS SIDE OF DIAPHRAGM

ILLUSTRATING PRINCIPLES OF VENTURI ARRANGEMENT

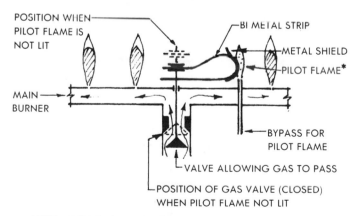

POSITION WHEN PILOT FLAME IS NOT LIT
BI METAL STRIP
METAL SHIELD
PILOT FLAME *
MAIN BURNER
BYPASS FOR PILOT FLAME
VALVE ALLOWING GAS TO PASS
POSITION OF GAS VALVE (CLOSED) WHEN PILOT FLAME NOT LIT

NOTE:- MAIN GAS VALVE WILL BE 'OPEN' ONLY WHEN THE PILOT FLAME HEATS THE BIMETALIC STRIP SUFFICIENT TO CAUSE THE STRIP TO BEND DUE TO DIFFERENTIAL EXPANSION OF THE 2 METALS COMPRISING THIS STRIP. THEREFORE WHEN PILOT NOT LIT, NO GAS CAN PASS TO MAIN BURNER.

* ALTERNATIVE METHOD: PIEZO SPARK IGNITER (FOR PILOT FLAME) AND ELECTRO-MAGNETIC FLAME FAILURE DEVICE

HOW IT WORKS

When a hot tap is turned on, the cold water flows in at 1 and passes through a Venturi tube 2 thus creating a differential pressure across a flexible diaphragm 5 via pipes 3 & 4. This moves the diaphragm which is fixed to a spring-loaded valve 6 and allows gas along pipe 10 to the burners 9 where the pilot flame ignites it(7). The cold water flows up to the finned heat exchanger 8 where it is heated on its way to the open hot tap. When hot tap is closed. water ceases to flow and valve 6 closes shutting off the gas supply to the burners if pilot light is not lit, no gas will be allowed to flow to the main burner in any case.

WATER BYELAW 46

Instantaneous heaters can be either mains fed or cistern fed but apparatus must not be subjected to a working pressure higher than that for which it is designed. See Byelaw and manufacturer's fixing instructions for details.

SAFETY FEATURES

The 'Venturi' ensures that gas cannot pass to the burner unless water is flowing through the appliance. Also no gas will be allowed to reach the same burner if the pilot light is not lit — this valve is closed by bi-metal strip or action of flame failure device.

ADVANTAGES

Heats water as and when user requires it, be it a cupful or several baths in quick succession. Not storage, therefore no standing losses; and no water need be heated that is not required. No storage space required, perhaps no feed cistern. Very convenient, economical, and neat in appearance.

FLOW RATES

These are sometimes considered to be a disadvantage as they are below those recommended for centralised systems, eg, bath 4 gal/min (0.30 litres/s). Heater of 100,000 Btu/h input produces about 1½ gal/min raised 80°F.

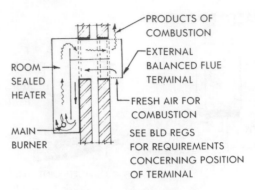

PRODUCTS OF COMBUSTION

EXTERNAL BALANCED FLUE TERMINAL

ROOM SEALED HEATER

FRESH AIR FOR COMBUSTION

MAIN BURNER

SEE BLD REGS FOR REQUIREMENTS CONCERNING POSITION OF TERMINAL

PRINCIPLE OF BALANCED FLUE

1. BEING MANUFACTURED AS A ROOM-SEALED APPLIANCE, AIR FOR COMBUSTION IS DRAWN FROM OUTSIDE, NOT FROM THE ROOM IN WHICH FIXED
2. FOR THE SAME REASON PRODUCTS OF COMBUSTION SHOULD NOT ENTER THE ROOM.
3. WITH THE AIR INTAKE AND FLUE OUTLET BEING IN CLOSE PROXIMITY, BOTH OPERATE UNDER SAME AIR PRESSURE CONDITIONS: THAT IS – BALANCED.

FLUES

In general, water heaters should be connected to a flue. One exception is a heater not exceeding a rating of 40,000 Btu/h and serving a sink only in a well-ventilated room. All modern multi-point and bath instantaneous heaters are 'roomed sealed' (ie balanced flue).

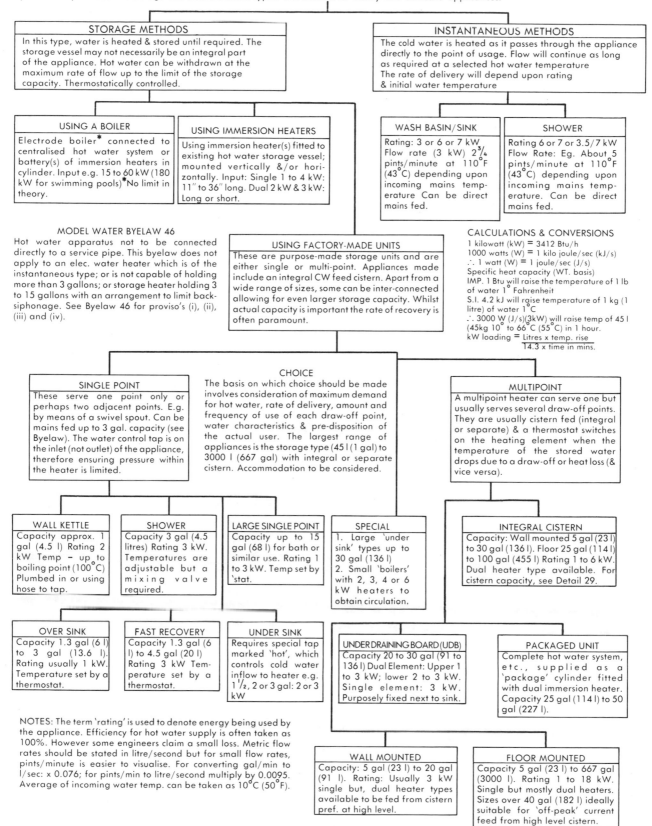

SELECTION OF APPLIANCES

A wide range of electric water heaters is available. These differ in design, construction, heating capacity, the method of application & installation. They may be broadly divided into storage and instantaneous types. This detail is for mainly with 'domestic' appliances.

STORAGE METHODS
In this type, water is heated & stored until required. The storage vessel may not necessarily be an integral part of the appliance. Hot water can be withdrawn at the maximum rate of flow up to the limit of the storage capacity. Thermostatically controlled.

INSTANTANEOUS METHODS
The cold water is heated as it passes through the appliance directly to the point of usage. Flow will continue as long as required at a selected hot water temperature. The rate of delivery will depend upon rating & initial water temperature

USING A BOILER
Electrode boiler* connected to centralised hot water system or battery(s) of immersion heaters in cylinder. Input e.g. 15 to 60 kW (180 kW for swimming pools)*No limit in theory.

USING IMMERSION HEATERS
Using immersion heater(s) fitted to existing hot water storage vessel; mounted vertically &/or horizontally. Input: Single 1 to 4 kW: 11" to 36" long. Dual 2 kW & 3 kW: Long or short.

WASH BASIN/SINK
Rating: 3 or 6 or 7 kW. Flow rate (3 kW) $2\frac{3}{4}$ pints/minute at 110°F (43°C) depending upon incoming mains temperature Can be direct mains fed.

SHOWER
Rating 6 or 7 or 3.5/7 kW Flow Rate: Eg. About 5 pints/minute at 110°F (43°C) depending upon incoming mains temperature. Can be direct mains fed.

MODEL WATER BYELAW 46
Hot water apparatus not to be connected directly to a service pipe. This byelaw does not apply to an elec. water heater which is of the instantaneous type; or is not capable of holding more than 3 gallons; or storage heater holding 3 to 15 gallons with an arrangement to limit back-siphonage. See Byelaw 46 for proviso's (i), (ii), (iii) and (iv).

USING FACTORY-MADE UNITS
These are purpose-made storage units and are either single or multi-point. Appliances made include an integral CW feed cistern. Apart from a wide range of sizes, some can be inter-connected allowing for even larger storage capacity. Whilst actual capacity is important the rate of recovery is often paramount.

CALCULATIONS & CONVERSIONS
1 kilowatt (kW) = 3412 Btu/h
1000 watts (W) = 1 kilo joule/sec (kJ/s)
∴ 1 watt (W) = 1 joule/sec (J/s)
Specific heat capacity (WT. basis)
IMP. 1 Btu will raise the temperature of 1 lb of water 1° Fahrenheit
S.I. 4.2 kJ will raise temperature of 1 kg (1 litre) of water 1°C
∴ 3000 W (J/s)(3kW) will raise temp of 45 l (45kg 10° to 66°C (55°C) in 1 hour.
$$\text{kW loading} = \frac{\text{Litres} \times \text{temp. rise}}{14.3 \times \text{time in mins.}}$$

SINGLE POINT
These serve one point only or perhaps two adjacent points. E.g. by means of a swivel spout. Can be mains fed up to 3 gal. capacity (see Byelaw). The water control tap is on the inlet (not outlet) of the appliance, therefore ensuring pressure within the heater is limited.

CHOICE
The basis on which choice should be made involves consideration of maximum demand for hot water, rate of delivery, amount and frequency of use of each draw-off point, water characteristics & pre-disposition of the actual user. The largest range of appliances is the storage type (45 l (1 gal) to 3000 l (667 gal) with integral or separate cistern. Accommodation to be considered.

MULTIPOINT
A multipoint heater can serve one but usually serves several draw-off points. They are usually cistern fed (integral or separate) & a thermostat switches on the heating element when the temperature of the stored water drops due to a draw-off or heat loss (& vice versa).

WALL KETTLE
Capacity approx. 1 gal (4.5 l) Rating 2 kW Temp – up to boiling point (100°C) Plumbed in or using hose to tap.

SHOWER
Capacity 3 gal (4.5 litres) Rating 3 kW. Temperatures are adjustable but a mixing valve required.

LARGE SINGLE POINT
Capacity up to 15 gal (68 l) for bath or similar use. Rating 1 to 3 kW. Temp set by 'stat.

SPECIAL
1. Large 'under sink' types up to 30 gal (136 l)
2. Small 'boilers' with 2, 3, 4 or 6 kW heaters to obtain circulation.

INTEGRAL CISTERN
Capacity: Wall mounted 5 gal (23 l) to 30 gal (136 l). Floor 25 gal (114 l) to 100 gal (455 l) Rating 1 to 6 kW. Dual heater type available. For cistern capacity, see Detail 29.

OVER SINK
Capacity 1.3 gal (6 l) to 3 gal (13.6 l). Rating usually 1 kW. Temperature set by a thermostat.

FAST RECOVERY
Capacity 1.3 gal (6 l) to 4.5 gal (20 l) Rating 3 kW Temperature set by a thermostat.

UNDER SINK
Requires special tap marked 'hot', which controls cold water inflow to heater e.g. $1\frac{1}{2}$, 2 or 3 gal: 2 or 3 kW

UNDER DRAINING BOARD (UDB)
Capacity 20 to 30 gal (91 to 136 l) Dual Element: Upper 1 to 3 kW; lower 2 to 3 kW. Single element: 3 kW. Purposely fixed next to sink.

PACKAGED UNIT
Complete hot water system, etc., supplied as a 'package' cylinder fitted with dual immersion heater. Capacity 25 gal (114 l) to 50 gal (227 l).

WALL MOUNTED
Capacity 5 gal (23 l) to 20 gal (91 l). Rating: Usually 3 kW single but, dual heater types available to be fed from cistern pref. at high level.

FLOOR MOUNTED
Capacity 5 gal (23 l) to 667 gal (3000 l). Rating 1 to 18 kW. Single but mostly dual heaters. Sizes over 40 gal (182 l) ideally suitable for 'off-peak' current feed from high level cistern.

NOTES: The term 'rating' is used to denote energy being used by the appliance. Efficiency for hot water supply is often taken as 100%. However some engineers claim a small loss. Metric flow rates should be stated in litre/second but for small flow rates, pints/minute is easier to visualise. For converting gal/min to l/sec: x 0.076; for pints/min to litre/second multiply by 0.0095. Average of incoming water temp. can be taken as 10°C (50°F).

The above is not the complete range of appliances available but is representative of the equipment most readily available. See manufacturers' literature for full details.

GENERAL NOTES

An immersion heater is an electric heating element designed for installation in a hot water storage tank or cylinder and will supply hot water for household storage needs. Available are lengths, loadings and sheath materials to suit every situation no matter what size storage cylinder or tank. An immersion heater is easy to install, requires no flue, is completely clean and silent in operation, takes no floor space, and will supply hot water, thermostatically controlled, at all times. Very useful in summer when other forms of heating are not required. For aggressive water supplies, it is important to select the correct sheath material if high maintenance costs are to be avoided, e.g. 'Monel' or titanium. Immersion heater(s) can be fixed horizontally but an alternative arrangement is the 'DUAL' type. It has two different length elements, each with its own thermostat. The short or 'sink' element is designed to heat a limited quantity of water for general household use, whilst the long or 'bath' element should only be switched on for periods when the 'whole' contents are required. Thus considerable savings can be effected. IN ALL CIRCUMSTANCES ANY TANK OR CYLINDER SHOULD BE WELL INSULATED.

IMMERSION HEATER ARRANGEMENTS

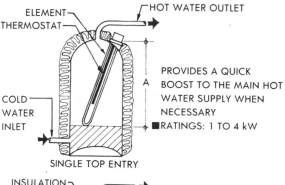

SINGLE TOP ENTRY

PROVIDES A QUICK BOOST TO THE MAIN HOT WATER SUPPLY WHEN NECESSARY
■ RATINGS: 1 TO 4 kW

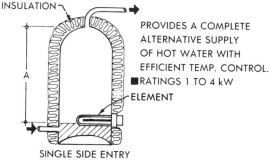

SINGLE SIDE ENTRY

PROVIDES A COMPLETE ALTERNATIVE SUPPLY OF HOT WATER WITH EFFICIENT TEMP. CONTROL.
■ RATINGS 1 TO 4 kW

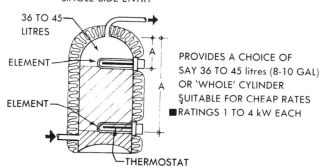

DOUBLE SIDE ENTRY

36 TO 45 LITRES

PROVIDES A CHOICE OF SAY 36 TO 45 litres (8-10 GAL) OR 'WHOLE' CYLINDER SUITABLE FOR CHEAP RATES
■ RATINGS 1 TO 4 kW EACH

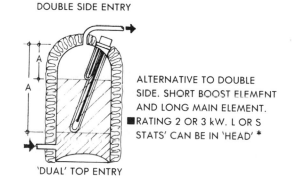

'DUAL' TOP ENTRY

ALTERNATIVE TO DOUBLE SIDE. SHORT BOOST ELEMENT AND LONG MAIN ELEMENT.
■ RATING 2 OR 3 kW. L OR S STATS' CAN BE IN 'HEAD' *

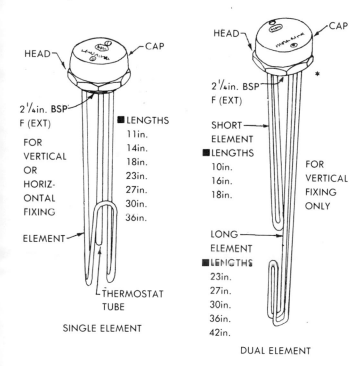

HEAD — CAP
2¼in. BSP F (EXT)
FOR VERTICAL OR HORIZONTAL FIXING
ELEMENT
THERMOSTAT TUBE

■ LENGTHS
11in.
14in.
18in.
23in.
27in.
30in.
36in.

SINGLE ELEMENT

HEAD — CAP
2¼in. BSP F (EXT) *
SHORT ELEMENT
■ LENGTHS
10in.
16in.
18in.
FOR VERTICAL FIXING ONLY
LONG ELEMENT
■ LENGTHS
23in.
27in.
30in.
36in.
42in.

DUAL ELEMENT

INSTALLATIONS TO SUIT DIFFERENT PURPOSES

1. Topping-up a fuel-fired hot water system — existing or new.
2. Summer time alternative to fuel-fired hot water system — existing or new.
3. All-electric water heating, designed as a new system or conversion using cylinder and separate cistern; integral cistern type; packaged unit; etc.

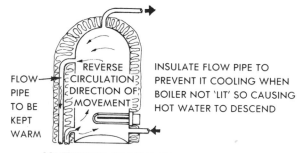

FLOW PIPE TO BE KEPT WARM
REVERSE CIRCULATION
DIRECTION OF MOVEMENT

INSULATE FLOW PIPE TO PREVENT IT COOLING WHEN BOILER NOT 'LIT' SO CAUSING HOT WATER TO DESCEND

CONTROLLING REVERSE CIRCULATION

LETTER 'A' INDICATES DEPTH OF HOT WATER AVAILABLE ACCORDING TO LENGTH (TOP ENTRY) OR POSITION (SIDE ENTRY) OF HEATER ELEMENT.

BRITISH STANDARD FIXING POSITIONS

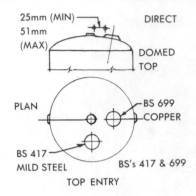

25mm (MIN)
51mm (MAX)

DIRECT

DOMED TOP

PLAN

BS 699 COPPER

BS 417 MILD STEEL

BS's 417 & 699

TOP ENTRY

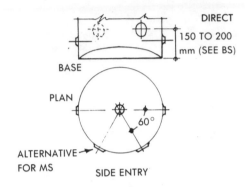

DIRECT

150 TO 200 mm (SEE BS)

BASE

PLAN

60°

ALTERNATIVE FOR MS

SIDE ENTRY

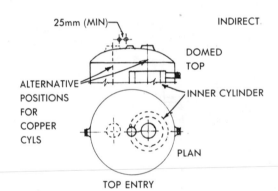

25mm (MIN)

INDIRECT

DOMED TOP

ALTERNATIVE POSITIONS FOR COPPER CYLS

INNER CYLINDER

PLAN

TOP ENTRY

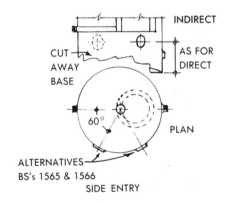

INDIRECT

CUT AWAY BASE

AS FOR DIRECT

60°

PLAN

ALTERNATIVES
BS's 1565 & 1566

SIDE ENTRY

FLANGES

SCREW-IN FLANGE FOR TOP ENTRY MOUNTING. FOR DIRECT CYLINDERS & TANKS ONLY

SCREW-IN FLANGE FOR HORIZONTAL (SIDE ENTRY) MOUNTING

SWEAT-IN FLANGE FOR VERTICAL FIXING FOR INDIRECT CYLINDERS

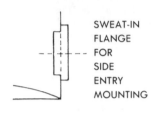

SWEAT IN FLANGE FOR TOP ENTRY MOUNTING FOR DIRECT CYLINDERS & TANKS ONLY

SWEAT-IN FLANGE FOR SIDE ENTRY MOUNTING

FLANGES All $2\frac{1}{4}$in. BSP F (INT)

'SWEAT' MEANS TO SOLDER

WARNING.: WHEN AN IMMERSION HEATER IS FITTED TO A HOT WATER OR COMBINED H.W & HEATING SYSTEM, DESIGN SHOULD BE SUCH THAT UNNECESSARY HEAT LOSSES & UNWANTED WATER MOVEMENT THROUGH PIPEWORK IS REDUCED TO THE MINIMUM.

THERMOSTATS CAN BE FITTED SEPARATELY FROM THE ELEMENT. FOR SIDE ENTRY, FIX 75mm ABOVE THE ELEMENT.

L = LONG. S = SHORT

SEE MANUFACTURERS LITERATURE

NOTES FROM BS CP 324. 202

A storage heater consists of a thermally-insulated vessel, one or more electric heating elements, thermostat(s) and pipe connections and is assembled by the manufacturer ready for installation on site. They should comply with BS843 as far as it applies. In electric water heating practice, the accepted method (Note CP dated 1951) is to use storage heaters in which water is steadily heated up to a pre-determined temperature and stored until required for use. The storage vessel should be located so that the pipe runs to the most frequently used outlets are as short as possible. Loss of heat increases in proportion to the length of pipe between the storage vessel and hot tap, since each time water is drawn, the pipe fills with hot water which then cools. Greatest aggregate of such losses occur from the pipe feeding the tap most frequently used — the sink (in dwellings).

MODEL WATER BYELAW 46

Electric storage heaters may connect direct to 'mains' if less than 3 gal. capacity. Ditto for 3 to 15 gal capacity if certain conditions regarding back siphonage are observed.

MODEL WATER BYELAW 51

The minimum of 25 gallons capacity does not apply to an electric storage heater under thermostatic control.

BS CP TYPES (324 202)

Storage heaters may be any one of the following types:

(a)   Non-pressure or open outlet type: The control tap is fitted to the inlet (not outlet) therefore heater not under pressure.

(b)   Pressure type: Connect to cistern placed at suitable height.

(c)   Cistern type: Incorporates own feed cistern with ball valve.

(d)   Dual-heater type: As for (b) but fitted with two heaters.

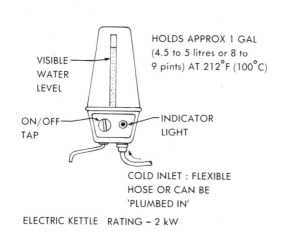

VISIBLE WATER LEVEL

HOLDS APPROX 1 GAL (4.5 to 5 litres or 8 to 9 pints) AT 212°F (100°C)

ON/OFF TAP

INDICATOR LIGHT

COLD INLET : FLEXIBLE HOSE OR CAN BE 'PLUMBED IN'

ELECTRIC KETTLE   RATING - 2 kW

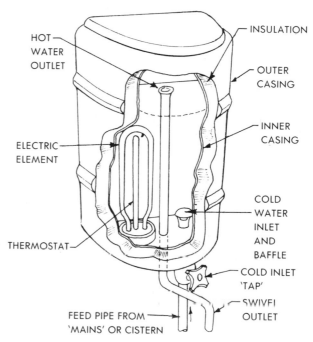

HOT WATER OUTLET

INSULATION

OUTER CASING

INNER CASING

ELECTRIC ELEMENT

COLD WATER INLET AND BAFFLE

COLD INLET 'TAP'

THERMOSTAT

SWIVEL OUTLET

FEED PIPE FROM 'MAINS' OR CISTERN

OPEN OUTLET TYPE (A)

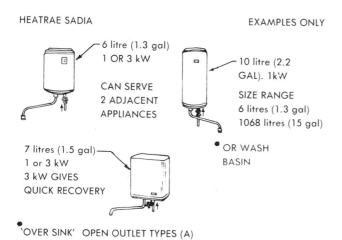

HEATRAE SADIA

EXAMPLES ONLY

6 litre (1.3 gal) 1 OR 3 kW

CAN SERVE 2 ADJACENT APPLIANCES

10 litre (2.2 GAL). 1kW

SIZE RANGE 6 litres (1.3 gal) 1068 litres (15 gal)

7 litres (1.5 gal) 1 or 3 kW 3 kW GIVES QUICK RECOVERY

OR WASH BASIN

'OVER SINK' OPEN OUTLET TYPES (A)

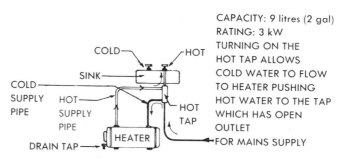

CAPACITY: 9 litres (2 gal) RATING: 3 kW TURNING ON THE HOT TAP ALLOWS COLD WATER TO FLOW TO HEATER PUSHING HOT WATER TO THE TAP WHICH HAS OPEN OUTLET FOR MAINS SUPPLY

COLD

HOT

SINK

COLD SUPPLY PIPE

HOT SUPPLY PIPE

HOT TAP

DRAIN TAP

HEATER

SANTON 'UNDER SINK' OPEN OUTLET TYPE (A)

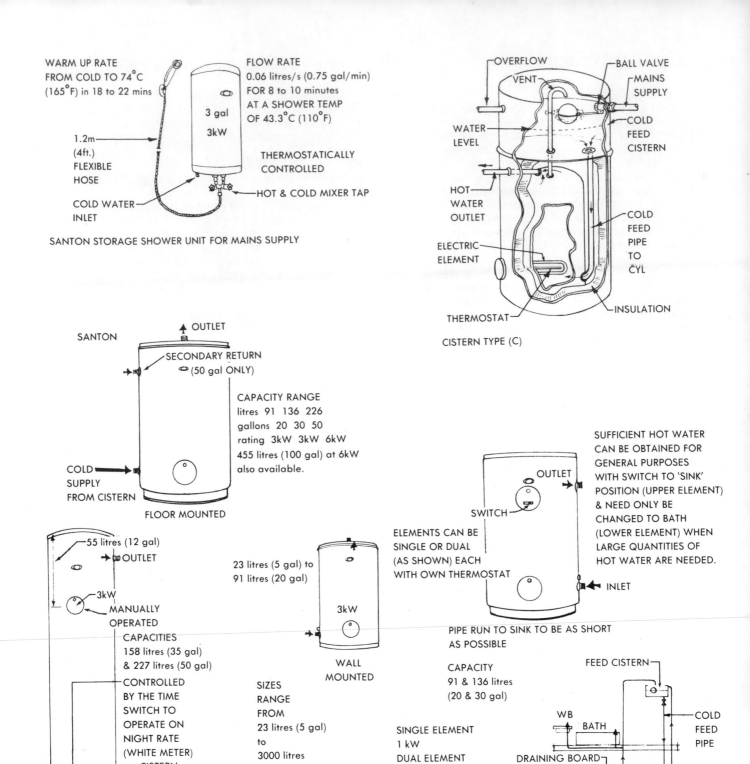

WARM UP RATE
FROM COLD TO 74°C
(165°F) in 18 to 22 mins

FLOW RATE
0.06 litres/s (0.75 gal/min)
FOR 8 to 10 minutes
AT A SHOWER TEMP
OF 43.3°C (110°F)

3 gal
3kW

1.2m
(4ft.)
FLEXIBLE
HOSE

THERMOSTATICALLY
CONTROLLED

COLD WATER
INLET

HOT & COLD MIXER TAP

SANTON STORAGE SHOWER UNIT FOR MAINS SUPPLY

OVERFLOW
VENT
BALL VALVE
MAINS
SUPPLY
WATER
LEVEL
COLD
FEED
CISTERN
HOT
WATER
OUTLET
ELECTRIC
ELEMENT
COLD
FEED
PIPE
TO
CYL
THERMOSTAT
INSULATION

CISTERN TYPE (C)

SANTON

OUTLET

SECONDARY RETURN
(50 gal ONLY)

CAPACITY RANGE
litres 91 136 226
gallons 20 30 50
rating 3kW 3kW 6kW
455 litres (100 gal) at 6kW
also available.

COLD
SUPPLY
FROM CISTERN

FLOOR MOUNTED

55 litres (12 gal)
OUTLET

3kW
MANUALLY
OPERATED

CAPACITIES
158 litres (35 gal)
& 227 litres (50 gal)

CONTROLLED
BY THE TIME
SWITCH TO
OPERATE ON
NIGHT RATE
(WHITE METER)

CISTERN
SUPPLY

3 kW

FLOOR MOUNTED

PRESSURE TYPES (B) ALL SUPPLIED FROM FEED CISTERN

23 litres (5 gal) to
91 litres (20 gal)

3kW

WALL
MOUNTED

SIZES
RANGE
FROM
23 litres (5 gal)
to
3000 litres
(667 gal)
FLOOR
MODELS

OUTLET

SWITCH

ELEMENTS CAN BE
SINGLE OR DUAL
(AS SHOWN) EACH
WITH OWN THERMOSTAT

SUFFICIENT HOT WATER
CAN BE OBTAINED FOR
GENERAL PURPOSES
WITH SWITCH TO 'SINK'
POSITION (UPPER ELEMENT)
& NEED ONLY BE
CHANGED TO BATH
(LOWER ELEMENT) WHEN
LARGE QUANTITIES OF
HOT WATER ARE NEEDED.

INLET

PIPE RUN TO SINK TO BE AS SHORT
AS POSSIBLE

CAPACITY
91 & 136 litres
(20 & 30 gal)

SINGLE ELEMENT
1 kW
DUAL ELEMENT
UPPER 1 to 3 kW
LOWER 2 to 3 kW
MUST BE CISTERN FED

FEED CISTERN

WB
BATH
COLD
FEED
PIPE
DRAINING BOARD
HEIGHT
SINK
'DUAL'
HEATER
SANTON

UNDER DRAINING BOARD (UDB) TYPE (D)

FOR FULL DETAILS SEE
MANUFACTURERS LITERATURE

94

INTRODUCTION

The idea of instantaneous electric water heating is by no means new. Many attempts both in the UK and overseas to market a suitable model over many decades failed because of non-acceptance by Water Authorities and/or Electricity Boards. Basically, control taps could not be repaired and some were electrically unsafe. Further progress appeared to be discouraged by Electric Authorities, in spite of vast improvements in design — the idea of intermittent use of numerous high rating appliances was not considered good. A control tap fixed external to the appliance (on the inlet) satisfied most Water Authorities. However, manufacturers persevered, there was obviously a demand and final acceptance as a method of water heating was acceptable. Ratings had to be increased (was 3kW), max now being 24 kW.

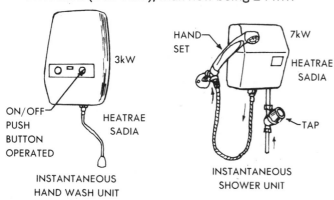

INSTANTANEOUS HAND WASH UNIT

INSTANTANEOUS SHOWER UNIT

HEATERS FOR HAND WASHING

It is sometimes desirable to fit a small water heater for hand washing or similar toilet purposes only, in a situation not convenient to the normal hot water supply. An electrical loading of 3 or 4 kW will give a supply of warm water at handwash temp at the rate of about 1½ litres (2.5-3 pints) per minute, suitable for such a situation. The amount delivered via the fine spray head on the swivel arm (giving a form of 'umbrella' type spray) is ample for hand washing. This heater is not recommended for use at the kitchen sink where greater amounts of water at higher temps are required. Safety is ensured by a pressure switch and thermal cutout.

HEATERS FOR SHOWERS

An electric loading of 6 kW, 7kW or 8.4 kW will give a continuous supply of warm water at showering temperature up to a maximum rate of approx. 3 litres (5 pints) per minute. The heater incorporates pressure switches which do not allow the element to be switched on until water is flowing and vice versa. Likewise, pre-set thermal cut outs safeguard against over heating. The heater can be installed with either a fixed shower head having vertical and horizontal adjustment, or alternatively an adjustable shower rose fitting on a flexible hose. No water fitting other than those supplied must be fitted to the permanently open outlet.

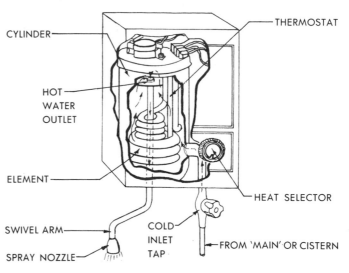

CUT-AWAY VIEW

MODEL WATER BYELAW 46

This Byelaw permits instantaneous electric water heaters to be connected directly to the service pipe but 3 proviso's are relevant (i) to be suitable for the pressure, (ii) water space enclosed, etc, (iii) discharge to be min ½in. above 'flood level' of san appl.

FORMULAE

$$\text{LITRE/HR} = \frac{\text{LOADING (kW)} \times 861.7}{\text{TEMP REQD (°C)} - \text{MAINS' TEMP (°C)}}$$

$$\text{GAL/HR} = \frac{\text{LOADING (kW)} \times 341.2}{\text{TEMP REQD (°F)} - \text{MAINS TEMP (°F)}}$$

SHOWER TEMP CAN BE ASSUMED TO BE 43°C (110°F) & INCOMING MAINS TEMP. 10°C (50°F)

HOT WATER FLOW RATES

kW	litre/min	litre/sec	gal/min	pint/min
3	1.31	0.022	0.284	2.28
4	1.74	0.029	0.379	3.03
6	2.61	0.044	0.569	4.55
7	3.05	0.051	0.663	5.31
9	3.92	0.065	0.853	6.82

SELECTION OF APPLIANCES

When inlet tap is turned on, cold water flows into the heat exchanger. The flow operates a pressure switch which activates the element and water flows rapidly over the element to the outlet. In most heaters the final temperature depends on the rate of water flow — slow for hot, fast for cold. Safety thermostat cuts out if temperature gets too high.

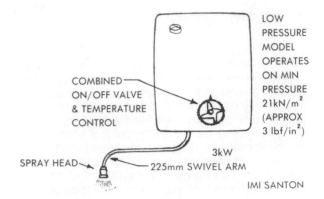

LOW PRESSURE MODEL OPERATES ON MIN PRESSURE $21 kN/m^2$ (APPROX $3 lbf/in^2$)

COMBINED ON/OFF VALVE & TEMPERATURE CONTROL

SPRAY HEAD

3kW

225mm SWIVEL ARM

IMI SANTON

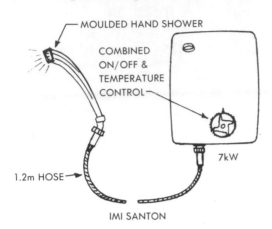

MOULDED HAND SHOWER

COMBINED ON/OFF & TEMPERATURE CONTROL

1.2m HOSE

7kW

IMI SANTON

RELEVANT DATA

Minimum pressure to operate: eg $100 kN/m^2$ (I bar) or $15 lbf/in^2$
Maximum pressure withstood: eg $1000 kN/m^2$ (10 bar) or $150 lbf/in^2$
Water supply: Mains or cistern fed providing pressure is within the limits specified (low pressure model available).
Ratings: in kW eg 3, 4, 5, 6, 7 (Stiebel Eltron: 9, 12, 18, 24 kW)
Multi-point eg 24 kW = 82,000 Btu (approx) at 100% effic.
Supplies 13 litres/min (about 3 gal/min) requires 415V 3-phase
Temperature. As heat input is fixed, reducing flow rate increases water temperature & vice versa.
Electrical: Check whether 13 AMP req; or separate 30 AMP; or 415V 3-phase. Amps = Watts ÷ volts eg 3000 ÷ 240 = 12.5A.

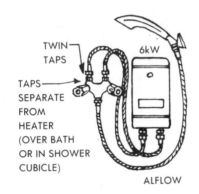

TWIN TAPS

6kW

TAPS SEPARATE FROM HEATER (OVER BATH OR IN SHOWER CUBICLE)

ALFLOW

ADVANTAGES CLAIMED

1. Plumbing kept to a minimum — cistern not necessary.
2. Economical — only uses electricity when operating
3. No waiting for water to be heated to required temperature.
4. Very clean operation : no dirt, fumes or flue.
5. Continuous supply for various purposes.
6. Occupies a very small amount of space.
7. Can be taken as 100% efficient.
8. Safety — sealed against spray, steam & condensation.
9. Requires only cold water supply and electrical connection if fitted over existing bath.
10. Regarded as ample water for showering.

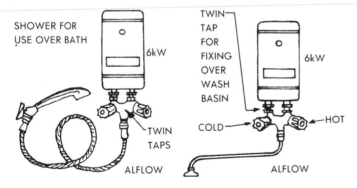

SHOWER FOR USE OVER BATH

6kW

TWIN TAPS

ALFLOW

TWIN TAP FOR FIXING OVER WASH BASIN

6kW

COLD

HOT

ALFLOW

CONTACT LOCAL WATER AUTHORITY AND ELECTRICITY BOARD TO ASCERTAIN ACTUAL REQUIREMENTS.

EXTENT OF INSULATION WORK TO BE UNDERTAKEN

All hot surfaces from which heat could be lost should be insulated, except those where the heat emitted serves a useful purpose, eg the warming where desired of kitchens, airing cupboards, bathrooms, etc. This recommendation applies in general to boilers, hot water storage vessels and all pipes forming part of a circuit whether freely exposed or run in a roof space under floors, in a chase, a duct or a cupboard. Pipes should not be left uninsulated in order to obtain increased natural circulation. (BS 5572).

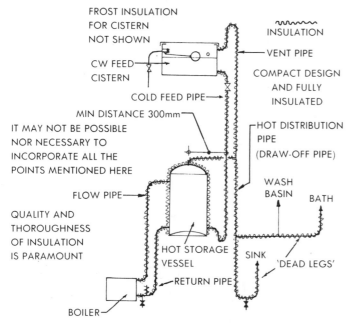

DESIGNING TO CONSERVE ENERGY

1. Primary circuits should be kept as short and direct as possible.
2. Do not oversize circuits: the larger they are, the greater the surface area.
3. Aim for as compact a design as the circumstances permit.
4. Position cylinder in as warm an environment as possible.
5. Place cylinder as near sink as possible: this appliance is often used the most.
6. Avoid the use of a secondary circulation, if at all possible.
7. Circs to towel rail to be kept as short as possible and well insulated.
8. Design to avoid reverse circulation.
9. Position all pipes in as warm situation as possible, e.g. under a boarded floor may be a very cold position due to air movement via wall cavity: avoid or increase insulation.
10. Keep draw-off pipes as short as possible and well within max. lengths.
11. Keep draw-off pipes to minimum sizes : smaller pipes have less surface area.
12. Dip cold feed pipe before entry to cylinder: this reduces I pipe circulation.

13. Continue vent pipe up to correct height: avoids overspill of hot water into cistern by surge, air bubbles, etc.
14. Take vent pipe horizontally from top of cylinder: the greater this distance, the greater the reduction in one pipe circulation in vent pipe.
15. Do not store more hot water than necessary.
16. Do not produce water hotter than needed to reduce standing losses and reduce scale formation.
17. Consider 'instantaneous' method as opposed to 'storage': the former has no standing heat losses.

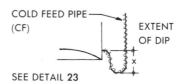

REDUCES HEAT LOSS BY ONE-PIPE CIRCULATION IN THE COLD FEED. GREATER DISTANCE x THE MORE EFFECTIVE IS DIP

DIPPING COLD FEED

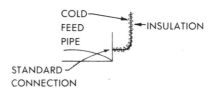

WHEN CYLINDER GETS HOT NEAR THE BOTTOM, THE WATER IN THE COLD FEED PIPE CAN GET AS WARM AS WATER IN PARTS OF VENT PIPE

INSULATING THE COLD FEED

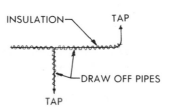

THE BENEFIT OF THIS INSULATION DEPENDS UPON THE PIPE LENGTH, SIZE, ENVIRONMENT, TEMPERATURE OF WATER CONTAINED, USAGE, ETC

INSULATING DRAW-OFF PIPES

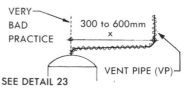

ONE PIPE CIRCULATION IN VENT PIPE CAN BE REDUCED IF THE PIPE IS HORIZONTAL FOR AT LEAST 300mm. GREATER x, GREATER THE EFFECT

TREATMENT OF VENT PIPE

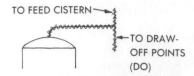

TO FEED CISTERN

TO DRAW-
OFF POINTS
(DO)

BENEFIT IS DERIVED FROM THE INSULATION OF THE VP. PARTICULARLY
IF VERY HOT WATER IS STORED OTHER FACTORS MAY BE RELEVANT

INSULATING THE VENT PIPE

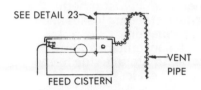

SEE DETAIL 23

VENT
PIPE

FEED CISTERN

VENT PIPE SHOULD BE CONTINUED UPWARDS TO THE RECOMMENDED
HEIGHT IF NOT, SURGE ETC MAY ALLOW HW TO ENTER CF CISTERN

HEIGHT OF VENT PIPE

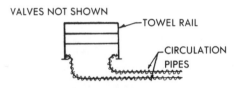

VALVES NOT SHOWN

TOWEL RAIL

CIRCULATION
PIPES

ALL CIRCULATION PIPES (BOTH PRIMARY & SECONDARY) SHOULD
BE INSULATED. AMOUNT OF BENEFIT DEPENDS UPON CIRCUMSTANCES

CIRCULATION PIPES

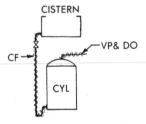

CISTERN

VP& DO

CF

CYL

AS EXPANSION WATER NORMALLY REACHES THE FEED CISTERN VIA CF
PIPE. THERE IS NO UNDUE RISE IN TEMPERATURE OF WATER IN CISTERN
CAUSED BY NORMAL EXPANSION

EXPANSION WATER

HEAT LOSSES FROM CIRCULATING PIPES						
HEAT EMISSION IN WATTS PER METRE RUN						
Temperature		Light gauge copper			Galvanised iron		
°C	°F	15mm (½″)	22mm (¾″)	28mm (1″)	15mm (½″)	20mm (¾″)	25mm (1″)
50	120	23	32	35	35	41	48
60	140	31	44	55	46	56	68
70	160	40	56	71	59	70	88
82	180	51	71	90	73	87	110

LOSS OF HEAT DUE TO RADIATION & CONVECTION PER
METRE RUN OF HORIZONTAL PIPE CONTINUOUSLY HOT
ASSUMPTIONS STILL AIR AT 16°C & PIPES BARE & DULL

INCREASE IN HEAT LOSS WITH INCREASE IN TEMPERATURE		
Water temperature		Loss of heat as a percentage of loss at 60°C (140°F)
°C	°F	
60	140	100%
65	150	117%
70	160	133%
77	170	151%
82	180	169%
88	190	189%
93	200	207%

HEAT LOSSES FROM 'DEAD LEGS'						
LOSS IN 1000 W HRS (UNITS) PER WEEK PER METRE RUN						
Temperature		Light gauge copper			Galvanised iron		
°C	°F	15mm (½″)	22mm (¾″)	28mm (1″)	15mm (½″)	20mm (¾″)	25mm (1″)
50	120	0.46	0.92	1.64	0.92	1.44	2.33
60	140	0.65	1.25	2.20	1.21	1.93	3.08
70	160	0.79	1.54	2.76	1.51	2.43	3.87
82	180	0.95	1.87	3.34	1.84	2.92	4.66

HEAT LOSS DUE TO THE PIPE & ITS WATER CONTENT COOLING
DOWN TO 16°C (60°F) AFTER EACH DRAW-OFF
IT IS ASSUMED THE PIPE IS USED 10 TIMES A DAY

IT MUST BE BORNE IN MIND THAT A H.W. SYSTEM IS USED ALL
THE YEAR ROUND AND ALTHOUGH THE WARMTH EMITTED
MAY BE CONSIDERED USEFUL IN COLD MONTHS, THIS MAY
NOT BE THE CASE FOR THE REST OF THE YEAR

NOTE FROM CP342 PART I

The hot water storage vessel should always be thermally insulated. Generally, where the storage vessel is installed in an airing cupboard, sufficient heat is emitted to keep the cupboard warm and dry; this may not be true for cased vessels or more heavily insulated factory produced units and a heating coil or other alternative means of heating may then be necessary. (Temperatures of 49°C (120°F) have been recorded in an airing cupboard housing an uninsulated cylinder — this high temperature is detrimental to certain fabrics eg. woollens. With a cylinder covered with an insulating jacket (25mm thick) experiments showed the cupboard temp reduced to 27°C (80°F) which is still considered warm enough for airing purposes. Airing cupboards should not be regarded as drying cupboards).

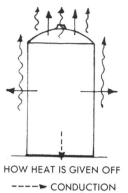

HOW HEAT IS GIVEN OFF

- - - -► CONDUCTION
———► RADIATION
∿∿∿► CONVECTION

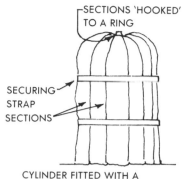

SECTIONS 'HOOKED' TO A RING

SECURING STRAP SECTIONS

CYLINDER FITTED WITH A SECTIONED LAGGING JACKET WITH PVC COVERING, FILLED WITH INSULATING MATERIAL

	Hot storage temperature			
°C	49	60	71	82
°F	120	140	160	180
Heat emission in watts per square metre	160	220	290	360
	(watts = joules per second)			

Loss of heat due to natural convection from a vertical surface. It is assumed that draught free air is at 16°C (60°F). Theoretical figures based on IHVE Guide & usage as at I Oct 73.

HEAT LOSSES FROM BARE CYLINDER SURFACES

TO PROVIDE EXTRA WARMTH IN AIRING CUPD (IF NEEDED) ONE SECTION OF THE LAGGING JACKET CAN BE TURNED BACK BARING A PORTION OF THE CYLINDER

JACKETS ARE NOT COSTLY BUT EVEN 'DIY' INSULATION CAN SAVE SOME ENERGY

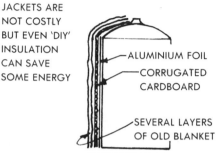

ALUMINIUM FOIL
CORRUGATED CARDBOARD
SEVERAL LAYERS OF OLD BLANKET

ANY INSULATION IS BETTER THAN NO INSULATION AT ALL. MANY ITEMS FOUND IN THE AVERAGE HOUSE PERHAPS UNWANTED OR WASTE MATERIAL WILL SERVE AS INSULATION

TYPICAL STANDING LOSSES IN 1000 WATT HOURS (UNITS) PER 24 HRS CYLINDER: 120 litres (28 gal nominal): TYPE BS 699/72 REF 7: GRADE 3

Nominal Thickness	Material	Stored Water Temperature		
		60°C(140°F)	71°C(160°F)	77°C(170°F)
25mm(1″)	Mineral wool	2.6	3.2	3.5
	Glass fibre	3.2	4.1	4.8
50mm(2″)	Mineral wool	2.0	2.5	2.8
	Glass fibre	2.0	2.5	2.9
75mm(3″)	Mineral wool	1.6	2.1	2.4
	Glass fibre	1.7	2.3	2.7

Figures based on tests with ambient temp of 21°C (70°F). Density of materials and efficiency of installation vary therefore use table as guide only.

HEAT LOSSES FROM JACKET LAGGED CYLINDER

THERMAL CONDUCTIVITY (k)

Material	Bulk Density kg/m³	'k' W/m°C
Urethane foam	30	0.02
Expanded ebonite	64	0.029
Expanded polystyrene	16-24	0.035-0.033
Foamed polyurethane	24-40	0.024 0.034
Glass fibre quilt	16-48	0.032-0.04
Mineral & slag wools	48	0.030-0.04
Wool, hair & jute fibre felts	120	0.036
Cork board (baked)	128	0.040
Insulating fibre building boards	240-400	0.053-0.065
Exfoliated vermiculite (loose)	80-144	0.047-0.058
Compressed straw slabs	369	0.086
Wood wool slabs	450	0.093
Polyester, glass fibre laminate	–	0.35
Copper	9000	400

DEFINITION OF COEFFICIENT OF THERMAL CONDUCTIVITY (K)

The heat flow in watts (joules/second) which takes place across a cube $1m^2$ in cross section & $1m$ in thickness, if the difference in temperature between the two faces is $1°C$ its dimensions are watts/metre per °C

State as W/m°C (or K = Kelvin)

(Note: Face to face, Not air to air) using

Imperial Units : $K = \dfrac{\text{Btu inch}}{\text{hour ft}^2\,°F}$

'k' deals with unit time, unit area, unit temperature & unit thickness of a homogenous slab of material.

'C' (thermal conductance) differs in as much as a specific thickness (L) of the uniform component or structure must be quoted.

'C' is expressed in $W/m^2°C$

Thermal conductance (C) = $\dfrac{K}{L}$

Conversions : Imperial to metric
$\quad$ x 0.144228 = W/m°C (k)

$\qquad$: Metric to Imperial

$\quad$ x 6.933467 = $\dfrac{\text{btu inch}}{\text{hour ft}^2\,°F}$ (k)

URETHANE FOAM INSULATION: IMI TRADEMARK 'HERCULAG'

'Herculag' was developed by IMI as an entirely new and improved method of insulating hot water cylinders. In addition to high efficiency and low bulk, further obvious advantages are — elimination of labour costs (no fitting of jacket) and permanence ie no settling, sagging or gapping as a sectional jacket may do. The insulation also protects the cylinder from damage during transit. Application of the foam to the cylinder is a 'sprayed on' process, the two component chemicals being brought together in the spray gun. The liquid begins to form its cellular structure within a few seconds & becomes firmly & permanently attached to cylinder.

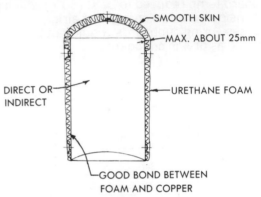

NOTE: EXTRA THICKNESS COVERING
UPPER PART OF CYLINDER WHERE THE
WATER IS THE HOTTEST

POINTS CONCERNING 'HERCULAG'

(i) Flame resistant additives cause it to exhibit low flame transmission and is classified as self extinguishing in ASTM D1692; complies with Class P in BS 476; and with Class Q in BS 4739.

(ii) Density if approx 30 kg/m³

(iii) 'k' value is given as 0.02W/m°C

(iv) Insulation performance meets the requirements of BS 5615 and Dept. of Environment.

(v) Cost — about the same as BS Sect. Jacket

(vi) Comparison of heat losses & savings. Copper cyl 900 x 450, holding 120 litres. heat loss: Unlagged cylinder: 11.2 kWh/day. Heat loss: Herculag or BS Jacket 3kWh/day.

RATE OF FLOW

Gallons per minute	Litres per second	Litres per minute	Cubic metres per minute	Cubic metres per hour
0.25	0.0189	1.1366	0.0011	0.0682
0.5	0.0379	2.2731	0.0023	0.1364
1	0.0758	4.546	0.0046	0.2760
2	0.1515	9.0929	0,0091	0.5455
3	0.2273	13.639	0.0136	0.8183
4	0.3031	18.185	0.0182	1.0911
5	0.3789	22.731	0.0227	1.3639
6	0.4546	27.277	0.0273	1.6366
7	0.5304	31.823	0.0318	1.9094
8	0.6062	36.370	0.0364	2.1822
9	0.6819	40.916	0.0409	2.4550
10	0.7577	45.462	0.0455	2.7277
11	0.8335	50.008	0.0500	3.0005
12	0.9092	54.554	0.0546	3.2733
13	0.9850	59.101	0.0591	3.5460
13.198	1.0000	60.000	0.0600	3.6000
14	1.0608	63.647	0.0637	3.8188
15	1.1365	68.193	0.0682	4.0916
16	1.2123	72.739	0.0727	4.3644
17	1.2881	77.285	0.0773	4.6371
18	1.3639	81.832	0.0818	4.9099
19	1.4396	86.378	0.0864	5.1827
20	1.5154	90.924	0.0909	5.4554
21	1.5912	95.470	0.0955	5.7282
22	1.6669	100.02	0.10002	6.00098
23	1.7427	104.56	0.1046	6.2738
24	1.8185	109.11	0.1091	6.5465
25	1.8943	113.66	0.1137	6.8193
26	1.9700	118.20	0.1182	7.0921
26.396	2.0000	120.00	0.1200	7.2000
30	2.2731	136.39	0.1364	8.1832
40	3.0308	181.85	0.1819	10.911
50	3.7885	227.31	0.2273	13.639
60	4.5462	272.77	0.2728	16.366
75	5.6828	340.97	0.3410	20.458
100	7.577	454.62	0.4546	27.277

For litre/second, multiply gal/min by 0.07577. For gal/min, multiply litre/second by 13.198. Litre to cubic metre ÷ 1000. m³ to litres x 1000.
CONVERSIONS
$1 \text{ yd}^3 = 0.765 \text{m}^3$. $1\text{m}^3 = 1.308 \text{ yd}^3$

VOLUME & MASS

ft³	m³	l(dm³)	lb	kg
1	0.0283	28.317	62.428	28.317
2	0.0566	56.635	124.86	56.635
3	0.0850	84.952	187.28	84.952
4	0.1133	113.27	249.71	113.27
5	0.1416	141.59	312.14	141.59
6	0.1699	169.90	374.57	169.90
7	0.1982	198.22	437.00	198.22
8	0.2265	226.54	499.42	226.54
9	0.2549	254.86	561.85	254.86
10	0.2832	283.17	624.28	283.17
11	0.3115	311.49	686.71	311.49
12	0.3398	339.81	749.14	339.81
13	0.3681	368.13	811.56	368.13
14	0.3964	396.44	873.99	396.44
15	0.4248	424.76	936.42	424.76
16	0.4531	453.08	998.85	453.08
17	0.4814	481.40	1061.3	481.40
18	0.5097	509.71	1123.7	509.71
19	0.5380	538.03	1186.1	538.03
20	0.5664	566.35	1248.6	566.35
21	0.5946	594.64	1310.9	594.64
22	0.6230	622.98	1373.4	622.98
23	0.6513	651.30	1435.8	657.30
24	0.6796	679.62	1498.3	679.62
25	0.7079	707.93	1560.7	707.93
26	0.7368	736.25	1623.1	736.25
27	0.7646	764.57	1685.6	764.57
28	0.7929	792.89	1748.0	792.89
29	0.8212	821.20	1810.4	821.20
30	0.8495	849.52	1872.8	849.52
31	0.8778	877.84	1935.3	877.84
32	0.9062	906.16	1997.7	906.16
33	0.9345	934.47	2060.1	934.47
34	0.9628	962.79	2122.6	962.79
35	0.9911	991.11	2185.0	991.11
35.315	1.0000	1000.0	2204.7	1000.0

For cubic feet to litres (dm³) multiply by 28.3168. for litres to cubic feed multiply by 0.03532. for lb to kg x 0.4536 for kg to lb x 2.20459.
1000kg = 1 tonne. 1 ton = 1016 kg

CAPACITY & MASS

Gallons	Litres	lb	kg	Gallons	litres	lb	kg
0.22	1	2.205	1	30	136.4	300	136.4
0.44	2	4.410	2	35	159.1	350	159.1
0.5	2.27	5	2.27	40	181.8	400	181.8
0.66	3	6.615	3	50	227.3	500	227.3
0.88	4	8.820	4	60	272.8	600	272.8
1	4.546	10	4.546	70	318.2	700	318.2
2	9.092	20	9.092	80	363.7	800	363.7
3	13.64	30	13.64	90	409.1	900	409.1
4	18.18	40	18.18	100	454.6	1000	454.6
5	22.73	50	22.73	200	909.2	2000	909.2
6	27.28	60	27.28	220	1000.0	2200	1000.0*
6.24(1ft³)	28.32	62.4	28.32	300	1363.8	3000	1363.8
7	31.82	70	31.82	400	1818.4	4000	1818.4
8	36.37	80	36.37	500	2273.1	5000	2273.1
9	40.91	90	40.91	600	2727.7	6000	2727.7
10	45.46	100	45.46	700	3182.3	7000	3182.3
15	68.19	150	68.19	800	3636.8	8000	3636.8
20	90.92	200	90.92	900	4091.4	9000	4091.4
25	113.7	250	113.7	1000	4545.96	10000	4545.96

SLIGHT INACCURACIES MAY APPEAR IN CERTAIN VALUES ABOVE. THESE ARE DUE TO THE INEVITABLE
'ROUNDING OFF' WHEN DEALING WITH SUCH LARGE NUMBERS OF DIGITS

CONVERSIONS
GAL TO LITRE x 4.546
LITRE TO GAL x 0.220

This table assumes
1 gal of water weighs
10lb, & 1 litre – 1kg

ACTUAL DENSITY
at 4°C (39.2°F) WATER
IS SAID TO WEIGH
999.9kg per m³
(This is usually
taken as 1000kg
per m³ or 1 tonne)
In Imperial units
this is quoted as
62.428 lb per ft³
and 1 gallon could
weigh 10.02lb

* 1 Tonne

TEMPERATURE CONVERSIONS
FAHRENHEIT TO CENTIGRADE OR CENTIGRADE TO FAHRENHEIT

°F		°C	°F		°C	°F		°C
28.4	-2	-18.9	93.2	34	1.1	158	70	21.1
32	0	-17.8	96.8	36	2.2	161.6	72	22.2
35.6	2	-16.7	100.4	38	3.3	165.2	74	23.3
39.2	4	-15.6	104	40	4.4	168.8	76	24.4
42.8	6	-14.4	107.6	42	5.6	172.4	78	25.6
46.4	8	-13.3	111.2	44	6.7	176	80	26.7
50	10	-12.2	114.8	46	7.8	179.6	82	27.8
53.6	12	-11.1	118.4	48	8.9	183.2	84	28.9
57.2	14	-10	122	50	10	186.8	86	30
60.8	16	-8.9	125.6	52	11.1	190.4	88	31.1
64.4	18	-7.8	129.2	54	12.2	194	90	32.2
68	20	-6.7	132.8	56	13.3	197.6	92	33.3
71.6	22	-5.6	136.4	58	14.4	201.2	94	34.4
75.2	24	-4.4	140	60	15.6	204.8	96	35.6
78.8	26	-3.3	143.6	62	16.7	208.4	98	36.7
82.4	28	-2.2	147.2	64	17.8	212	100	37.8
86	30	-1.1	150.8	66	18.9	215.6	102	38.9
89.6	32	0	154.4	68	20	219.2	104	40

°F		°C	°F		°C	°F		°C
222.8	106	41.1	287.6	142	61.1	352.4	178	81.1
226.4	108	42.2	291.2	144	62.2	356	180	82.2
230	110	43.3	294.8	146	63.3	359.6	182	83.3
233.6	112	44.4	298.4	148	64.4	363.2	184	84.4
237.2	114	45.6	302	150	65.6	366.8	186	85.6
240.8	116	46.7	305.6	152	66.7	370.4	188	86.7
244.4	118	47.8	309.2	154	67.8	374	190	87.8
248	120	48.9	312.8	156	68.9	377.6	192	88.9
251.6	122	50	316.4	158	70	381.2	194	90
255.2	124	51.1	320	160	71.1	384.8	196	91.1
258.8	126	52.2	323.6	162	72.2	388.4	198	92.2
262.4	128	53.3	327.2	164	73.3	392	200	93.3
266	130	54.4	330.8	166	74.4	395.6	202	94.4
269.6	132	55.6	334.4	168	75.6	399.2	204	95.6
273.2	134	56.7	338	170	76.7	402.8	206	96.7
276.8	136	57.8	341.6	172	77.8	406.4	208	97.8
280.4	138	58.9	345.2	174	78.9	410	210	98.9
284	140	60	348.8	176	80	413.6	212	100

CENTIGRADE TO FAHRENHEIT: $x \times \frac{9}{5} + 32$. FAHRENHEIT TO CENTIGRADE: $32 \times \frac{5}{9}$. TEMP INTERVAL $°F \times \frac{5}{9} = °C$. $°C \times \frac{9}{5} = °F$. DEGREE KELVIN (K) IS THE ONLY TRULY ACCEPTABLE SI SCALE FOR SCIENTIFIC PURPOSES BUT CENTIGRADE (CELSIUS) IS PERMITTED FOR MANY PURPOSES

HEAT FLOW RATE

Btu/hour	kWh
1.0	0.0002931
100	0.02931
1000	0.2931
1706	0.5
2000	0.5862
3000	0.8793
3412	1.0
4000	1.1724
5000	1.4655
6824	2.0
10000	2.931
10236	3.0
13648	4.0
15000	4.3965
17060	5.0
20000	5.862
20472	6.0
23884	7.0
25000	7.3275
27296	8.0
30000	8.793
30708	9.0
34120	10.0
35000	10.2585
37532	11.0
40000	11.724
40944	12.0
44356	13.0
45000	13.1895
47768	14.0
50000	14.655
51180	15.0
54592	16.0
55000	16.123
58004	17.0
60000	17.586
61416	18.0
75000	21.9825
85300	25.0
100000	29.31

BRITISH THERMAL UNIT PER HOUR = 2.931×10^{-1} Watt
WATTS = JOULES PER SECOND

QUANTITY OF HEAT

Btu	kJ	MJ
1.0	1.05506	0.00106
100	105.506	0.1055
1000	1055.06	1.0551
1706	1799.93	1.7999
2000	2110.12	2.110
3000	3165.17	3.165
3412	3599.87	3.59987*
5000	5275.28	5.2753
6824	7199.73	7.1997
10000	10550.60	10.5506
10236	10799.59	10.7997
13648	14399.46	14.3995
15000	15825.9	15.8259
17060	17999.32	17.9993
20000	21101.2	21.1012
20472	21599.19	21.5992
23884	25199.05	25.1991
25000	26376.4	26.3764
27296	28798.92	28.7989
30000	31651.8	31.6518
30708	32398.78	32.3988
34120	35998.65	35.9987
35000	36927.1	36.9271
37532	39598.51	39.5985
40000	42202.4	42.2024
40944	43198.38	43.1984
44356	46798.24	46.7982
45000	47477.7	47.4777
47768	50398.11	50.3981
50000	52753.0	52.7520
51180	53997.97	53.99797
54592	57597.84	57.5978
55000	58028.3	58.0283
58004	61197.7	61.1977
60000	63303.6	63.3036
65000	68578.9	68.5789
68240	71997.29	71.9973
85300	89996.62	89.9966
*100000	105506.0	105.506
102360	107995.9	107.9959

ONE Btu EQUALS 1.0551 x 10³ JOULES●
(OR x 1.0551 for kJ). 1 kW = 3.6MJ
*ONE THERM (100,000 Btu) = 1.055 x 10⁻¹GJ

1 inch = 25.4mm. 1 foot = 0.3048m 1 yard = 0.9144m. 1 Metre = 3.2808 ft.

k = KILO:x 10³. M = MEGA:x 10⁶. G = GIGA:x 10⁹

PRESSURE CONVERSIONS

lbf/m²	ft 'head'	m 'head'	N/m²	kN/m²	bar	m bar
14.5	33.5	10.2	100000	100.000	1.0000	1000
		9	88233	88.233	0.88233	980
		8	78430	78.430	0.78430	784
10.0		7	68626	68.626	0.68626	686
	20.0	6	58822	58.822	0.58822	588
		5	49018	49.018	0.49018	490
5.0		4	39215	39.215	0.39215	392
	10.0	3	29411	29.411	0.29411	294
		2	19607	19.607	0.19607	196
1.0	2.0	1	9804	9.804	0.09804	98
1.424	3.281	1.0	9804	9.804	0.09804	98
1.302	3.0	0.9	8823	8.823	0.08823	88
		0.8	7843	7.843	0.07843	78
1.00	2.3	0.7	6863	6.863	0.06863	69
0.868	2.0	0.6	5882	5.882	0.05882	59
		0.5	4902	4.902	0.04902	49
		0.4	3921	3.921	0.03921	39
0.434	1.0	0.3	2941	2.941	0.02941	29
		0.2	1961	1.961	0.01961	20
		0.1	980	0.980	0.00981	10
	inches	mm				
0.434	12	304.8	2989	2.989	0.02989	30
	11					
	10	250	2451	2.451	0.02451	25
0.325	9	225	2206	2.206	0.02206	22
	8					
0.253	7	175	1715	1.715	0.01715	17
	6					
0.180	5	125	1225	1.225	0.01225	12.5
	4					
0.108	3	75	735	0.735	0.00735	7.5
	2					
0.036	1	25	245	0.245	0.00245	2.5
	1.0	25.4	249	0.249	0.00249	2.5
	0.9					
	0.8	21.0	205.8	0.2058	0.002058	2.1
	0.7	18.0	176.4	0.1764	0.001764	1.8
	0.6	15.0	147.0	0.1470	0.001470	1.5
	0.5	12.0	117.6	0.1176	0.001176	1.2
	0.4	9.0	88.2	0.0882	0.000882	0.9
	0.3					
	0.2	6.0	58.8	0.0588	0.00588	0.6
	0.1	3.0	29.4	0.0294	0.000294	0.3
		mm(exact)				
	0.10	2.54	24.9	2.540		0.249
	0.09	2.2	22.0	2.244		0.22
	0.08	2.0				
	0.07	1.8	18.0	1.836		0.18
	0.06	1.6				
	0.05	1.4	14.0	1.428		0.14
		1.2				
	0.04	1.0	9.807	1.00		0.098
	0.03	0.8				
	0.02	0.6	6.0	0.612		0.06
		0.4				
	0.01	0.2	2.0	0.204		0.02

l bf/m² = 6.895 x 10³ or 6894.76 N/m² or 6.895 kN/m²
INCHES WATER HEAD (4°C) x 2.491 for mbar
FOOT WATER HEAD (4°C) x 2.989 for kN/m² or 29.89 for mbar

H INTRODUCTION TO CALCULATIONS

DAILY DEMAND & HOT WATER STORAGE

SEE DETAIL 13
FOR SIZES

STORAGE VESSELS PREFERABLY
CYLINDRICAL & FIXED VERTICALLY

USING SI UNITS
Values taken from Guide Book B (CIBS)

<u>MAXIMUM DAILY DEMAND</u>

5 PERSONS AT 115 litres/PERSON = 575 litres $(0.575m^3)$
(THESE FIGURES SERVE AS A GUIDE WHEN
CALCULATING RUNNING COSTS & ESTIMATING
COLD WATER STORAGE CAPACITY).

<u>HOT WATER STORAGE</u>

5 PERSONS AT 30 litres/PERSON = 150 litres $(0.15m^3)$
EXAMPLE OF CYLINDER SIZE : BS699 TYPE REF 9
166 litres EXTERNAL DIAMETER: 450mm HEIGHT
OVER DOME: 1200mm. DIRECT TYPE

USING IMPERIAL UNITS
Values taken from BS CP342

<u>MAXIMUM DAILY DEMAND</u>

5 PERSONS AT 25 GAL/PERSON = 125 GAL $(20ft^3)$
(THESE FIGURES SERVE AS A GUIDE WHEN
CALCULATING RUNNING COSTS & ESTIMATING
COLD WATER STORAGE CAPACITY).

<u>HOT WATER STORAGE</u>

5 PERSONS AT 10 GAL/PERSON = 50 GAL $(8ft^3)$
EXAMPLE OF CYLINDER SIZE: BS699 TYPE REF 10
44 GAL (PERHAPS TOO SMALL) OR REF 11, 56 GAL
EXT. DIAM. 20in. APPROX. HEIGHT OVER DOME : 59in. DIRECT

BOILER POWER & WARM-UP TIME

BOILERS MAY BE INDEPENDENT
OR FITTED TO ROOM HEATER. A
RANGE BOILER MAY ALSO BE USED

<u>BOILER POWER</u> (Based upon 1 hr time factor)

5 PERSONS ALLOWING 0.7kW/PERSON = 3.5 kWh
ie. 5 PERSONS ALLOWING 11 litres/PERSON RAISED TO
55°C (FROM 10°C to 65°C). CALCULATION VIZ:

$$\frac{5 \times 11 \times 55 \times (4.187 \times 1000)}{3600} = 3518Wh \text{ or } 3.5kWh$$

EXAMPLE OF SIZING A HOT WATER SYSTEM   DETAIL 36
MEDIUM RENTAL HOUSE FOR 5 PERSONS

NOTE: HEAT REQ TO RAISE TEMP OF 1 litre OF WATER 1°C
= 4.187 J(w/s)
TIME REQUIRED TO HEAT CYLINDER CONTENTS

$$\frac{\text{HEAT CONENT OF CYL}}{\text{BOILER POWER}} = \text{TIME (IN HOURS)}$$

$$\text{eg } \frac{150l \times 1.163 \times 55°C}{3.5 \times 100} = 2\frac{3}{4}\text{hrs (approx)}$$

<u>BOILER POWER</u> (Based upon 1 hr time factor)

5 PERSONS ALLOWING 3.0 GAL/PERSON = 15 GAL/HR
ie 5 PERSONS ALLOWING 3 GAL/PERSON RAISED
100°F (FROM 50°F TO 150°F) ASSUMING 1 GAL WEIGHS 10 lb
5 x 3 x 100 x 10 = 15,000 Btu
(therefore 1 GAL IS 'EQUAL' TO 1000 Btu)

NOTE: HEAT REQ TO RAISE TEMP. OF 1lb of WATER 1°F = 1 Btu
TIME REQUIRED TO HEAT CYLINDER CONTENTS

$$\frac{\text{HEAT CONTENT OF CYL}}{\text{BOILER POWER}} = \text{TIME (IN HOURS)}$$

$$\text{e.g. } \frac{50 \text{ GAL} \times 10lb \times 100°F}{15000} = 3.3 \text{ hrs (approx)}$$

COLD WATER STORAGE

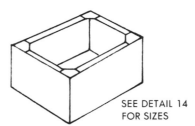

SEE DETAIL 14
FOR SIZES

FEED CISTERN
USED FOR SUPPLYING COLD
WATER TO H.W. APPARATUS
& NO OTHER PURPOSE

<u>CAPACITY OF COLD FEED CISTERN</u>

MINIMUM: EQUAL TO CYLINDER CAPACITY = 150 litres
BS 417 TYPE REF SCM 230. CAPACITY TO WATER
LINE: 159 litres (WL TO BE 114mm FROM TOP EDGE)
DIMENSIONS: LENGTH 736mm. WIDTH 559mm
DEPTH 559mm
WEIGHT: 150 kg of WATER + 35 kg CISTERN
(GRADE A) + WEIGHT OF COVER, SUPPORTS, ETC
IF WATER AUTHORITY REQUIRE STORAGE TO COVER
24 HRS SUPPLY, THEN CISTERN TO HOLD 450 litres
ACCORDING TO TABLE 2 OR 575 litres WHEN
CALCULATED AS PER TABLE 1. (NOT USUALLY
REQUIRED FOR DWELLINGS).

<u>CAPACITY OF COLD FEED CISTERN</u>

MINIMUM: EQUAL TO CYLINDER CAPACITY = 50 GAL.
BS 417 TYPE REF. SCM 320. CAPACITY TO WATER
LINE: 50 GAL. (WL TO BE APPROX 4.5in. FROM TOP EDGE).
DIMENSIONS: LENGTH 36 in. WIDTH 24 in.
DEPTH 23 in.
WEIGHT: 500lbs of WATER + 95lb CISTERN (GRADE A)
+ WEIGHT OF COVER, SUPPORTS, ETC.
IF WATER AUTHORITY REQUIRE STORAGE TO COVER 24 HRS
SUPPLY THEN CISTERN TO HOLD 100 GAL
ACCORDING TO TABLE 2 OR 125 GAL. WHEN
CALCULATED AS PER TABLE 1. (NOT USUALLY
REQUIRED FOR DWELLINGS).

MODEL WATER BYELAWS (51)

Minimum capacity of hot water storage vessel:- 25 gal unless heated only under thermostatic control by electricity, gas or oil. (38) No minimum capacity stated for cistern acting as feed cistern only.

CP342 Pt I Hot storage vessel: allow for 10 gal (45 litres)/person with a min of 30 gal (136 litres). Off-peak elec: min 50 gal (227 litres). Independent boiler: to be sized to heat contents of storage vessel to 65°C (150°F) in max 2½ hrs plus all other loads. Cistern: if used only as feed cistern — at least equal to capacity of the hot storage vessel.

CP342 Pt 2. refers to information in 'IHVE' Guide Book.

HOT WATER DEMAND, STORAGE & BOILER POWER

BUILDING TABLE 1		Maximum daily demand per person		Storage per person at 65°C		Boiler power per person to 65°C	
		litre*	gal•	litre*	gal•	kW*	gal•
SCHOOLS AND COLLEGES	Boarding	115	25	25	5	0.7	2.5
	Day	15	3	5	1	0.1	0.3
DWELLING HOUSES	Low rental	70	–	25	–	0.5	–
	Medium rental	115	25	30	10	0.7	4.0
	High rental	140	30	45	10	1.2	4.0
	Factories	15	3	5	1	1.2	0.4
FLATS – BLOCKS	Low rental	70	15	25	5	0.5	1.5
	Medium rental	115	25	30	7	0.7	2.5
	High rental	140	30	45	7	1.2	3.0
HOSPITALS	General	135	30	30	6	1.5	5.0
	Infectious	225	50	45	10	1.5	5.0
	Infirmaries	70	15	25	5	0.6	2.0
	Infirm with laundries	90	20	30	6	0.9	3.0
	Maternity	230	50	30	7	2.1	7.0
	Psychiatric	90	20	25	5	0.7	2.5
	Nurses homes	135	30	45	10	0.9	3.0
	Hostels	115	25	30	7	0.7	2.5
HOTELS	First class	135	30	45	10	1.2	4.0
	Average	115	25	35	8	0.9	3.0
	Offices	15	3	5	1	0.1	0.4
	Sports Pav. with Spray Showers	35	8	35	8	0.3	1.0

VALUES TAKEN: • FROM CP 342 (1950) AND * FROM 'IHVE' GUIDE BOOK B.
NOTE: HOT WATER DEMAND IS GIVEN PER DAY OF 24 HOURS ON THE DAY OF HEAVIEST DEMAND DURING WEEK: FOR BOILER POWER GIVEN IN GALLONS – 1 GAL 'EQUALS' 1000 Btu. THE BOILER POWER SHOULD ALSO INCLUDE FOR HEAT LOSSES FROM TOWEL RAILS, PIPES, ETC
LOW RENTAL MAX 88m² (950ft²) MEDIUM 88m² to 140m². HIGH OVER 140m² (1500ft²) OF FLOOR AREA

PROVISION OF STORAGE TO COVER 24 HRS INTERRUPTION OF SUPPLY (COLD WATER)

TYPE OF BUILDING	PER	LITRES*	GALLONS
Dwelling houses & flats	Resident	90	20
Hostels	Resident	90	20
Hotels	Resident	135	30
Offices without canteens	Head	35	8
Offices with canteens	Head	45	10
Restaurants	Head/meal	7	1½
Day schools	Head	30	6
Boarding schools	Resident	50	20
Nurses homes & med quarters	Resident	115	25
Factories (from CP3 Ch VII)	Employee	–	10

TABLE 2 (CP310 except *)

THE RELATION BETWEEN HW STORAGE & 'BOILERS' IS COMPLEX & CIRCUMSTANCES MAY ALTER THEIR OPTIMUM RELATIONSHIP

BRITISH STANDARD CYLINDER CONNECTIONS FLOW & RETURN
1in. NOMINAL
DIRECT MS: 73 litres (16) to 136 litres (30) COPPER: 74 litres (16) TO 120 litres (26)
INDIRECT MS: 109 litres (24) TO 123 litres (27) COPPER: 96 litres (21) TO 117 litres (26)
1¼in. NOMINAL
DIRECT MS: 159 litres (35) TO 241 litres (53) COPPER: 144 litres (32) TO 166 litres (37)
INDIRECT MS: 159 litres (35) COPPER: 140 litres (31) TO 162 litres (36)
1½in. NOMINAL
DIRECT MS: 332 litres (73) TO 441 litres (97) COPPER: 200 litres (44) TO 255 litres (56)
INDIRECT MS: 227 litres (50) TO 273 litres (60) COPPER: 190 litres (42) TO 245 litres (54)
2in. NOMINAL
DIRECT COPPER: 290 litres (64) TO 450 litres (99)
INDIRECT MS: 364 litres (80) TO 455 litres (100) COPPER: 280 litres (62) TO 440 litres (97)

(FIGURES IN BRACKETS ARE GALS)

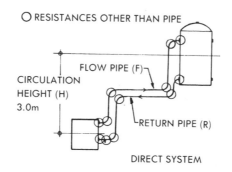

○ RESISTANCES OTHER THAN PIPE

FLOW PIPE (F)

CIRCULATION HEIGHT (H) 3.0m

RETURN PIPE (R)

DIRECT SYSTEM

RELEVANT DATA
FLOW TEMPERATURE: 66°C (150°F)
RETURN TEMPERATURE: 50°C (122°F)
DESIGN TEMP DIFFERENCE: 16°C (MAX 22°C)
CYLINDER CAPACITY: 370 LITRE (81 GAL)
RECOVERY OR WARM-UP TIME: 2.5 HOURS
WEIGHT OF WATER AT 66°C: 979.9 kg/m³ (Drf)
WEIGHT OF WATER AT 50°C: 988.0 kg/m³ (Dr)
CIRCULATION HEIGHT: 3.0m
MEASURED LENGTH OF CIRCS (F & R): 10.0m
EQUIVALENT LENGTH ie RESISTANCES
OTHER THAN PIPE (ESTIMATED): 30.0m (EL)
EFFECTIVE LENGTH = MEASURED + EQUIVALENT
See table 1 •

STEP	EXPLANATION	CALCULATION
1. CALCULATE CIRCULATING PRESSURE (CP)	9.81 (Dr - Df) x CIRC HEIGHT (H) = N/m²	9.81 (988.0 - 979.9)• x 3.0m = 238.38 N/m²
2. OBTAIN EFFECTIVE LENGTH OF CIRCS (F + R)	MEASURED LENGTH (m) + EQUIVALENT LENGTH (m) (THE LATTER SHOULD BE CALC- ULATED. ESTIMATED HERE)	LENGTH AS MEASURED =10.0m EQUIV. (ESTIMATED) =30.0m EFFECTIVE LENGTH = 40.0m
3. 'ALLOWABLE' MAXIMUM PRESSURE LOSS IN N/m² PER METRE RUN	$\dfrac{\text{CIRC PRESSURE}}{\text{EFFEC LENGTH}}$	$\dfrac{238.38}{40}$ =5.96 N/m² m say 6 N/m² m
4. CALCULATE HEAT FLOW RATE (Q) (See Detail 36)	Q = l/h x °C (F & R DIFF) x $\dfrac{4.187 \times 1000}{3600}$	Q = $\dfrac{370 \times (66°-10°) \times 1.163}{2.5}$ =148 x 56 x 1.163 = 9640 W (J/s) PLUS OTHER LOSSES (THESE SHOULD BE CALCULATED): ASSUME 10% OF Q THEREFORE 964 W TOTAL Q = 10604 W (J/s)
5. CALCULATE WATER FLOW RATE	LITRE (kg)/SECOND = $\dfrac{Q}{\text{F \& R DESIGN TEMP DIFF} \times 4187}$	$\dfrac{10604}{16 \times 4187}$ = 0.158 l/s say 0.16 l/s (1 LITRE WEIGHS APPROX 1 kg)
6. SELECT PIPE SIZE FROM CHART 1	USE 6N/m² (VERT SCALE) & 0.16 litres/s (HORI SCALE)	42mm (1½in.) APPEARS SATISFACTORY

NOTES FROM THE CP'S REGARDING PRIMARY CIRCULATION PIPES
CP342 (1950) IN NO CASE SHOULD THE DIAMETER OF THE PIPES BE LESS THAN 1in.
CP342 Pt 1 NOMINAL BORE OF THE PIPES SHOULD NOT BE LESS THAN 1in. (25mm)
CP342 Pt 2 SHOULD BE SIZED FOR TEMPERATURE DROP NOT EXCEEDING 22°C
CP403 101 INDEPENDENT BOILER: MIN 1in. PIPES WITH BOILER TAPPED 1¼in.... BACK
BOILER FOR INDIRECT: CAN BE REDUCED TO ¾in.... UNDESIRABLE TO HAVE RAPID CIRCULATION
FOR SMALL BOILER OUTPUT: CP310 MIN 1in. & PREFERABLY (SPECIALLY IF WATER HARD) 1¼in.

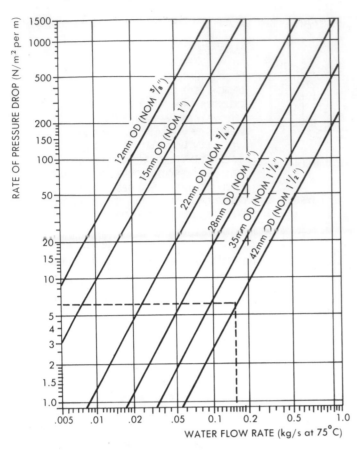

CHART 1   FLOW OF WATER IN COPPER PIPES (BS2871 Pt 1 'X')

DENSITY OF WATER	
TEMP. °C	DENSITY kg/m³
0.01	999.8
4	999.9
10	999.7
12	999.4
14	999.2
16	998.9
18	998.6
20	998.2
22	997.7
24	997.2
26	996.7
28	996.2
30	995.6
32	995.0
34	994.3
36	993.6
38	993.0
40	992.2
42	991.4
44	990.6
46	989.8
48	988.9
50	988.0
52	987.2
54	986.2
56	985.2
58	984.3
60	983.2
62	982.1
64	981.1
66	979.9
68	978.9
70	977.7
72	976.6
74	975.4
76	974.3
78	973.1
80	971.8
82	970.6
84	969.3
86	968.0
88	966.7
90	965.3
92	964.0
94	962.7
96	961.2
98	959.8
100	958.3

TABLE 1

EASY SIZING OF PRIMARY CIRCULATION PIPES

(i)   THE FOLLOWING TABLE SHOWS THE F & R DIAMETER (INCHES) REQUIRED FOR A RANGE OF CONDITIONS NORMALLY OCCURRING. OTHER CASES SHOULD BE CALCULATED

(ii) 'H' IS THE VERTICAL HEIGHT FROM MID-BOILER LEVEL TO MID CYLINDER LEVEL (SEE SKETCH).

(iii) 'L' IS THE TOTAL MEASURED LENGTH (F + R) PLUS AN ALLOWANCE IN TERMS OF LENGTH FOR ALL OTHER RESISTANCES ie EFFECTIVE LENGTH

EXAMPLE AS ABOVE: H = 3 & L = 10 therefore $\frac{L}{H} = \frac{10}{3} = 3.3$

ALLOWING FOR CIRCULATION OF 30 GAL/HR, THE PIPE SIZE INDICATED IS 1in. HOWEVER, USING L AS 40 L/H =13.3

H AND THE REQUIRED PIPE SIZE CAN BE READ OFF AS 1½in

SIZES

NOMINAL BORE	OD COPPER PIPES	Value of L/H	15	20	25	30	35	40	45	50	60	75	100 ◄ gal/hr
			4.35	5.8	7.25	8.7	10.15	11.6	13.1	14.5	17.4	21.8	29.3 ◄ kWh
		2	¾	¾	1	1	1	1	1	1¼	1¼	1¼	1½
½in.	15mm	3	¾	1	1	1	1	1¼	1¼	1¼	1¼	1¼	1½
¾in.	22mm	4	¾	1	1	1	1¼	1¼	1¼	1¼	1½	1¼	1½
1in.	28mm	6	1	1	1	1¼	1¼	1¼	1¼	1½	1½	1¼	2
1¼in.	35mm	8	1	1	1¼	1¼	1¼	1½	1½	1½	1½	2	2
1½in.	42mm	10	1	1¼	1¼	1¼	1½	1½	1½	1½	2	2	2
2in.	54mm	15	1	1¼	1¼	1½	1½	1½	2	2	2	2	2

TABLE 2   BOILER OUTPUT FROM 10°C (50°) TO 66°C (150°F) gal/hr & kWh (GAL/HR ALSO REPRESENTS BOILER OUTPUT IN 1000's OF Btu/hr)

FITTING OR APPLIANCE	RATE OF FLOW (COLD OR HOT)	
	l/sec	gal/min
Flushing cistern	0.12	1.5
Wash basin tap	0.15	2.0
Basin spray tap	0.04	0.5
Bath tap (19mm)	0.30	4.0
Bath tap (25mm)	0.60	8.0
Shower (nozzle)	0.12	1.5
Sink tap (13mm)	0.20	2.5
Sink tap (19mm)	0.30	4.0
Sink tap (25mm)	0.60	8.0
Urinal (per stall)	0.004	0.05

FLOW RATES
TABLE 1

DWELLINGS & FLATS	LOADING UNITS
WC flushing cistern	2
Wash basin	1.5
Bath	10
Sink	3 to 5
OFFICES	
WC flushing cistern	2
Wash basin	1.5
WB (used in rapid succession)	3
SCHOOLS & INDUSTRIAL BUILDINGS	
WC flushing cistern	2
WB (used in rapid succession)	3
Shower (with nozzle)	3
Public Bath	22

LOADING UNITS
TABLE 2

COPPER				GALV. MILD STEEL			
Nom Bore (in)	Metric OD (mm)	Metre run of pipe		Nom Bore (mm)	Metre run of pipe		
		Elbow	Tee		Galv. elbow	Bend	Tee
1/2	15	0.5	0.6	15	0.5	0.4	1.2
3/4	22	0.8	1.0	20	0.6	0.5	1.4
1	28	1.0	1.5	25	0.7	0.6	1.8
1 1/4	35	1.4	2.0	32	1.0	0.7	2.3
1 1/2	42	1.7	2.5	40	1.2	1.0	2.7
2	54	2.3	3.5	50	1.4	1.2	3.4

LOSS OF HEAD IN PIPE FITTINGS EXPRESSED IN
EQUIVALENT PIPE LENGTHS
TABLE 3

BS fitting	0.075 l/s	0.12 l/s	0.15 l/s	0.20 l/s	0.22 l/s	0.30 l/s	0.35 l/s	0.47 l/s	*
1/2" bib tap	0.185	.365	0.52	0.75	1.1	1.8	–	–	
3/4" bib tap	–	–	0.21	0.33	0.45	0.75	1.1	1.4	
1" bib tap	–	–	–	–	–	0.45	0.70	0.90	
1/2" pillar tap	0.24	0.40	0.52	0.70	0.80	–	–	–	
3/4" pillar tap	–	–	0.24	0.30	0.40	0.50	0.70	–	

LOSS OF HEAD IN METRES THRO' DRAW OFF TAPS
TABLE 4
       * DISCHARGE RATE

*PSD PROBABLE SIMULTANEOUS DEMAND

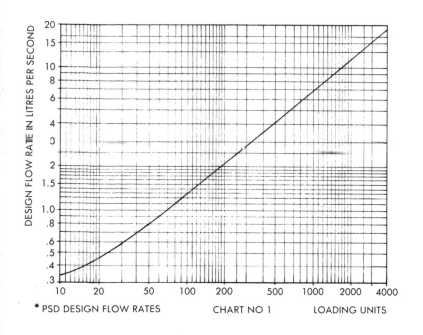

* PSD DESIGN FLOW RATES   CHART NO 1   LOADING UNITS

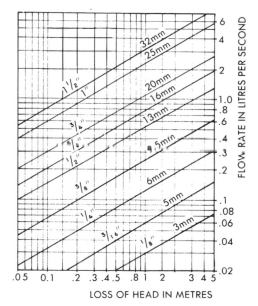

LOSS OF HEAD IN METRES

HEAD LOSS THROUGH BALL VALVE ORIFICES

CHART NO 2

NO BALL OR STOPVALVE IN THE
EXAMPLE: CHARTS 2 & 3 NOT USED

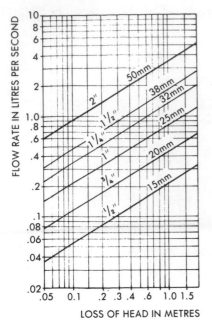

CHART NO 3 HEAD LOSS THRO'STOPVALVES

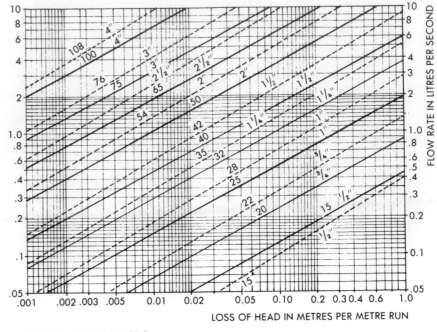

COPPER, LEADS & PLASTIC -----
GALVANISED STEEL ————

CHART NO 4   PIPE SIZING GRAPHS

USING A DEMAND UNIT METHOD

HOT WATER SUPPLY FOR FIVE FLATS

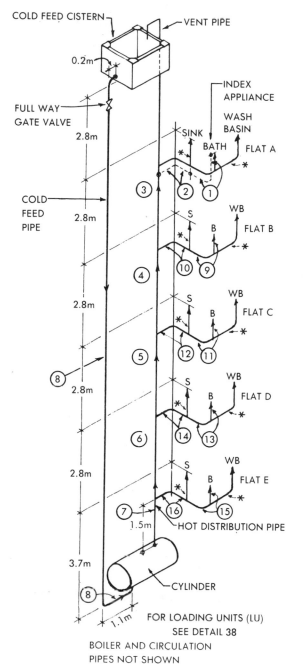

COLD FEED CISTERN
VENT PIPE
0.2m
FULL WAY GATE VALVE
2.8m
INDEX APPLIANCE
WASH BASIN
SINK
BATH   FLAT A
③ ② ①
COLD FEED PIPE
2.8m
S   WB
B   FLAT B
⑩ ⑨
④
2.8m
S   WB
B   FLAT C
⑫ ⑪
⑤
⑧
2.8m
S   WB
B   FLAT D
⑭ ⑬
⑥
2.8m
S   WB
B   FLAT E
⑦ ⑯   ⑮
1.5m HOT DISTRIBUTION PIPE
3.7m
CYLINDER
⑧
1.1m   FOR LOADING UNITS (LU)
SEE DETAIL 38
BOILER AND CIRCULATION
PIPES NOT SHOWN

THE PREPARATORY WORK INCLUDES

(i) An accurate drawing of the layout to allow pipe lengths to be scaled off, head available to be measured; appliances located; identification of pipe fittings & valves etc.

(ii) flats to be lettered for easy reference

(iii) pipes to be numbered in a sequence allowing for recognition of the INDEX CIRCUIT i.e. from the tap least favourably situated, along the entire 'main' pipe run back to the source of supply. In this example, the bath tap in Flat A is chosen as the INDEX APPLIANCE, hence the numbering 1 to 8 back to the cistern. Other branches are numbered in order of 'importance'.

(iv) Ascertain the 'head' available at the various draw-off levels. This is a vertical measurement using the worst situation, ie, from underside of cistern to approx. draw off level. (Flat A appliances have the least available head (2.8m) and the longest distance for the water to travel — cistern to taps).

(v) Some assumptions can be made to reduce the number of pipes to be sized. An example is — pipes marked with asterisk can be assumed to be ½in. (15mm); they are short branches; the bend to WB can be large radius, & taps are ½in. in any case. Steps like this are left to the discretion of the designer.

Maximum Possible (100%)		Probable simultaneous Demand		Maximum Possible (100%)		Probable simultaneous Demand	
l/sec	gal/min	l/sec	gal/min	l/sec	gal/min	l/sec	gal/min
UP TO 0.91	UP TO 12	100% OF maximum possible		6.14	81	2.80	37
				7.12	94	2.96	39
1.06	14	0.99	13	8.11	107	3.18	42
1.21	16	1.10	14.5	9.32	123	3.41	45
1.36	18	1.21	16	10.76	142	3.64	48
1.52	20	1.33	17.5	12.35	163	3.94	52
1.74	23	1.44	19	14.25	188	4.24	56
1.97	26	1.55	20.5	16.37	216	4.62	61
2.27	30	1.71	22.5	18.79	248	4.93	65
2.65	35	1.82	24	21.67	286	5.38	71
3.03	40	1.97	26	24.93	329	5.83	77
➡ 3.49	46	2.12	28	28.64	378	6.44	85
4.02	53	2.27	30	32.96	435	7.20	95
4.62	61	2.43	32	37.89	500	7.88	104
5.38	71	2.58	34	over37.9	over500	20% of max	

PROBABLE SIMULTANEOUS DEMAND: TABLE ADAPTED FROM CP342

PROBABLE SIMULTANEOUS DEMAND (PSD) OR LOAD FACTOR

To design for 100% simultaneous demand may be necessary in certain cases but for many schemes, a much lower figure can be used with the economic advantage of reduced pipe sizes etc. There are many methods of estimating PSD, producing a wide variety of answers from 10% to 100% *in the extreme*. Out of the 15 hot water taps comprising this layout, how many are likely to be ON at the same time — *for design purposes?*

Using the LOADING UNIT METHOD as presented in CP310 & the IoP publications, 99% satisfaction is quoted, ie for only 1% of the time will the assumptions be wrong therefore *acceptable*.

PROCEED AS FOLLOWS: LU per flat — washbasin 1.5; bath 10.0 sink; say 4.0 therefore TOTAL = 15.5 LU. Assuming only two taps on per flat at any one time, total LU could be 14 (bath & sink). Taking 16 LU per flat & using PSD curve (Detail 38) the PSD flow rate for each stage can be read of thus:

Pipe(s) supplying Flat A	② & ③	16 LU	0.41 l/sec PSD flow
Pipe(s) supplying Flats A&B	④	32 LU	0.60 l/sec PSD flow
Pipe(s) supplying Flats A,B&C	⑤	48 LU	0.78 l/sec PSD flow
Pipe(s) supplying Flats A,B,C&D	⑥	64 LU	0.95 l/sec PSD flow
Pipe(s) supply All Flats	⑦ & ⑧	80 LU	1.10 l/sec PSD flow

FLOW RATE IF ALL APPLIANCES ON AT THE SAME TIME (SEE DETAIL 37

wash basin	0.15 l/s	Therefore for 5 flats the flow rate for the
bath	0.30 l/s	whole building could be 0.65 x 5
sink	0.20 l/s	= 3.25 l/s (IF ALL TAPS ON AT THE SAME
PER FLAT	0.65 l/s	TIME)

$$\text{PERCENTAGE DEMAND} = \frac{1.10}{3.25} \times \frac{100}{1} = 34\% \text{ round up : } 40\%$$

(Table indicates nearer 60%)

If 40% is accepted then only 2 flats out of the 5 need to be considered for actual pipe sizing & the designer would concentrate on the 2 flats in the worst situation: with least head viz: A & B. On the other hand, the PSD percentage may be increased to provide a 'safety margin' eg using Table: 60%: Flats A, B & C) and certain engineers may even take 100% (all flats).

LU: LOADING UNIT(S)

112

| CLIENT | A.N. Other Ltd | | | JOB No | 237/B/49 |
| PROJECT | Flat Development E (5 storey) | | | DATE | 1 Jan 1980 |

LOCATION	Cairnscourt, Merebrook, W.Glam	DETAILS
		Service	Centralised Hot Water Supply
		Tube & Joint	BS 28711 Pt.1 Table X & 'M' cap joint
WATER AUTHORITY	Welsh Water	Other Information	For duct detail see Drg 9D/CC

1	2	3	4	5	6	7	8	9	10	11	12	13
	From Chart 1		From Chart 4			LENGTH IN METRES			HEAD IN METRES			
Pipe No	Loading Units (total)	Flow Rate (l/sec)	Estimated Pipe size (nom)	Head Loss m/m run	Actual Pipe (m)	Resistances (EL) (m)	Effect Total (m)	Consumed (column 5 x 8)	Running Total (m)	Head Available (m)	Revised Head loss	Final Pipe Size (mm)
1	11.5	0.35	19mm	0.110	1.5	1 x 19mm tee = 1.0 / 1 x 19mm elbow = 0.8	3.3	0.363 / 0.50ø	0.863			22.OD
2	16	0.41	25mm	0.040	1.2	1 x 25mm tee = 1.5 / 1 x 25mm elbow = 1.0	3.7	0.148 / 0.70•	1.711			28 OD
3	16	0.41	25mm	0.040	2.8	1 x 25mm tee = 1.5	4.3	0.172	1.883			28 OD
4	32	0.60	32mm	0.026	2.8	1 x 32mm tee = 2.0	4.8	0.125	2.008			35 OD
5	48	0.78	32mm	0.040	2.8	1 x 32mm tee = 2.0	4.8	0.192	2.200			35 OD
6	64	0.95	38mm	0.024	2.8	1 x 38mm tee = 2.5	5.3	0.127	2.327			42 OD
7	80	1.10	38mm	0.029	1.5	1 x 38mm tee = 2.5	4.0	0.116	2.443			42 OD
8	80	1.10	50mm	0.0075	19.0	3 x 50mm elbows = 6.9	25.9	0.194	2.637	2.8*		54 OD
9		Same as pipe No 1						0.863				22 OD
10	16	0.41	19mm	0.145	1.2	1 x 19mm tee = 1.0 / 1 x 19mm elbow = 0.8	3.0	0.435 / 0.70•	4.635	5.6		22 OD
11		Same as pipe No 9						0.863				22 OD
12		Same as pipe No 10						1.135	6.633	3.4		22 OD
13	ø	Same as pipe No 9						0.863				22 OD
14		Same as pipe No 10						1.135	8.631	11.2		22 OD
15	ø	Same as pipe No 9						0.863				22 OD
16		Same as pipe No 10						1.135	10.629	14.0		22 OD

NOTE

As the available range of commercial pipe sizes is limited the arithmetical accuracy need not be to a high degree. Faced with need for economy coupled with an acceptable performance standard, a designer may make a decision to select a pipe size knowing full well that his calculations indicate it marginally under-sized. Alternatively he may select the next size larger which will probably deliver two or three times the required rate of flow. He may then be accused of being too generous. The pipe sizes selected in this example should be accepted as one solution. If a pipe is oversized in one section of the layout, a pipe elsewhere may be undersized (to a degree) without necessarily affecting the overall performance.

PROCEDURE (Refer to charts, tables, drawings & notes on Details 38 & 39)

COLUMN I. Pipe numbers for identification sequence not critical. Designer adopts a method to suit own ideas. Various theories exist. See Detail 39.

COLUMN 2. Insert summation of loading units for all appliances to be served by each individual pipe as numbered in Col I. See details 38 and 39.

COLUMN 3. Insert probable simultaneous demand flow rates in litres/sec as read off from PSD design curve (Detail 38) using LU for each pipe in turn.

COLUMN 4. Based upon information in Col 3 & Chart 4 (Detail 38), estimate a suitable pipe size. Experience produces a more proficient designer. If the wrong size pipe is selected it will soon become apparent when values in Cols 10 & II are compared. Adjust pipe size if necessary.

COLUMN 5. Using flow rate (Col 3) & estimated pipe size (Col 4), read off head loss in metres per metre run for each pipe situation and insert in this column. Note choice of 'smooth' or 'rough' pipe.

COLUMN 6. Insert measured pipe length, scaled off from drawing.

COLUMN 7. Resistances attributed to pipe fittings (elbows, tees, etc) in terms of equivalent (EL) pipe length are recorded in Col 7. These values are obtainable from Table 3 on Detail 38.

COLUMN 8. Effective lengths ie a summation of Col 6 (measured length) & Col 7 (EL) are put in this column.

COLUMN 9. Calculate 'head consumed' by multiplying 'head' loss in metres per metre run (Col 5) by the effective length (Col 8) and insert 'head' loss caused by the presence of taps, valves, etc should also be inserted in this column (see Table 4 Detail 38). An alternative to this method is to allow for taps etc, in terms of EL using Col 7.

COLUMN IO. This is for the running total of all items appearing in Col 9 in terms of 'head' loss. This total can be compared at various stages with head available in Column II which should not be exceeded.

COLUMN 12. Used if any pipe size has to be adjusted: larger or smaller.
COLUMN 13. For the final paper size selected.

EXPLANATORY NOTES
ø this is the loss of 'head' in metres through a ¾in. bath pillar tap discharging .30 litre/sec
• this is the loss of 'head' in metres through a ½in. sink pillar tap discharging .20 litres/sec. (See Table 4 on Detail 38)
* this is the approx head available at the level of the taps in Flat A. It will be noticed that the estimated head 'consumed' at this level, based upon the various assumptions made, is about 0.2m less than the 'head' available, therefore design flow rates should be possible. At Flat B level, the difference is about 1 m, at C level about 1.7m; D level about 2.5m and so on, indicating an increasing balance of 'head' available which will ensure adequate flow rates throughout.

It might be possible to reduce these pipe sizes as ample head appears available. (Not recommended here)

REMINDERS
A throughway gate valve is used on the cold feed pipe & losses are assumed to be negligible. The same applies to the entry and exist from cylinder. Pipes to WB & branch to sink (not numbered) to be 15mm (½in.) & losses assumed negligible.

THIS DETAIL MUST BE STUDIED IN CONJUNCTION WITH DETAILS 38 and 39 No 3 CONTAINS THE TABLES & CHARTS FOR SIZING HOT & COLD WATER SERVICES, AND 39 DEALS WITH THE FIRST STAGES OF A PIPE SIZING PROBLEM. THESE 3 SHEETS PRESENT A DIGEST OF A COMPLEX PROCEDURE WITH MANY DIFFERING THEORIES.

Published by Building Trades Journal

Titles available:

Arbitration for Contractors
Builders' Reference Book 12th edition
Building Regulations 1985 Explained
Buyers' Guide 1987
Construction Case Law in the Office
Contract Joinery
Guide to Estimating Building Work 1986/87
Site Carpentry
Techniques of Routing
The Small Contractors' Guide to the Computer
Builders' Detail Sheets (Consolidated)
Drainage Details
Hot Water Details
Sanitation Details (Consolidated)

Practical Guide Series
Alterations & Improvements
Basic Bookkeeping
Bricks & Brickwork
Builders' Questions & Answers
Day Work Rates 1986/87
Estimating for Alterations & Repairs
Groundworks and Foundations
Repair & Maintenance of Houses
Roofing
Setting Out on Site
Sub-Contracting
Windows
Construction News Books
Bonus Calculations
Construction News Annual Financial Review
Understanding JCT Contracts

For further details on the above titles or for a booklet on prices etc. please ring
the BTJ Books Department, telephone number 01-935 6611.